Pleasure and the Arts

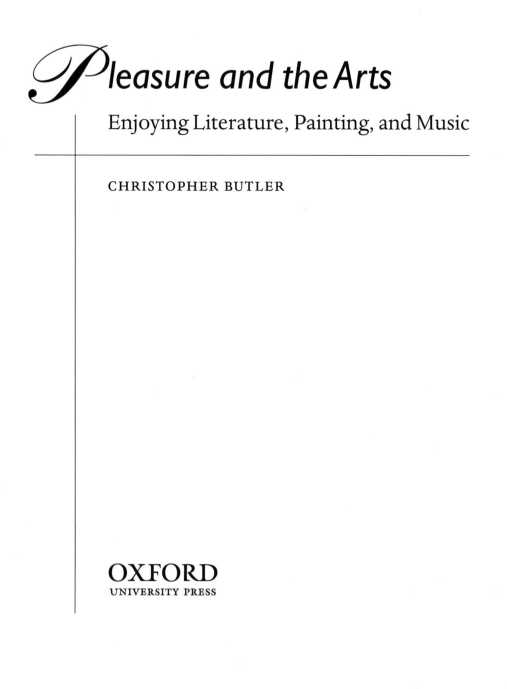

Pleasure and the Arts

Enjoying Literature, Painting, and Music

CHRISTOPHER BUTLER

OXFORD

UNIVERSITY PRESS

OXFORD

UNIVERSITY PRESS

Great Clarendon Street, Oxford OX2 6DP

Oxford University Press is a department of the University of Oxford.
It furthers the University's objective of excellence in research, scholarship,
and education by publishing worldwide in

Oxford New York

Auckland Bangkok Buenos Aires Cape Town Chennai
Dar es Salaam Delhi Hong Kong Istanbul Karachi Kolkata
Kuala Lumpur Madrid Melbourne Mexico City Mumbai Nairobi
São Paulo Shanghai Taipei Tokyo Toronto

Oxford is a registered trade mark of Oxford University Press
in the UK and in certain other countries

Published in the United States
by Oxford University Press Inc., New York

© Christopher Butler 2004

The moral rights of the author have been asserted

Database right Oxford University Press (maker)

First published 2004

British Library Cataloguing in Publication Data

Data available

Library of Congress Cataloging in Publication Data

Data available

ISBN 0-19-927248-4

10 9 8 7 6 5 4 3 2 1

Typeset by SNP Best-set Typesetter Ltd., Hong Kong
Printed in Great Britain
on acid-free paper by
Biddles Ltd., King's Lynn, Norfolk

Don't take it as a matter of course, but as a remarkable fact, that pictures and fictitious narratives give us pleasure, occupy our minds.

Wittgenstein, *Philosophical Investigations*, sect. 1, para. 524

This book is dedicated to those who taught me
in particular to Alan Mould and Alastair Fowler

and to the memory of

Bill Barron, Geoffrey Elcoat,
and Isaiah Berlin

Acknowledgements

Making a book comes after writing it, and my friends in the Oxford University Press have as always combined demanding intellectual standards with a close attention to detail; Sophie Goldsworthy commissioned some reports of exceptional length and intellectual generosity which helped me to rethink a good part of my text; Elizabeth Prochaska managed the early stages of production and breezed in to Christ Church to take a photograph of me for the jacket which I hope looks as editor- (and reader-) friendly as I felt; Rowena Anketell copy-edited and was tolerant of the odd missing verb, let alone comma; Sandra Assersohn was an admirably persistent and inventive picture researcher; Sue Tipping produced an elegant and negotiable design; and Frances Whistler, an incomparable scholarly editor, saved me from many errors, was immensely helpful in making decisions about pictures, and proved to be a penetrating and witty critic of captions and titles.

There is an implicit bit of autobiography even in an academic book, and I wouldn't have enjoyed my life or the works of art described in this book half so much if I had not had the extraordinary good luck to have inspiring teachers: at Brentwood School, Bill Barron (English), Alan Mould (History), Geoffrey Elcoat (French); and at Oxford, Alastair Fowler and Isaiah Berlin. They are of course no more personally responsible than anyone else who has helped me for the views I express below, but they did a good deal to help me to come by them, and I can't help hoping that they would by and large approve of what follows, because the standards and the values of great teachers always extend far beyond them in the activities of their pupils.

C.B.

Contents

List of Illustrations

Introduction

We worry a good deal about the moral and political significance of the arts. But this seems to me to be far too easy. Anyone can think up or obey political or moral principles and apply them to art, and many do. Such arguments are parasitic on those which we have all the time, and they often just *use* art to make familiar moral or political points which are usually believed in by the critic on grounds quite other than the examination of art. For example, if you already know that patriarchy abuses women by displaying their bodies for the male's pleasure, then it can hardly come as a great surprise to be told that Titian's Venus of Urbino is somehow 'implicated' in this system and therefore somehow bad.[1] It is the fate of the pleasure the picture can give that interests me.

This is not a book about the relationship between morality and pleasure, or the arts and censorship, or the views of religious or political groups on pleasure. That is another kind of endeavour. I have tried to make a case for the many kinds of pleasures which we can expect to derive from the canonic works of the culture we have inherited, and from the more ephemeral and more popular culture which surrounds us, and which ranges from high to fairly low. The pleasures I am interested in are those which are in various ways intrinsic to the procedures by which works of art are made for us. Of course I have ethical principles, and a liberal view of politics, which make it worthwhile for me to write about pleasure in the first place. The argument that follows will reflect to some degree my belief that the autonomous and uninterfered-with cultural development of individuals is of supreme importance; that only in a culture in which different views in different works of art peacefully compete and debate with one another can progress be made; and that only a tolerant pluralism in art and in criticism is acceptable, since those ideologies and belief structures which seem to have all the answers, or even too many of them, are always a threat to our humanity.

I have found it difficult to formulate the principles which underlie this very preliminary account of the ways in which we might all enjoy works of art (including the Titian), or at least those works which fall into the categories of fiction, musical work, painting, and film-making, which make up the examples which follow. There are surprisingly few books on the subject. We don't always pay enough conscious attention to the pleasure we take in the arts, and to what we might learn, of a relatively non-trivial and even moralizing kind, from that. The training of our sensibility, and our learning to appreciate *whole* works of art, can be a far more subtle and difficult process than the expression of our moral intuitions or principles when we are confronted by the provoking *parts* of them or of their politically incorrect historical contexts.

In what follows, then, I try to give an account of some of the ways in which the arts can be enjoyed, and this book is for anyone who wants to reflect on the pleasures they get from them. There are parts of my argument which plunge a bit into the philosophical substructure, but I hope that I have emerged from this with formulations which are intelligible to any art lover.

I give a trusting account of our pleasures, in the first instance. This because I am primarily concerned with what I am calling the 'phenomenology' of first-person reports about the enjoyment of art. I will quote plenty of them below, for the interesting reason that such first-person accounts are authoritative, at least about the pleasures they report. Many critical remarks of course contribute to this phenomenology. I will therefore report the responses of others, and my own, and I won't stop to quarrel too much with those whom I believe to have had the 'wrong' ones. The first five chapters, then, develop a positive account of the arts and our enjoyment.

This is not a work of philosophical aesthetics, though I hope that it is informed by the thoughts of some of the best thinkers in that field. Only in the final chapter will I look at some rival conceptions and theories of pleasure, most of which I don't like, because they are too reductive, and also argue for the positive view that we can very happily relate to works of art as to human individuals.

There are at least two popular commonplaces about pleasure: the first of these is that 'Tastes in the arts are just subjective and you can't argue about them' (*De gustibus non est disputandum*). But I solicit agreement, and so I use the pronoun 'we' here unrepentantly, despite the reservations that might be felt by any reader who is not sympathetic to what they may take to be my class, gender, origins, or supposed social position. And by 'we' I mean men and women, though I have avoided a half-and-half distribution of the personal pronoun in what follows. And I hope that my interpretation of art will be acceptable to homosexual as well as to heterosexual readers; though it is obvious that it is around these two major differences that significant variations in subjective response can sometimes be apparent. This is because works of art help to create and imply broadly based interpretative communities for whom particular pleasures are available and significant. The audience for Mapplethorpe's 'X-Portfolio' is in this respect rather different from that for Edward Weston's nude studies of women. I also have a more philosophical criterion in mind. When I say 'we believe x', I also mean to suggest that if somebody didn't assent to my proposition, we (again) might feel that there was some kind of conceptual or psychological problem faced by the dissentient. My use of 'we' is therefore thoroughly and explicitly normative. I am trying to articulate what I believe 'reasonable persons' might come to agree about, while recognizing also that they often reasonably and passionately differ, and of course that I might be wrong.

This 'philosopher's we', which appeals to a common rationality, means that I am not directly concerned in this book with the differences there may be in the psychological responses of women as opposed to men, or indeed homosexual as opposed to heterosexual persons. Most of my arguments and examples are intended to be directed to everyone, though I have no doubt that the bias of some of them will indicate to some readers a better acquaintance with and enjoyment of male heterosexual interests than other kinds. Where this happens I hope that I admit it, by using the first-person pronoun.

But there is a further question—in appealing to a universal or at least rational 'we', I argue for an understanding and appreciation of works of art and persons through narrative and situation rather than through 'identification'. This has the consequence that differences of gender or sexual orientation do not usually go beyond the capabilities of our reason to convey them. (Though some horrors do indeeed go beyond reason.) Even if it is supposed that they are part of an 'essential' (i.e. not culturally formed) or intrinsic or intuitive or even genetically programmed difference in response between men and women, the same processes of understanding are going to be as relevant here as for other kinds of experience. It is possible to specify, more or less well, the differences in point of view of women and men situationally. Of course the situation, and the direction of attention of female painters, for example like Artemisia Gentileschi and Berthe Morisot, was demonstrably different, and in very interesting and significant ways, from that which affected the men of their time.[2] But to understand their work as near as is possible from their point of view, we need that information, and indeed to learn appropriate, more understanding emotional responses to it. A huge amount of this work has been done for us all by feminist critics of the arts. And the same goes for differences of sexual orientation. That is the best we can do; we cannot completely identify with a member of the other gender or orientation, any more or less than we can completely understand what it is to be any other person. Of course the strength of the sympathies which arise between *groups* who have had a common experience is the greater. But I stress throughout that we enjoy art as individuals through our own predispositions, moods, and experiences. So the difficulties which men have in understanding painters like Gentileschi and Morisot are not different in principle from their attempt to understand what it means for a woman to make love to a man, or even more likely, what it is like to be accused as Gentileschi was, or to develop as a woman painter in a domesticating culture, as did Morisot. Men can never have the exact sensational and emotional experience of these women, and can never feel that intimate solidarity with others which arises because they have had the same experience. But this argument is entirely symmetrical, as between women and men. Here the arts can help us all; and indeed our understanding of the role of such immediate sensational and deeply emotional experiences and, so far as is possible, our participating in them in imagination is an immensely important part of our non-verbal enjoyment of art, as I shall argue.

Many people think they may have to differ, to return to the *de gustibus* idea, when something as 'subjective' as pleasure as sensation is at issue. The *Oxford English Dictionary* indeed defines pleasure as something seen from a particular point of view, as 'the condition of consciousness or sensation induced by the enjoyment or anticipation of what is *felt or viewed as* good or desirable'. We tend furthermore to think that pleasures take place 'within' individuals, and that the individual's sincere judgement that he is enjoying something is somehow irrefutable. We have a peculiar authority in reporting our own pleasures and pains, even if we are often inaccurate in describing them. But the fact that all my bodily or intellectual pleasures (like sneezing or orgasms, or thrills to James Bond, or insights into Dorothea Brooke) take place 'in me' shows that this kind of subjectivity is not peculiar to pleasure alone. I have all my most generally negotiable thoughts, as well as my most pleasurable ones, 'in me' too. And I have important subjective feelings invested in such general thoughts. I agree with David Hume that reasoning is or should be accompanied by the calmer emotions, because all of our thoughts are full of affect. The 'problem of subjectivity' in relation to works of art surely arose partly in an attempt to distinguish (private) bodily sensations and emotions from (shareable) thoughts (this bothered Keats). But it also arises from a more general cultural attitude—how individualist (or relativist) do we *want to be* about our pleasurable experiences, and the ways in which we describe them to others?

Subjectivist views of pleasure can confuse two separate issues then. The first is that of our 'right to feel as one likes', and to be authoritative about our own states of feeling, and to form our own taste. We are in general willing to concede this kind of prerogative to others, and particularly in artistic contexts, which we presumably (and wrongly) think do not matter as much as arguments, say, about how we 'really' feel about our parents, or about how we are going to vote.

The second issue follows on from the first: it concerns the degree of objectivity we might actually be able to achieve in talking about the nature of our pleasures in the arts. The extraordinary and enduring appeal of masterworks to thousands of people leads one to suspect that something more generally significant than an essentially private sensation, like a tickle or a sneeze, or an 'aesthetic emotion' might be involved here. But even something that the individual can only experience 'in him/herself'—such as the taste of ice cream, a kiss, or the sight of a good sunset—is not *ipso facto* beyond discussion in general terms. Many of us are enjoying the same sort of thing when we look at a Rembrandt or a Monet, and with very good reason. A belief in subjectivist limitations can prevent us from looking at what actually happens in such cases. The arguments we have all had as we come out of the cinema, about the sheer enjoyability of the film we have seen, seem to me to be quite impassioned enough for this kind of tolerance of 'subjectivity'—or the thought that 'it's just my opinion'—to be doing no more than provide us with a moral escape route, which is largely irrelevant to the understanding of our pleasurable responses to works of art.

Of course there are plenty of pleasures which remain subjective in the sense that they arise from the individual's more or less private associations (such as 'that character (in a film) horrifies me because she is is just like my Aunt Maud', or 'I really enjoy that picture or car because *I* possess it, and because I could pay £20,000 for it'). (There is some doubt whether it is really the picture which is being enjoyed in such cases.)

Another support for the dictum 'It's just subjective' is often enough: 'It's just a state of feeling'. This tells us a good deal more about our beliefs about our feelings and their supposed idiosyncrasy and privacy in general, than it does about our emotional responses to the arts, or the ways in which, as I shall try to show, such feelings are *also* negotiable beliefs. Our pleasures are indeed very largely bound up in states of feeling, but this does not mean that they have nothing to do with that proper cognitive work in relation to works of art, which so often just leads us back into the familiar duelling grounds of interpretation and of our moral and political beliefs.

I accept the current view that works of art are made out of forms of discourse which always have a more or less explicit social dimension, which surrounds and transcends or supplements any simply individualist notions of creativity, and that the conventions which typically structure works of art have a social history and hence a political significance. Indeed, despite what I have written above, we will frequently bump up against the boundaries we sometimes put between our pleasure and morality—for example, in discussing sentimentality and erotic art. This interaction between the languages of art and the languages of society is not in dispute. But in writing about 'our' pleasure in works of art, I am going to assume they are typically enjoyed in a rather more limited social context, of privacy and self-cultivation (and not just as an aspect of middle-class leisure). This is a very different mental activity from, say, an academic attempt at the historical reconstruction of the social conditions under which Raphael's *Transfiguration* or Beethoven's Ninth or Virginia Woolf's novels came into existence. I therefore treat the works I am concerned with here as most often being enjoyed by an audience which encounters them in the concert hall, on the CD player, in the museum, or in the pages of the illustrated art book, on TV, in the cinema, in the theatre, or in (usually) silent and private reading. From there, and through that, audiences and works of art of course promote many interactions with our conception of the world, past or present. Interpretation typically makes such mediations, hence the current concentration on the institutional and social contexts for art. But I am primarily concerned here with art as it is understood in the intimate context of private personal enjoyment (though this is often amplified by public participation, as when we laugh with others in the theatre or jump about at a rock concert, or endure Arsenal in the rain, as Nick Hornby has amply desomstrated in his novel, *Fever Pitch*). I am only secondarily concerned then with the ethics and politics of interpretative mediation, though I argue that the interpretative assumptions we bring to the private enjoyment of works of art have very important effects on us as individuals.

I shall argue in what follows that our pleasurable feelings and emotions are in fact very complicated modes of understanding the world, and that it is a combination of feeling and understanding which gives us pleasure. The pleasure of a work of art is very far from being just the emotional icing on the cake, or something that is merely added to it as an inducement to us to take on something serious (despite the fact that another awful old tag—*docere cum delectare* (teach while pleasing)—suggests that it is). It is the nature of the 'cum' here which needs to be carefully looked at, so that we can attempt to understand the *interactive* relationships between emotion and understanding in pleasure.

I also want to see how pleasure arises from specific works of art, and that this specificity matters to us; that is why my discussion will be led by examples. If what is said about *them* is convincing, any more general theory will matter far less, because the partial truth that resides in the *de gustibus* dictum surely is that our pleasures are very various indeed, and that works of art allow us to repeat them, in response to their quite remarkable expression of an individuality which is worth getting to know.

I also wish to offer some ideas about pleasure as a supremely worthwhile *motive* for a deep and lifelong engagement with the arts, and as a part of our response to them, which, if we paid a closer attention to it, by being appreciators as well as interpreters, might release in us yet more pleasurable experiences, as the appetite grows by what it feeds on.

This is a book about our enjoyment of the arts; but it may be of interest at least to allude to the broader context of these. Ornstein and Sobel[3] refer to a study done at Stanford which reported on what thrills people. The results are interesting: musical passages 96 per cent, a scene in a movie, play, ballet, or book 92 per cent, great beauty in nature or art 87 per cent, physical contact with another person 78 per cent, climactic moment in opera 72 per cent, sexual activity 70 per cent, nostalgic moments 70 per cent, watching emotional interactions between other people 67 per cent, viewing a beautiful painting, photograph, or sculpture 67 per cent, moments of inspiration 65 per cent, something momentous or unexpected happening 63 per cent, seeing or reading about something heroic 59 per cent, sudden insight, understanding, solution to a problem 57 per cent, success in a competitive endeavour 49 per cent, particular fragrances 39 per cent, physical exercise 36 per cent, parades 26 per cent. It is notable how many of these are essential to the effects of art, as we will see below, and how many of them are indeed specific to the experience of art. (And since nostalgic moments score 70 per cent, the reactions of one of the publisher's readers for this book, that there seemed to be rather a large number of elegiac examples, may be explained by these findings. Or it may just be me.) Ornstein and Sobel also report that healthy robust and vital people don't lead bland stress-free lives, but 'They expect good things of the world. They expect that things will work out well; they expect that their world will be orderly; they expect that other people will like and respect them. And most important *they expect pleasure in much of what they do*.'[4] I hope that this book may reinforce some of these expectations, and not just for the 'healthy and robust'.

Notes

1. Cf. Rona Goffen (ed.), *Titian's Venus of Urbino* (Cambridge: CUP, 1997), 10, 13, 16, 17, 38, 90.
2. Cf. e.g. Mary D. Garrard, *Artemisia Gentileschi* (Princeton: Princeton UP, 1989), and Kathleen Adler and Tamar Garb, *Berthe Morisot* (London: Phaidon, 1987).
3. Robert Ornstein and David Sobel, *Healthy Pleasures* (Reading, Mass.: Perseus Books, 1989), 58, reporting Avram Goldstein, 'Thrills in Response to Music and Other Stimuli', *Physiological Psychology*, 8/1 (1980), 26–9.
4. Ornstein and Sobel, *Healthy Pleasures*, 5.

1 | *J*okes, Poems, Understanding

A friend of the Diracs [P. A. M. Dirac, then Lucasian Professor of Mathematics at Cambridge] had been surprised to find Dirac reading *A Passage to India* and thought it might be interesting to bring the two taciturn old men together. A tea was arranged, and an introduction effected. There was a long silence and then Dirac spoke: 'What happened in the cave?' Forster replied: 'I don't know.'[1]

Animals and Men

Noah finally managed to land his Ark on Mount Ararat and, when he'd let down the gangplank, the animals started to leave, led by two giraffes. Two lions followed, then two tigers. Then came four gnus.

A man standing on the shore said to Noah, 'Why so many?'
And Noah said, 'Well, there's some good gnus and some bad gnus . . .'[2]

How does this not very good but typical joke work to amuse us? It's the pun in the punchline on 'news/gnus' which does the trick of releasing our response. The thought of the gnus' sexual misbehaviour (amongst the animals who after all have been chosen to restock a drowned world) motivates the pun on 'bad gnus' by giving us a sexual snigger factor, and the anachronistic use of a cliché phrase gives the joke a veneer of wit, by bringing an excessively well-worn genre (the Noah joke) within sight of the contemporary.

Or look at a Gary Larson cartoon of a dog being interviewed in a TV studio. He is being asked about the remarkable (and ludicrous) fact that he is a talking dog. The interviewer asks him, 'So tell us Buffy, how long have you been a talking dog?' So far so good, and the incongruity of the situation is apparent as soon as we get a general grasp of the image. But, just in front of the dog, we can see a teleprompter, which reads, 'Well, Jim, I've been talking for some time now.' So, we infer, the dog *reads* as well, and we are amused by the fact that in this fantasy world, human beings are stupid enough to have interested themselves in what is by far the less remarkable of the dog's abilities. (The teleprompt message I think works like the pun in the joke above—we first read the pictorial situation as a whole, in the light of its subtitle, and then the punchline or trigger for the joke operates when we *focus* more narrowly, on the message to the dog.)

Another Gary Larson cartoon is subtitled 'Horse Hospitals'. In it horses lie on beds in a hospital ward, their broken legs bandaged and raised on supports. Between the beds, human doctors walk as usual, with clipboards for medical notes in their hands but, anomalously, with rifles under their arms. And when we focus on the background we can see, from left to right, an elbow, a gun, a bed with curtains drawn round it, and above it the word 'BLAM!' Larson makes us think as we laugh, about the incongruity of the conceptual relationships, between our consenting to the shooting of a horse with a broken leg on a race course, and the implications of the legalized killing (euthanasia) of human beings within a hospital.

In these jokes, we are made to match and contrast the conceptual frameworks we use for animals and for human beings. (We all fear death in hospital, but not so much for animals.) The oddity of our own hospital doctors deliberating in this way over the medical condition of horses reminds us of something that may be paradoxical about our attitudes. (Why shouldn't we kill off human beings when they become useless too?)

There can also be visual jokes: my fourth animal is a goat, as made up by Picasso—*The Goat* (1950)—out of various *objets trouvés*.[3] He uses a palm branch for the backbone, a wicker basket for the ribcage, and terracotta milk jars to make the udders, all of which are vaguely 'appropriate' to their new functions, so that there is something like a visual pun.[4] This goat strikes me as very comic. Its humour again arises from the way in which we think of the relationship between men and animals. It has a comic relationship to a 'real' goat, but it also

Fig. I Picasso, *The Goat* (1950). An animal
with a metaphorical bread basket and jarring
udders.

conveys its own expression—through caricature, it suggests the anthropomorphic characteristics of sturdy independence.

It is a brilliant case of ad hoc metaphoric adaptation, as Picasso was well aware. His comment on his animal sculpture was 'I achieve reality through the use of metaphor': 'My sculptures are plastic metaphors', for like his paintings, it 'shouldn't be a *trompe l'oeil* but a *trompe l'esprit*. I'm out to fool the mind rather than the eye. And that goes for sculpture too. I make you see reality because I used the metaphor.'[5]

This sudden, surprising getting of the point in humorous material is most obviously enjoyable when it gives rise to the seemingly involuntary and 'helpless' autonomic effect of laughter. My analysis above has already suggested some of the characteristics that make for this effect. Our bringing together of two apparently incongruous conceptual frameworks gives us a pleasure in understanding a relationship (in the Larson case, between the shooting of horses after the Grand National and human hospitals). I am inclined to agree with Arthur Koestler that jokes often bring about a 'clash of two mutually incompatible codes, or associative contexts, which explodes the tension' of their narrative for us.[6] The most obvious and the most frequent example of this, from inspiring to dreadful, is the pun, but Koestler gives us an example from Chamfort: a husband finds his wife in bed with a bishop, and immediately walks across the bedroom to the window, and blesses the people in the street outside it. The stereotypical roles and social codes of 'husband' and 'bishop' are made to cross; but it is the witty aplomb of the husband, in provoking that crossover (saying, 'If you do my job, I'll do yours'), which is the cause of our pleasure.

In analysing a joke's effects then, we are looking at a mental process which is very like that involved in understanding metaphor. We are (1) experiencing a tension between competing 'codes', 'frameworks', or 'matrices' (terminology varies a good deal here); (2) focusing on the 'link' or focal concept, the word, or situation which is 'bisociated' (to use Koestler's term) with both 'mental planes' or frameworks (typically to be found in the 'punchline'); (3) by doing so, we release the emotive tensions or charge of the joke. For example:

> 'What is Sacramento?'
> 'The stuffing in a catholic olive.'

The competing codes here are those used to denote or describe (1) towns, (2) cocktail food, and (3) the sacrament of communion (so there are already more than Koestler's two, but food, sacred and profane, are the two most basic). One turns into the other (one is tempted to say 'transubstantiates') when we focus on the bisociating word, 'catholic', which doesn't immediately or obviously fit into its context, and makes the olive Eucharistic, by picking up anaphorically on 'Sacramento' in a way that makes it, too, then metamorphose (as the words of the joke then come into line with the conceptual schema demanded by 'catholic') from a term for a town, to the word for 'sacrament under the appearance (accidents) of pimento'. It becomes an ad hoc 'portmanteau-word'. 'Sacramento' is thus described as the 'appropriate' stuffing for a (metaphorized and transubstantiated) 'catholic' olive (an assertion which is in itself a bit bizarre and even stupid).[7] Once this bit of 'making strange' has taken place in our heads, we may also have the thought that even the approved forms of the Eucharist can be seen as more or less peculiar, because some of the emotional tension released here comes from a long history of religious conflict and taboo about the 'kinds' in which the Christian communion can be made.

Even this very clumsy analysis shows that for jokes, as for metaphors, the two-frameworks-joined-by-an-ambiguous-concept model would need elaboration to be strictly convincing. As in metaphors, both 'sides' relate to one another in very complicated and interactive ways, and there tend to be awkward third terms about.[8] But however such complexities may work out, it is obviously some kind of wordplay, some punning ambiguity (between sacrament–Sacramento–pimento) which works the rhetorical mechanism of the joke.

The key to success for such jokes seems to be a play on some kind of conceptual and emotional tension in the audience concerning the situation. (So Chamfort's 'Bishop' joke mixes religion and sex, the horse hospital turns on our fear of dying, and the Christmas card saying 'We wanted a girl' violates a pious state of mind by breaking a taboo, against speaking disrespectfully of the Christian Holy Family.) Our narrative expectations for what is 'proper' to happen in scenes of flagrante delicto or the stories of Noah's Ark, and the Christmas Nativity, are subverted (along with our 'politically correct' sympathetic attitudes). This can arouse and release a tension in the hearer, between the socially imposed effort of sustaining 'correct' thinking and the sudden ease of wish-fulfilment within the liberated context of joke-telling.[9] The storytelling genre of the joke thus 'allows' us to express and to feel more or less repressed sadistic or 'politically incorrect' attitudes, sexual desires, and so on. And so:

> How many Jewish sons does it take to change a light bulb?
> Only one. But it's all right, I can sit in the dark.

Jokes like this, and a fortiori comedies like those of Wilde, Stoppard, Ayckbourn, are very effective cognitive traps. When we laugh at a stereotypical or prejudiced joke (about stupid Irishmen, pregnant Catholic women, Jewish sons, and so on) our pleasure shows that we have indeed *ipso facto* seen the prejudiced point, and sympathized with it enough to be amused by it. Thurber's cartoon about the Angry Woman, who says: 'Well if I called the wrong number, why did you answer the 'phone?', only works if we accept, not just its glorious (il)logic, but also to some degree the stereotype of the ignorant bullying woman, and the way she is likely to look.

The joke therefore gives us our pleasure in a rhetorical structure whose suddenness and surprise seem to involve us in a peculiarly creative act of thinking, which juxtaposes conceptual frameworks, in a double-minded, unstable equilibrium, so that conventionally accepted relationships between belief and emotion are disturbed, as for example in the plays of Oscar Wilde and Tom Stoppard. As Cecil

Graham puts it: 'The world is perfectly packed with good women. To know them is a middle class education.'[10] This emotional and conceptual instability contrasts with the integrative effects of metaphor in serious contexts. Indeed, if a 'seriously intended' metaphor allows its conceptual fields to be too incongruously related to one another, an unintended comedy creeps in, as for example when the poet Crashaw ludicrously describes the weeping eyes of St Theresa as 'portable baths, compendious oceans'. The joke, with its dependence on a liberating conceptual relativism, is essential to the tradition of comedy and satire. It can exploit ambiguities which are of a serious, even philosophically engaging kind. (Larson's cartoons very often do this, by taking anthropomorphic projection to absurd extremes, and using it to cast a critical light on human behaviour.) In this way jokes flatter our understanding, particularly as they so often encourage us to enjoy our superiority to those who are less apparently worldly wise, or liberated.

What I have said above about jokes can help us to see what is involved in the pleasures of understanding a poem, where once more we so often have the pleasure of matching apparently incongruous conceptual frameworks, to make an implicative sense which is satisfying to us (and often resolves the ambiguity and doesn't usually involve the irrationality and error of the joke). We enjoy the 'puzzle aspect' of the poem, as we work out what it means, and (temporarily perhaps) master it, so that we think we understand it, to some degree or another. In doing this we don't just work through the language of the poem—we bring into play a large amount of cultural knowledge, activate allusive structures, and so on.

For example, in Cummings's 'ponder, darling'[11] where, if we grasp the poem's genre (one of which is that of the seduction poem), we can appreciate the way in which the thoughts we might anticipate in such a poem are economically and wittily expressed.

> (ponder, darling, these busted statues
> of yon motheaten forum be aware
> notice what hath remained

> —the stone cringes
> clinging to the stone, how obsolete
> lips utter their extant smile. . . .
> remark
>
> a few deleted of texture
> or meaning monuments and dolls

The competent reader here negotiates the complex and paradoxical relations between witty expression and seductive attitudes (sensual, bodily). This can also involve a sense of the relationship between the poetic tradition and Cummings's individual talent, when we read the poem as a more or less successful literary (and seductive) performance—a variation on a known (*carpe diem*) theme.

> resist Them Greediest Paws of careful
> time all of which is extremely
> unimportant) whereas Life
>
> matters if or
>
> when the your- and my-
> idle vertical worthless
> self unite in a peculiarly
> momentary
>
> partnership (to instigate
> constructive
>   Horizontal
> business. . . . even so, let us make haste
> —consider well this ruined aqueduct
>
> lady,
> which used to lead something into somewhere)

Indeed, this apparently informal and demotic and irreverent poem is very artfully rhetorically structured. The pleasures of understanding it can include those of seeing how the overall logical syntactic structure of the poem, for example the imperatives, 'ponder', 'mark', 'resist' at the opening, are antithetical to the 'let us make haste'; as the narrator's main aim turns on a sexual proposition, which ironically contrasts the busted statues, as resisting 'Them Greediest Paws of careful | time', with his companion, whom he hopes won't resist his attempts to get *his* hands on her. All through, there is a contrast between monumental verticality and 'Horizontal [sexual] | business', and the values of serious 'study' as opposed to those of 'play'.

At a slightly more sophisticated level, we may get pleasure from the way the poem is structured around verbs which jokily metaphorize the non-verbal, and inanimate, statues and ancient world, as if they were a readable text. Hence there are a few statues '*deleted* of *text*ure'.

(These remarks are no more than some rather obvious suggestions—other readers may well make much more of the poem.)

As we read and interpret, we make other types of relationship with the poem. (I will just indicate some of these here, and discuss them more fully in later chapters.) We can get pleasure in reading Cummings through a sympathetic identification with the aims of the implied narrator of the poem—with his ironic superiority, his way with cultural knowledge (in his references to 'yon motheaten forum' and so on). There is a mock-heroic, high culture–popular culture inversion here from the start. *If* we accept this, we can take pleasure in Cummings's version of demotic speech, as when he points to 'these busted statues', which also makes a joke through a sexual pun. This will involve, for many male readers at least, an identification with some typical sexual imperatives. (At a more reflexive level, the thought might cross the reader's mind that the whole poem is as much a clever seductive strategy for us, as it is for its fictional audience. It positively demands not just a cognitive identification with the speaker's strategy, but the 'liking' and intimacy which typically arise from the telling of a joke.)[12]

This intimacy is enhanced by the fact that the poem is also a bit of a fantasy for men. This (often suppressed or disguised) fantasy level of enjoyment is one of the most discussed in literary criticism, but I will for the time being offer an uncritical, common-sense definition of fantasy, as centred on wish-fulfilment, by 'imagining something that you would like to be the case, but which actually isn't, and enjoying the thoughts and feelings that that imagining arouses'. We (if we are males) may have the pleasure here of the fantasy of succeeding in a witty propositioning, and of being about to make love, which is also presented as a pleasurable subversion of the demands of High Cultural Values, implicit in the suggestion that these tourists (like so many others) would really rather be making love in the present than contemplating the monuments of the past.[13] And a woman may more or less enjoy the fantasy of being spoken to in this way.[14] This poem plays on the notion that the official culture represses our attempts at a spontaneous and instinctive sexual enjoyment. In using a metaphorical indirection to suggest these sexual facts, the poem allows the repressed to break through, as in the joke. (What is, for example, 'peculiarly momentary' about the 'partnership' proposed? And is there a final displaced sexual pun on the ruined aqueduct which used to 'lead something into somewhere'?)

Although I shall have more to say about intimacy and fantasy later (in Chapter 6) I want to note that the distinction between reality and fantasy is a fundamental one. Children are taught as soon as possible to distinguish between the two,[15] and they are particularly taught this in relation to art—stories, movies, TV programmes, etc. (This doesn't mean that they—or adults—always succeed in making this distinction.) The reality-testing part of our understanding of fictions is built into our response to the arts right at the beginning, partly no doubt as a form of emotional self protection—('they are just acting', 'the animal didn't really die', etc.), but it continues right through, so that fantasy falls into a specifically learned realm of our pleasurable artistic experience, in interaction with truth or realism or likeness to life.

My theme so far has been that literary and visual works of art can provoke a particular type of understanding, which gives us pleasure in new-connection-making structures, which are very often, perhaps primarily, metaphorical. This is one of the consequences for our pleasure of the kind of claim made by Kant when he gives poetry the highest rank amongst the arts, because

It expands the mind; for it sets the imagination free, and offers us, from among the unlimited variety of possible forms that harmonise with a given concept, though within the concept's limits, that form which links the exhibition of the concept with a wealth of thought to which no linguistic expression is completely adequate, and so poetry rises aesthetically to ideas.[16]

Kivy glosses this as a 'quickening, mind enhancing satisfaction'.[17] This is not a new thought. Shelley similarly believes that 'Poetry . . . awakens and enlarges the mind itself by rendering it the receptacle of a thousand unapprehended combinations of thought.' It also, for him, 'lifts the veil from the hidden beauty of the world., and makes familiar objects to be as if they were not familiar'.[18] T. S. Eliot, in making the same kind of claim, adds the thought that the work of art unifies and makes coherent: 'When the poet's mind is perfectly equipped for its work, it is constantly amalgamating disparate experience; the ordinary man's experience is chaotic, irregular, fragmentary. The latter falls in love, or reads Spinoza, and these two experiences have nothing to do with each other, or with the noise of the typewriter or the smell of the cooking; in the mind of the poet these experiences are always forming new wholes.'[19]

To the Lighthouse

In Virginia Woolf's *To the Lighthouse* (1927) a number of modernist techniques are deployed to create such effects. Its associative psychology (expressed through a stream-of-consciousness technique) and its depth of literary allusion combine in a work which has 'taught its reader to take account of symbols and symbolic patterns of recurrence in the smallest of details as perhaps the most important generators of meaning in the work'.[20] The many meanings of the lighthouse as symbol,[21] or of the skull in Part II, and of the comic familial conflicts aroused by James's 'Oedipus complex' (from the perspective of a writer sceptical of Freud) are just three of many such elements.

But Woolf aimed at a particular kind of pleasurable understanding—an *'epiphanic'*, immediate, instantaneous, revelatory apprehension of something deeply significant[22]—which penetrates through our everyday discursive understandings, and strikes us in a way that they cannot match. She works towards this experience for one of her characters, Lily Briscoe, who in the third part of the novel, which takes place after the First World War, returns to the holiday house of the first part, to paint a picture, from the same position as she had occupied ten years before. She seems to be trying to complete a picture which contains 'Mrs Ramsay sitting on the step with James'.[23] But the 'revelation' she then has is wonderfully poised between the nature of the object to be depicted and the nature of art in giving it order. As she sees through the window that someone has come into the drawing room behind the steps, she fears that that may disturb the design of her canvas, and thinks that

One wanted [she thought], dipping her brush deliberately, to be on a level with ordinary experience, to feel simply that's a chair, that's a table, and yet at the same time, It's a miracle, it's an ecstasy. The problem might be solved after all. (272)

The 'problem' is a traditional one, and many paintings that Woolf would have known aim at getting us to realize the nature of something in the external world, often by a very direct sensuous appeal (which parallels the extraordinary specificity of Woolf's writing). Rilke had very similar feelings about Cézanne's apples, which for him 'cease to be edible altogether, that's how thinglike and real they become, how simply indestructible in their stubborn thereness'.[24]

As Lily paints, Virginia Woolf faces the literary problem of describing her painting in relation to the narrative movement of her novel as a whole. On 3 September 1926 she wrote in her diary about the problems of carrying on from this point, and ending her novel. She wants to describe Lily completing her painting, and the widowed Mr

Ramsay, setting foot at last on the lighthouse rock which he had apparently refused to visit in the first part of the novel:

At the moment I'm casting about for an end. The problem is how to bring Lily and Mr R. together and make a combination of interest at the end. I am feathering about with various ideas. The last chapter which I begin tomorrow is In the Boat: I had meant to end with R. climbing on to the rock. If so, what becomes of Lily and her picture? Should there be a final page about her and Carmichael looking at the picture and summing up R.'s character? In that case I lose the intensity of the moment. If this intervenes between R. and the lighthouse, there's too much chop and change, I think. Could I do it in a parenthesis? So that one had the sense of reading the two things at the same time? I shall solve it somehow, I suppose.[25]

This is a brilliantly revealing passage of reflection about one of the central techniques of modernist writing, for we do indeed have the pleasure of seeing that these two actions come together at the end of the novel, and of realizing that Lily finishing her painting and Mr Ramsay at last stepping on to the lighthouse island both have a huge, and similar, symbolic resonance for the story as a whole. Because they occur at the same time, they achieve a typically modernist effect of simultaneity, in a kind of transcendence (so far as that is possible in language) of ordinary linear narrative. They also achieve a marvellous tension and ambiguity, because they are contrasting metaphors for each other, of completing an action, making an end; and they both memorialize the dead Mrs Ramsay in the act, so that the whole episode is suffused with an elegiac emotion.[26]

The conclusion of the novel is double: getting 'to the lighthouse' and completing the painting. Both are achieved by a very simple gesture. The first action is simply a step onto the island: 'as he sprang, lightly like a young man, holding his parcel, onto the rock' (280). Even this description manages a doubleness, as the old man Mr Ramsay is momentarily young, cast back to an earlier period, and it is that earlier period (of the novel) which he is now redeeming by taking James to the island. The second of these is the placing of a simple mark on canvas, and what is more an abstract one: what it 'is' or represents,

Mrs Ramsay, or the lighthouse, or maybe merely an abstract mark—which makes a formal reconciliation giving the canvas a 'significant form'[27]—it is up to the interpreter to decide.

Both of these actions can be seen as gestures of memory and reconciliation,[28] acknowledgements of the dominating presence in memory of a dead person, who was alive to us too, in the first part of the book. Mrs Ramsay is painfully absent for Lily and the Ramsay family; but she has also been present in quite distinct ways to the memory of the characters and of the reader in this third part of the work. This demanded, for an artist as conscious of literary tradition as Virginia Woolf, an elegiac generic structure. By these means the book comes to an emotionally satisfying final understanding, which triumphantly shows how Virginia Woolf solved the problem she set herself at the outset, of giving a final order and intelligibility to her novel. She allows us to think that she has succeeded in this, by the reflexive parallel she encourages through the book between Lily as woman painter and herself as woman writer. They have both (pluperfectively) 'had their vision' in the larger artistic sense: without actually or literally seeing Mrs Ramsay at all. The famous and highly wrought conclusion of the novel is and is like the completion of the painting, as the one element that it has needed all along is put into place, and a reconciling balance between Lily Briscoe and Mrs Ramsay is finally achieved.

She looked at the steps; they were empty; she looked at her canvas; it was blurred. With a sudden intensity, as if she saw it clear for a second, she drew a line there, in the centre. It was done; it was finished. Yes, she thought, laying down her brush in extreme fatigue, I have had my vision. (281)

Understanding

My hypothesis, which will be further tested and elaborated in all that follows, is that we all have a drive to explore and understand, whose satisfaction gives us much of the pleasure we get from Cummings's poem and Woolf's novel. This is particularly well satisfied by narrative, which arouses our interests and motivations and desires. It is made enjoyable in art by what I am going to call a 'provocative rhetoric', which contributes to an 'ordering effect'.[29] Many of the typical dynamic temporal processes involved in the narrative sequencing of artworks bring together these elements (most of which will concern us in more detail in later chapters): for example, erotic models of tension and release, threatened overload leading to clarity, the complexity and tension of a situation finally resolving in lyric expansion (as we shall see in the final Trio of *Der Rosenkavalier*), a calm complex ordering (as in the *Art of Fugue*), a perpetual variation based on an underlying repeated order (as in the Diabelli Variations, and much jazz), a subjective expansion into a 'timeless' state (as in some abstract painting), and most obviously and popularly, in narratives where agents and their actions lead us through suspense (or through absurd setbacks) to 'success', in the thriller, and the comic story.

At this stage I will treat these distinctions in a very simple way. I hope to make them far better exemplified (and indeed more problematic) in what follows. What lies behind our pleasure here is a *drive to understanding*, along with (what is not quite the same thing) curiosity, an intellectual hunger to explore. This 'urge to find meaning'— following mental schemata involving purpose, ends, and the causality that narrative tracks—can cause pleasure or frustration, and is a built-in feature of brain function.[30]

And so for example, we can sketch a plausible process of our understanding of the Larson dog cartoon, or a film, or a fiction. We begin with a 'first visual analysis of textures, lines and figure' (in the Larson case, 'what have we here? A dog on a chair?'). Then we do some memory-searching, calling up of networks of associations ('what do I know about dogs and about TV interviews?'). This leads to the construction of a narrative scene or universe within an imagined world ('what is going on here?'), and this will arouse us, as we readjust our 'affect appraisal' and labelling of the situation ('something odd is going on here'—'oh I see the joke, the dog can read, how surprising and absurd'). Such reactions can be more or less pleasurable, as we smile, laugh, commiserate with others, and have feelings about human activities of various kinds such as TV interviewing.

This urge to find meaning is the end result of a great deal of adaptive evolution, and brings with it an (often indirect) desire for the acquisition of knowledge; that is, the truth. This is a vital part of our experience of works of art.[31] Our understanding of them involves the evolutionary need for truth, both within and outside the work. It's an achievement of a particular and rather odd kind to detach oneself from the beliefs we rely on, as Wittgenstein pointed out.[32] *The default is to want to know. Not knowing is frustrating.* Hence the peculiar satisfaction given to us by truthful works of art, which for many would include, for example, the moral commentaries of George Eliot and the attention to objects in the paintings of Chardin.[33]

The pleasurable component in the arts cannot, however, centre on the satisfaction of our curiosity and the extension of our knowledge alone (or on its subsequent usefulness to us), for stories and works of art are frequently repeated, and still engage us with no significant loss of affect—Beethoven's Ninth is nearly always exhilarating. Particularly in the case of art, we remain gripped by the familiar, though it has to be realized that our attention is more often secured by our learning about *new aspects* of works of art. The greatest works allow most generously for such variations. (Think of the many ways in which 'Embraceable You' can be sung by different singers, and improvised on by different jazz musicans, let alone the different ways of 'doing' *King Lear*, and the inexhaustibility of Rembrandt's self-portraits as a sequence.)

Artworks, whose unchanged identity over time we make great efforts to preserve, can therefore offer the security of the familiar (even at the same time as they continue to provoke deep conceptual challenges, as in tragedy). There are many Western films, and those (like Clint Eastwood's *Unforgiven*) which deviate from the secure formula are easy to spot. This conventional familiarity no doubt usually helps to balance out the intense arousal and suspense caused by violence in this genre, with the sense that one is nevertheless in the relatively predictable and morally ordered world of the 'Western'. (Auden said much the same about the 'guilty vicarage' of the 1930s detective story.)

I am trying to get here at the pleasurable *within the mental process* of our acquiring certain kinds of meaningful understanding from works of art. However, even if it is true (as Aristotle and others believed) that 'all men by nature desire to know', that doesn't make *all* learning a form of entertainment, or inherently pleasurable.[34] We often acquire very painful knowledge through the arts, and I will look at the paradox of our enjoying the painful in the next chapter. Of course we don't *always* enjoy making inferences; for example, when we conclude from the mess in our house that we have been burgled. For pleasure, the pay-off of inference has to serve our *interests*. That is why a man may enjoy the Cummings poem more than a woman. Our cognitions may be motivated by preferences for such goods as 'food, security, erotic gratification, and social acceptance'.[35]

When we fill in the gaps in narrative, or work out metaphors, we make inferences in the generally 'safe' context of art. A detective story baffles and frightens as it goes along, but the genre promises resolution: in many novels we will be allowed to know whether a relationship 'worked out' or not. Elizabeth finally comes to an understanding with Darcy—as do the heroines of her many Mills and Boon successors.[36] The enjoyable work of art tends to make our experience more coherent rather than more disordered, baffling, confusing, obscure, perplexing, puzzling (though there are plenty of deliberately frustrating postmodernist exceptions to this). And so the work of art is at least the 'site' of enjoyable inference-making, and this may be one of its defining (or at least typical) characteristics.[37] The 'bisociative' mechanism of jokes, the metaphoric modelling in Cummings, and the parallel between the two actions with which *To the Lighthouse* concludes are all support for this hypothesis.

Within this context, narrative structure has a very special status for our understanding. The joke, for example, usually has a 'surface pattern' or narrative sequence, which runs through 'situation'

(Noah), 'problem' (the four gnus), 'response' (curious man on bank), and 'result/evaluation' (there are good gnus and bad gnus). There is a typical problem–solution pattern within the narrative here.[38] There are all sorts of possible refinements for this kind of account (given the experimentation and sophistication of all kinds of literature through history) but some such model will underlie all narrative from the point of view of our understanding and satisfaction. These inference-licensing narrative schemata (and their associated affects) are *basic mental models*.[39] What we find in particular cases will depend on all sorts of differences in knowledge and cultural background, but it is not so much the diverse content of literary works I am concerned with here, as their constant pleasure-giving structures.

I am going to argue that nearly all our pleasurable responses with respect to *all* the arts can be seen as derived from or deviating from an essentially narrative comprehension. I therefore believe that the following cannot possibly be true: 'When a ballet is not narrative or representational in any way, we are not asked to see in the body of the dancer anything but itself.' [40] Whatever this body does, it will express and suggest some kind of rationalizing narrative to the viewer (including just saying 'look at me' or 'this is how we dance'). The need for narrative (and hence for some kind of representative realism) is the default. And so, as we shall see, where there is no easily accessible narrative, for example in abstract painting and in 'absolute' music, there is a special problem in explaining the grounds for our pleasurable emotional responses.

This 'narrative attitude' is part of our basic posture of involvement with the world, *along with its wished-for and feared outcomes*, because we have developed our mental abilities through a long evolution in order to implement our preferences. Narratives are not just conclusion-providers. They are process-oriented, and they usually bring about some kind of disequilibrium to get going. There has to be a lack, of knowledge, of power, of goods . . . which gives rise to various desires, things that we want in and from the narrative: for Cummings's narrator to continue to charm us, and for us to interpret the final aqueduct image as a satisfying reinforcement of his sexual invitation, or for Lily to complete her picture and Mr Ramsay to get to the lighthouse, or for the 'great fish' in *Jaws* to mete out a 'bloody death for those who don't matter' while 'safety for the good guys' is suspensefully assured.[41] You can't enjoy the narrative without at some level wanting the shark to gobble up human beings. That is what provides the story. And the same goes for *Moby Dick*. And so on. I agree with Grodal that this wanting cannot be reduced to Freudian notions of desire, because our preferences within narrative (such as for avoiding danger, removing an opponent, for social recognition, sexual gratification, food, shelter, and so on) are located in different and indeed divergent sociobiological needs, and so cannot intelligibly or usefully be subsumed under a single label such as a unitary, sex-driven 'desire'.[42]

Narrative fictions simulate reality because the interests they arouse in us can then be more or less satisfied or not satisfied by what happens next as the text activates wishes (and fears) about new states of affairs. Many of us find it difficult to accustom ourselves to works of art which don't have this kind of involving narrative. The rather different pleasures of being in a non-purposive state (or in a very long-term purposive state as in Proust and Wagner), or in a very repetitive and calm state of mind, or in a narrative which impedes itself by perpetual self-contradiction, rather than being pulled along within a narrative process, can seem to frustrate some of our basic needs. Examples are Stockhausen's meditative *Stimmung*, much abstract painting, much of the French New Novel and its postmodernist successors, and the minute repetitive happenings in the music of Reich. Such works seem to demand a special, detached, 'meditative' trance-like or 'transcendental' state of mind, beyond our everyday wishes and wants, which it takes a particular, mystical, contemplative, academic, or 'theoretically informed' discipline to achieve.

Mass art on the other hand is much more accessible, and its basic reliance on intelligible narrative simply shows that it is 'designed for fast pick up by relatively *untutored* audiences'.[43] (This doesn't make it bad.) It is usually comprehensible 'virtually on the first go round'. For a mass audience, puzzlement and perplexity are not so good unless they carry the longer term assurance of a familiar narrative genre (as in Agatha Christie films, or the narratives of Stephen King which involve a basic question with a basic answer). Avant-garde art can behave in a very different way; indeed it is often enough designed to problematize or frustrate mass consumption. Hence the burgeoning questions of Robbe-Grillet and Resnais's *L'Année dernière à Marienbad*, the opacity of William Gass, or the many comic contradictions in Donald Barthelme's short stories.

These considerations remind us that what makes our experience of a work of art pleasurable is the fact that, however complex our understanding of it may be, it is ordered and controlled not just by its more or less demanding underlying conceptual and narrative frameworks, but on the 'surface' by the *provocative rhetoric*, which largely orders and controls our response.[44] This is most obvious in the ways that narratives can engage interest and create expectations, which they may or may not satisfy, and so on. Explanations of jokes are far from funny. They are far too slow for one thing, though you may still sense the funniness behind the explanation, and be mildly amused. It's like the difference, as Cohen points out, between knowing or believing that a work is good (e.g. 'important') and actually liking it (i.e. the experience of it).[45] It is the rhetorical mechanism of the joke (its achievement of an intellectually surprising timing) which accounts for our pleasure in it, as we locate the part of the picture that triggers the comic paradox. We laugh at jokes, and enjoy works of art, *as we get their point*: as they come together (but not only at this final point, of course). Our enjoyment stems from the way in which their rhetorical structures, the timing of the release of the point, retains our interest and controls our understanding. That is what stand-up comics, as well as poets, are very good at doing.

One of the distinctions I am concerned with in what follows is that between the *communicability* of thoughts which give pleasure ('that's not a goat's tummy, it's a—literal—bread basket') and the *provoking* of that pleasure by the way in which the thought is brought to us (the presence of the literal basket was slyly disguised by Picasso). This is an important distinction: the work of art can communicate X so that you understand it (as we may do a proposition) but how does it communicate X in such a way as to get us to feel Y-ish *about* X? (Satisfied, in a deep way, that *To the Lighthouse* ends with Mr Ramsay on the island.) Obviously something more than the bare proposition is necessary—it will be organized rhetorically, as in the 'seductive' ordering as well as intention of Cummings's poem, from bust to aqueduct.

For there is a big difference (as ordinary conversationalists, let alone poets know) between our saying something or writing a poem to communicate our feelings (to let others know that we feel something) and our provoking our audience's emotional response in the desired way. I may be showing you pictures which I tell you I enjoy, and so be showing you some of the *sources or causes* of pleasure in me. But I need not, at the same time (even by explaining or pointing out certain features), be *ipso facto* provoking a similar pleasure in my audience at those features. The picture itself has to get to work on you. Its provocative rhetoric has to work for you too.[46]

This provocative quality in art leads us on to the theme of my next chapter—that of feeling—but I wish to emphasize here the way in which the rhetorical presentation of narrative can get us to enjoy certain types of conceptual-ordering effects. In *To the Lighthouse*, for example, how does the paragraphing of the 'Time Passes' section, and its bracketed sentences (within one of which Mrs Ramsay dies), contribute to such effects? We like to satisfy our curiosity, to come to recognize something (someone we want to see, like Rembrandt, or realizing the nature of the thing as it is, as Lily Briscoe thought she did); to get things clear, and to feel superior by our understanding (typically so, in jokes and comedy). In particular we like putting an end to the tension or frustration of *not* having understood something (as when we conquer elementary mathematics or irregular verbs, come to the punchline, arrive at what might be a workable concept of pleasure, or get to the end of a detective story). Many of our pleasures indeed come from our conquering, or getting relief from, uncomfortable beliefs and bad feelings.

We like to feel that we are (somehow) in control of an experience by understanding it. I am inclined to say this for Foucauldian reasons, in so far as the ability to make and to comprehend a textual description is so often the expression of authority, mastery, and control in the real world. The pleasurable effects of understanding thus very often come from our belief (with its associated feelings) that we have mastered a problem, or overcome a difficulty. We can also of course get satisfaction from thoughts about the likely utility of our new knowledge. (Once I seem to have mastered and come to enjoy some of the conventions for *Così fan tutte*, I can go on to *Don Giovanni*.) We can also enjoy the spreading of understanding, by entering an interpretative community, and becoming 'part of the conversation'. On the other hand, if evaluative demands on our response intrude—write a report, write an essay—the effort and external control become pretty evident. (Often enough, interpretative demands overcome the 'ludic' experience; hence Oscar Wilde's joke to his examiners when translating one of the Gospels about not wanting to stop because he wanted to know how the story came out.)

The relationship of feeling to this type of understanding is often fairly obvious in the Hollywood movie, as Bordwell points out:

When we bet on a hypothesis, especially under the pressure of time, confirmation can carry an emotional kick; the organism enjoys creating unity. When the narrative delays satisfying an expectation, the withholding of knowledge can arouse keener interest. When a hypothesis is disconfirmed, the setback can spur the viewer to new bursts of activity. The mixture of anticipation, fulfilment and blocked or retarded or twisted consequences can exercise great emotional power.[47]

Though we can be disappointed. Maybe *Citizen Kane* is like a Borges labyrinth without a centre; and it is not too difficult to raise baffling and frustrating doubts about the conclusion of James's *The Turn of the Screw* or *The Figure in the Carpet*. The substitutive pleasures of interpretation may at this point try to come in to save us. It is indeed the desperate recourse to even the most bizarre of interpretations by critics, which tends to confirm my thought that some people cannot be satisfied until they feel they are in control. Hence the general alarm caused by Derrida, and others, who suggested *inter alia* that the metaphorical nature of language ensures that we never really master anything. But this can only seem a plausible thesis so long as you don't consider too many cases in which a pro tem controlling understanding does indeed seem to be arrived at, for example in most of science, or when Chardin paints a pot, or Furtwängler conducts Beethoven, or T. S. Eliot gets (on Christian assumptions) to the climactic end of the *Four Quartets*, which so cunningly orchestrates the symbols, themes, and rhythms of the earlier parts of the poem.

Indeed our arrival at a final point of illumination, or understanding, or simple conviction, is one of the greatest pleasures offered by art. (What would we give to understand fully the allegory behind Botticelli's *Primavera*?) The point of 'vision' in *To the Lighthouse* is expanded in many literary works, obviously enough in the philosophical conclusion of Wordsworth's *Prelude*, or the last volume of *A la recherche du temps perdu*, but the same effects may derive from any book which pleasurably enlarges the mental horizons of its readers, as Jonathan Rose so eloquently shows in his account of the responses of British working-class readers to literature of all kinds, especially Ruskin.[48] These culminating expansions of our understanding are also to be found in many musical works, as in Isolde's *Liebestod*, or the astounding conclusion of Bruckner's Eighth Symphony, where

The coda begins calmly in C minor, and rises steadily to its famous culmination: with the full orchestra in brilliant fortissimo, the main themes of the four movements combine in a sonic panoply. First comes the Scherzo theme in the horns, along with the trumpet fanfares that punctuated the opening pages of the Finale, and as the music triumphantly reaches the tonic major in m 697, two horns recall the sighing motive from the Adagio theme and trombones add a variant of the main theme of the first movement that is recast so as to ring a C major triad. It is, quite literally, a moment of stunning glory.[49]

(I will have a good deal more to say that is rather less technical about the ways in which we understand music of this kind in the following chapters.)

It will be obvious to the reader from the examples I have cited that any attempt to separate cognitive from affective responses to art is doomed (for example, the feeling of 'sudden superiority' which Hobbes said was caused by the joke). The distinction between them may help to clarify the nature of the different elements involved, but it cannot do justice to the complex phenomenology of our experience. So we now need to look more closely at emotion and its interdependence with understanding.

Notes

1. Walter Gratzer (ed.), *Eurekas and Euphorias: The Oxford Book of Scientific Anecdotes* (Oxford: OUP, 2002), 70–1.
2. Fred Metcalf (ed.), *The Penguin Dictionary of Jokes* (Harmondsworth: Penguin, 1994), 22.
3. Cf. Elizabeth Cowling and John Golding (eds.), *Picasso: Sculptor/Painter*, exh. cat. (London: Tate Gallery, 1994), no. 118, illus. p. 151.
4. This visual punning is common in advertising: cf. the study by Charles Forceville, *Pictorial Metaphor in Advertising* (London: Routledge, 1996).
5. Picasso, cited in Cowling and Golding (eds.), *Picasso*, 145 (from Gilot and Lake, *Life with Picasso* (Harmondsworth: Penguin, 1966)). The *Observer* newspaper ('Who's acting the giddy goat?' Sunday 13 Feb. 1994) had the clever idea of asking Rosalind Renshaw, a judge for the British Goat Society, to look back from Picasso to reality in assessing *The Goat*. She saw it as 'not a wonderful specimen' but 'anatomically it seems to be absolutely spot on. Its feet are correct. Its tail is correct'. (But the eyes were too round.) And 'The udder is simply dreadful and I would guess this is a Mediterranean, as opposed to an English, goat. In the Mediterranean they tend to milk the goats from behind. In England we're far too proper—you could catch all sorts of other things as well as the milk—and so one milks from the side.' It is old and skinny and the udder is beginning to go. Indeed 'the udder is a definite no no. A divided udder like that is something that breed-

ers like myself have been trying to breed out for along time—with some success. This poor animal would go right to the bottom of the line.' She 'looks a little bit arrogant' but then 'goats are very self possessed creatures'.

6. Arthur Koestler, *The Act of Creation* (London: Hutchinson, 1964), 35. But this incongruity view of jokes, which I develop here, does not apply to all cases of laughter, as Noël Carroll argues in his *Beyond Aesthetics* (Cambridge: CUP, 2001), 325.

7. The joke comes from Ted Cohen in Eva Shafer (ed.), *Pleasure, Preference and Value* (Cambridge: CUP, 1983), 125. The analysis is mine. Cf. also Ted Cohen's *Jokes* (Chicago: Chicago UP, 1999), 35, where he scrupulously acknowledges the authorship of this joke by Richard Bernstein. Carroll insists in his analysis of jokes (*Beyond Aesthetics*, 326) that jokes license fantasy and error: 'in fact it is the mark of a joke in the interpretation, that it will generally require the attribution of an error.' I am indebted to Cohen's seminal article for a number of the ideas of this chapter.

8. Cf. Eva Feder Kittay, *Metaphor: Its Cognitive Force and Linguistic Structure* (Oxford: OUP, 1987), 258–99.

9. Freud's insights into jokes depend on this idea. Koestler says the joke 'deflates anger apprehension and pride', Bergson postulates 'a momentary anaesthesia of the heart' and so sees laughter as a corrective punishment inflicted by society on the unsocial individual, and McDougall sees the joke as an antidote to sympathy, 'a protective reaction shielding us from the depressive influence of the short-comings of our fellow men'. Koestler, *Act of Creation*, 51, 53. Such remarks suggest a moral bias in interpreting jokes, with which I am not concerned. They abound in the literature.

10. Wilde, *Lady Windermere's Fan*, Act III. On the other hand women of the kind of Mrs Erlynne are 'most useful. They form the basis of other people's marriages'. Again, if you laugh you are caught. For an excellent study of the subversive elements in Wilde's plays see Sos Eltis, *Revising Wilde: Society and Subversion in the Plays of Oscar Wilde* (Oxford: OUP, 1996).

11. E. E. Cummings, *Complete Poems 1904–62*, ed. George G. Firmage (New York: Liveright, 1994), 258.

12. Cf. Ted Cohen, *Jokes*, 128–9.

13. It is thus a comic extension of 'Love among the Ruins' by Browning. There are of course plenty of fantasized love poems written from the point of view of a woman, though not so many, perhaps, from the point of view of a female seducer.

14. Cf. Ita Daly's response to Marvell's 'To his Coy Mistress' as reported in Niall McMonagle (ed.), *Lifelines: Letters from Famous People about their Favourite Poem* (Dublin: Town House, 1992), i. 94: 'It is sensuous witty and wise. I share its philosophy and admire its execution'.

15. As Victor Nell notes in *Lost in a Book* (New Haven: Yale UP, 1988), 54.

16. Immanuel Kant, *Critique of Judgement*, sect. 53, tr. W. J. C. Meredith (Oxford: OUP, 1952), 192.

17. Peter Kivy, *Philosophies of the Arts* (Cambridge: CUP, 1997), 95.

18. P. B. Shelley, *Defence of Poetry*, in *Works* (1930), 116.

19. T. S. Eliot, 'The Metaphysical Poets' (1921), in his *Selected Essays* (London: Faber, 1951), 287. His *The Waste Land* and *Four Quartets* are two utterly different virtuosic demonstrations of just such possibilities.

20. Stevie Davies, *Virginia Woolf: To the Lighthouse* (London: Penguin, 1989), 87.

21. There are any number of interpretations of the symbolic meaning of the lighthouse. It 'is' the feminine creative principle; the rhythm of joy and sorrow; the individual as unique and as part of the flux of history; it is Eden and heaven; the third stroke of its light is the Holy Ghost; it is a synthesis of time and eternity; it also stands for the phallic, for male authority, patriarchal time, and so on.

22. An example of this in Woolf comes from *A Sketch of the Past*: 'The second instance was also . . . in the garden at St Ives. I was looking at the flower bed by the front door; "That is the whole" I said. I was looking at a plant with a spread of leaves; and it seemed suddenly plain that the flower itself was a part of the earth; that a ring enclosed what was the flower; and that was the real flower; part earth; part flower. It was a thought I put away as being likely to be very useful to me later.' Virginia Woolf, *Moments of Being*, ed. Jeanne Schulkind (London: Grafton Books, 1989), 80.

23. Virginia Woolf, *To the Lighthouse* (Oxford: OUP, 1992), 217. Further page references are given in the text.

24. Rainer Maria Rilke, *Letters on Cezanne*, ed. Clara Rilke (London: Jonathan Cape, 1988), 33: letter of 8 Oct. 1907.

25. Virginia Woolf, *Diaries*, vol. iii. *1925–30*, ed. Ann Olivier Bell (Harmondsworth, 1982), 106: 5 Sept. 1926. And later, on 13 Sept.: 'And this last lap, in the boat, is hard, because the material is not so rich as it was with Lily on the lawn. I am forced to be more direct and more intense. I am making some use of symbolism, I observe; and I go in dread of 'sentimentality' (ibid. 109–10).

26. At the same time as making a conclusion for the book, they sustain one of Virginia Woolf's most important philosophical themes. As Morris Beja puts it, in reading Woolf we have to grasp 'two fundamental truths: that when the true nature of reality is perceived, an intuitive union takes place between the subject and the object, that is between the person knowing and the thing being known; and that, because the nature of reality is largely a matter of subjective interpretation, objects are very complex, and nothing can be said to be simply one thing'. Morris Beja (ed.), *To the Lighthouse: A Casebook* (London: Macmillan, 1970), 220.

27. 'Heaven be praised for it, the problem of space remained, she thought, taking up her brush again. It glared at her. The whole mass of the picture was poised on

that weight. Beautiful and bright it should be on the surface, feathery and evanescent, one colour melting into another like the colours on a butterfly's wing; but beneath the fabric must be clamped together with bolts of iron' (Woolf, *To the Lighthouse*, 231). On 'significant form' see below, Ch. 5.

28. And one can add to this the allusive effect of Lily's perception of Mr Carmichael's gesture as he stands by her: 'He stood there as if he were spreading his hands over all the weakness and suffering of mankind; she thought he was surveying, tolerantly and compassionately, their final destiny. Now he has crowned the occasion, she thought, when his hand slowly fell, as if she had seen him let fall from his great height a wreath of violets and asphodels which, fluttering slowly, lay at length upon the earth' (Woolf, *To the Lighthouse*, 281).

29. By a provocative rhetoric, I do not mean mere rhetorical cliché without thought (the wind of newspapers and politicians) or even an evident self-regarding virtuosity. The pianist whose speedy scales and thumping double octaves do nothing but distort the real structure and spirit of the work he or she is playing, the actor who is honkingly actorish, and the painter who is all surface and no depth are all too well known, and they just have the wrong *kind* of rhetoric, even if they can be useful reminders to us of what technique can do.

30. The innateness of this 'drive to understanding' is perhaps most obvious in the case of the dream: cf. J. Allan Hobson's work on dreams, e.g. his *The Dreaming Brain* (New York: Basic Books, 1988). In sleep there is a *random* activation of the brain, but the dream process tries to make sense of it. The synthesis we are driven to make of this in our reports is seen by Hobson as a narrative activity concerned with causal relationships. What is more, 'The human mind is designed to see dream causality even when it could not possibly be present'. Hobson describes an experiment in which a number of dream reports were cut in two at a scene change, given new partners, and then mixed with a number of continuous dream reports. Readers of the reports could not tell the difference between the two kinds. They all seemed equally coherent. 'Even highly trained, practising psychoanalysts failed the dream-splice detection test if a scene change was involved.' Hobson, *Dreaming* (Oxford: OUP, 2002), 156–7. For a further account see Owen Flanagan, *Dreaming Souls* (Oxford: OUP, 2000), esp. 56–7, 127–61.

31. On the role of truth as presupposed in this book, see Bernard Williams, *Truth and Truthfulness* (Princeton: Princeton UP, 2002), esp. 232–69. Williams emphasizes the role of narration in making sense of things, ibid., 233 ff.

32. 'Make the following experiment: say "it's cold in here" and *mean* "It's warm in here". Can you do it? And what are you doing as you do it? And is there only one way of doing it?' Ludwig Wittgenstein, *Philosophical Investigations*, tr. G. E. M. Anscombe (Oxford: Blackwell, 1958), 140. So much for any real 'suspension of disbelief' in reading. What we are doing is hypothesizing.

33. When Diderot sees Chardin's *Jar of Olives* (1760) he says 'the porcelain vase is really made of porcelain' and that 'these biscuits need only be picked up and eaten' (cited in Pierre Rosenberg, *Chardin* (London: Royal Academy, 2000, 288). My concern here is not with asking whether Chardin was any more or less *correct* in his representation of jugs but with our pleasurable reaction to a painting that seems to us so 'truthful' (by the performance of an illusion) and through that to involve us in an intimacy with Chardin's 'integrity' of vision. This is not a naive response, any more than the effect here is easily achieved (cf. below, Ch. 2).

34. As Francis Sparshott, *The Theory of the Arts* (Princeton: Princeton UP, 1982) 134, points out. Understanding theories of pleasure descend from Aristotle, *Poetics*, 1448^{b}13. He believes that our enjoyment of imitation is inborn, 'though a thing itself is disagreeable to look at, we enjoy contemplating the most accurate representations of it . . . the reason for this lies in another fact: learning is a great pleasure, not only to philosophers but likewise to everyone else. . . . He enjoys looking at these representations, because in the act of studying them he is learning—identifying the object by an inference' (*Aristotle on the Art of Fiction*, tr. L. J. Potts (Cambridge: CUP, 1959), 20–1).

35. According to Torben Grodal, *Moving Pictures: A New Theory of Film Genres, Feelings and Cognition* (Oxford: OUP, 1997), 87. Everyone has their list. For Freud—money, fame, and the love of women.

36. For a very interesting study of the distribution and appeal of such popular books, including Mills and Boon, see Joseph McAleer, *Popular Reading and Publishing in Britain, 1914–1950* (Oxford: OUP, 1992), esp. 74 ff. for an account of readers' responses.

37. Berlyne in his experimental aesthetics claimed to establish that collative variables, that is the correlation and comparison of two or more sources, 'constitute the crux of the aesthetic phenomenon' (1973, as reported by Nell, *Lost in a Book*, 175 ff). The elements Berlyne saw as important for this were novelty, complexity, surprisingness, ambiguity, and puzzlement.

38. Cf. Delia Chiaro, *The Language of Jokes: Analysing Verbal Play* (London: Routledge, 1992), 50. There have been many attempts to define the basics of all narrative and its structure, e.g. Labov reports that in 'natural narratives'—the oral stories of ordinary people—there is a six-step structural pattern closely corresponding to narrative literature, from an *abstract* which briefly encapsulates the point of the story, through an *orientation*, to a recounting of the *complicating action*, a *resolution*—which offers an *evaluation* that explains why the story was worth telling—and a *coda* to leave the listener with a feeling of satisfaction and completeness. Cf. Mary Louise Pratt, *Towards a Speech Act Theory of Literary Discourse* (Bloomington, Ind.: Indiana UP, 1977), 38–51. All of these typical structures of course invite subversion by literary persons, and even for those for

whom narrative has to keep to an effective recipe, like the writers of Hollywood movies.

39. Cf. Grodal, *Moving Pictures*, 81 ff. on 'Narratives as Basic Mental Models'. Cf. also Turner's argument in *The Literary Mind* (Oxford: 1996), 140 ff. that story is basic. 'Grammar results from the projection of story structure. Sentences come from stories by way of parable' (ibid. 141) and 'sentences are small stories' (ibid. 161). Cf. also Mark Turner, *The Body in the Mind* (Chicago: Chicago UP, 1987), 18–140 and 171–2. And Roger Schank and Robert Abelson, *Scripts, Plans, Goals and Understanding* (Hillsdale NJ: Lawrence Erlbaum, 1977).

40. Karl Berger, *A Theory of Art* (Oxford: OUP, 2000), 20.

41. Wayne C. Booth, *The Company We Keep: An Ethics of Fiction* (Berkeley and Los Angeles: University of California Press, 1988), 203.

42. Cf. Grodal *Moving Pictures*, 101; and below, pp. 181–96.

43. Noel Carroll, *A Philosophy of Mass Art* (Oxford: OUP, 1998), 192.

44. In Raphael's *School of Athens*, e.g., the canonic philosophers for the Renaissance period are seen in dialogue with one another, and so arranged, in a composition that the viewer must consider, according to their relative importance. Cf. Marcia Hall (ed.), *Raphael's School of Athens* (Cambridge: CUP, 1997), 9–10.

45. Ted Cohen, *Jokes*, 121.

46. This is not to say that I can't help you to enjoy the pictures—that is, make remarks about them that may help you to appreciate them. I owe my appreciation of this vital distinction to Biljana Scott.

47. David Bordwell, *Narration in the Fiction Film* (Madison: University of Wisconsin Press, 1985), 39–40.

48. Jonathan Rose, *The Intellectual Life of the British Working Class* (New Haven and London: Yale UP, 2002).

49. Benjamin M Korstvedt, *Bruckner: Symphony No. 8* (Cambridge: UP, 2000), 47–8.

2 | *Emotions and Narrative*

Richard Strauss's opera *Der Rosenkavalier* comes to a dramatic climax in the Trio of its last act, which is one of the most extraordinary examples of the way in which music can allow the characters in an opera to express their different emotions simultaneously, while held together by the musical structure. Strauss's librettist, Hugo von Hofmannsthal, was very well aware of the importance of the handling of emotional effect at this point. Here are his comments on the end of the last act:

> The end must be very good, or it will be no good at all. It must be psychologically convincing and at the same time tender, the words must be charming and easy to sing, it must be properly split up into conversation and again into numbers, it must provide a happy ending for the young people and yet not make one too uncomfortable about the Marschallin. In short, it must be done with zest and joy[1]

The Trio turns on the Marschallin's renunciation of her affair with the young Octavian, so that he can marry a young girl, and on her general understanding of the relationship between age and experience and youth, while Octavian and Sophie both in different ways express a rather naive amazement at what is happening to them.

At the opening of the sequence, the situation has all the complexity one might expect from a comedy of cross-purposes. Sophie is coming to see that she has been released from the nightmare of the boorish Baron Ochs's courtship of her ('Mein Gott, es war nichts mehr als eine Farce'—'My God, it was just a farce'). Octavian is acutely embarrassed at the thought that his lover the Marschallin has been the witness of his attachment to Sophie (which, like that of Tristan to Isolde, he has already displayed for the audience, but not to her, in a second-act duet).[2] He stumbles away, 'Befiehlt Sie, dass ich—soll ich nicht—die Jungfer—der Vater' ('Do you wish that—should I not—the young lady—her father'). The Marschallin understands these two confused young people all too well (just as she has previously asserted her aristocratic control over Ochs's farcical predicament earlier). 'Geh Er doch schnell and tu Er, was Sein Herz Ihm sagt' ('Go and do as your heart bids you'), she tells Octavian. There is a great complexity of motivation and feeling behind this remark, which at the least is a proclamation of freedom for Octavian. But Sophie is in despair. She thinks she has been left in 'empty air' ('leere Luft'). The Marschallin has virtually to order the confused Octavian to go over and pay court to her ('Geh Er und mach Seinen Hof'). He tries to launch into some kind of a self-justifying proclamation to her: 'Ich schwör Ihr' ('I swear to you') but she cuts him off: 'Lass Ers gut sein' ('Let it be').

At this point the Marschallin expresses her immensely poignant reflections on the situation—and her point of view surely becomes dominant at this point. She takes the place, in a way, of a narrator for this episode: she knows that she saw this coming, and indeed the passage here refers back, in its words and its musical themes, with an aching nostalgia, to an earlier part of the opera, when she repeats her phrase

> Heut oder morgen oder den ubernächsten Tag.
> Hab ich mirs denn nicht vorgesagt?
> Das alles kommt halt über jede Frau.
>
> (Today or tomorrow or the day after that.
> Have I not told myself?
> It comes to every woman.)

Octavian continues to persuade Sophie of his love—and ends up poised between the two women—Sophie stands in the doorway, uncertain whether to go or to stay. She thinks that the Marschallin wishes to speak to Octavian, but it is she who has to undergo interrogation: 'So schnell hat Sie ihn gar so lieb?' ('Have you come to love him so quickly?') Her 'pale face' gives her away. The orchestral accompaniment to these extraordinary interactions is given a depth and complexity (for those who know and remember the music well in this way) by repeating and varying themes and phrases from the music we have heard earlier on, for example in warm and sweeping statements of a phrase which is used throughout the opera 'in connexion with the Marschallin's melancholy over her fading youth and the inevitable loss of Octavian which this will bring with it'.[3] The Marschallin then makes it clear that she will mediate with Sophie's father, Faninal, and at this point Octavian turns to her:

> 'Marie Theres', wie gut Sie ist.
> Marie Theres', ich weiss gar nicht—
>
> (Marie Therese, how good you are.
> Marie Therese, I just don't know . . .)

And her reply (with an 'indefinable expression', according to the stage directions) is 'Ich weiß auch nix. | Gar nix' ('I don't know anything either. Not a thing'). Octavian wants to follow her.

But she makes him stay where he is, and the dialogue I have summarized gives way to the Trio, in which all three voice their mixed feelings simultaneously. This is what the Marschallin says in the Trio:

> I vowed to myself to love him in the right way, so that I would love even his love for another! I truly didn't believe that I would have to bear it so soon! Most things in this world are unbelievable when you hear about them. But when they happen to you, you believe them, and don't know why. There stands the boy and here I stand, and with that strange girl he will be as happy as any man knows how to be.[4]

While the Marschallin is singing this, Sophie is rather confusedly expressing her awe, the holiness of the feelings she feels, and her gratitude to the Marschallin: 'I want to understand, yet not understand'

('Möcht alls verstehen und möcht auch nichts verstehen'). But by the end of her utterance she also comes to a climactic certainty that will echo Octavian's (and be repeated at the end of their subsequent duet together). She says, 'I see only you and know only this: I love you!' And he, after asking himself if he dare ask for her, also says 'I . . . see only you, feel only you, Sophie and know nothing but that I love you.'

All these thoughts and feelings, as expressed by the words of the text, and all to do with the coming to a final understanding of the situation, are emotionally reinforced or mirrored or supplemented and transformed by the expressivity of Strauss's instrumental accompaniment to them. (I realize that all these verbs point to different and potentially contradictory effects.) This is because the musical themes here make a very extensive and emotional transformation or metamorphosis of earlier music from very different contexts—and in doing so they express the emotional changes in the characters, as the Marschallin comprehends a final loss, and the lovers a new happiness.[5]

The extent to which the listener needs to be *consciously* aware of all these musical relationships, or whether he or she can just trust to a subconscious association of themes with the emotional effects associated with them from earlier on, is a matter which it is very difficult to resolve.

One of the many things we can enjoy in this Trio is the expression of emotional interrelationships which are reinforced by the movement, the binding articulation, the harmonies, and the emotional expressivity of the orchestral music which accompanies it. The differing thoughts of the characters are brought together into a musical unity, by a melody and harmony which reflects and reinforces our own understanding of the common predicament expressed by the text, and gives it a huge emotional expansion. But the notion of 'reinforcement' here is a problematic one. According to Roger Scruton, the orchestra in the pit acts 'like a chorus' 'responding to what occurs on stage' so that 'when the characters sing, they attach their feelings to the musical line, borrow the great force of sympathy with which the orchestra surrounds their action, and project their emotions into our hearts'.[6] There is an immense awareness of differences in feeling, as well as of the reconciliation of divergent human purposes (so suitable to the end of a comedy), because the three women's voices so sublimely combine in musical harmony.

For the accompaniment does two things, and the balance between the two varies from one vocal work to another. It provides its own emotional structure—the one it would have if we didn't hear the words, in an orchestral arrangement.[7] This sense of an independent musical structure is more obvious, say, in Mozart's operas and in Beethoven's *Fidelio*, where the work divides up into discrete numbers with clear generic conventions, than it is in through-composed work like this by Wagner and Richard Strauss. But there is always a trade-off between these two tendencies, and the orchestral accompaniment *also* reinforces the words as it accompanies them (like the music for a film scene).[8] Since it can't make statements in language of its own, this reinforcement, mirroring, supplementing, and transformation has an essentially emotional impact. We understand the scene 'under its aegis'. The emotions that music expresses 'alone', without words, are always in some sense vague, but the literary presence of a dramatic action seems to give those emotions *specificity* (or a referent—an object or situation on which to concentrate them). And the musical procedures involved in the accompaniment will express the *intensity* and *dynamics* of the emotions involved—aggressive, contained, calm, agitated, expansive, and so on.

And of course in opera this music doesn't *just* accompany action, as it seems to do in most films. The musical structure is firmly in charge and is variously accommodated to the much freer narrative structure of drama (which often has to give way to it, as for example in the simplification of plot in the many operas based on Shakespeare).

None of these emotions are simple.[9] We may think of our emotions as pretty pure states but most of them come to us mixed (as indeed they do to the Marschallin and Octavian, and significantly less so to the innocent Sophie). This is because a single situation can arouse a wide range of emotions: such as

disgust—'he left me because I am such an awful person'—
and anger—'why did he leave me the bastard',
and anxiety—'how will I cope now that he's gone?'
and the nostalgic loss of past happiness—'O how I miss the good times
we had.'[10]

The Marschallin expresses a far less overt (and far less aggressive) range of this situation-induced family of emotions. What we enjoy in such emotional expressions are its blends (as we can enjoy the conceptual blending of metaphor) from the pure and simple to the extremely complex.

Emotions are not just difficult to list and to categorize for critics and clinicians; they are often very difficult to name, even as they occur in ordinary experience. We have a current, culturally determined, rather limited ability to *specify* the emotions we feel. This may just be due to the non-availability of a wide range of linguistic labels for particular feelings, and may be misleading. For there are indeed plenty of different emotional states; but artists in particular go to work to give us an extraordinary variety of mixtures and combinations of them, as we have already partly seen. There is a disjunction then between the conceptual accessibility of our emotion states, and the variety and specificity of their combination in experience. This is a disjunction which contrasts with our ability to distinguish objects in the external world—and hereby lies a clue to the discrimination of emotions, for we can often only refer to the emotion we feel by pointing to its situation or external causes. 'It's the feeling you get from . . .', say, Prufrock's concluding speech, a Chopin waltz, or Cézanne's Mont St Victoire. Or an early morning run, presents at Christmas, or heavenly descanting choirboys. All this gives some plausibility to T. S. Eliot's account of the 'objective correlative', which is most important for the idea that we can rely on the poet and painter and opera composers to find ways of presenting us with objects and situations so that they can indeed provoke a (strong and precise) emotional response in us.

This reliance is often eloquently expressed by those introducing their favourite poem in the *Lifelines* anthologies: Flo McSweeney tells us that her poem by John Cooper Clarke 'captures perfectly the desolation and loneliness of a suburban housewife', and Iris Murdoch that Auden's 'Out on the Lawn' is a 'marvellously elegiac song full of magisterial images, [which] expresses both fear and hope. It also conjures up, with great tenderness and feeling, a particular occasion. This connection of vast moral vistas with individual situations is typical poetic magic'.[11]

This provocative dynamic sequencing of emotions within narrative enhances our sense of its being concerned with matters of value. Ultimately it is these emotional responses which count for our pleasure or pain; it is our emotions and moods, apart from physical pain, that contribute most to our sense of the happiness, and the sadness of our lives. In general, it is some emotionally laden interest or desire which reinforces and focuses the value which knowledge or understanding has for us. And so if we want to be able to think of Sophie and Octavian as 'happy ever after', that wish is sturdily reinforced (if only through fantasy) by their childish, rather sentimental, Mozartean duet, which comes just after the Trio we have looked at. It is the emotional state that such an understanding of their duet can put us in, that most counts for *our* pleasure.

Indeed our primary attachment to many works of art is surely an emotional one. I think of the thrilling romantic poise and expansion and bravado of Rachmaninov's Third Piano Concerto, or the aching nostalgia of the first movement of his Third Symphony, the triumph of the climactic conclusion to Sibelius's Second, the sheer fresh feeling of Monet's fields full of flowers, the pathos of his lonely child in an apartment, the rhythmical exultation of Matisse's *La Danse*, the monumental calm of some of Renoir's bathers, and the comedy of Picasso's caricature.

Indeed many of us go to the (representational) arts, and most particularly to mass art, for an intensification or a memory-reviving or a nostalgic evocation of many of the pleasures upon which we would *like* to be able to rely in our everyday lives, as any anthology of love poetry, or the Ella Fitzgerald *Song Books*, will show—think of the envy, sense of loss, and nostalgic evocation of past happiness which can be provoked by 'These Foolish Things'.

Such pleasures, for example my pleasure at the prospect of the pearly accuracy and harmonious tones of an Impressionist painting (as in Monet's versions of the dawn on the Seine, discussed below in Chapter 3), arise from a cultural situation in which pleasures outside art, of the contemplation of the beauties of the sunrise, a love of the countryside, and so on, are all already culturally 'in place' for me, just as our conventional beliefs about 'young love', at least in more innocent times, are for *Der Rosenkavalier*.[12] This is not to deny that works of art, like Impressionist paintings, can arouse in us all sorts of *new* beliefs and emotions, which can then be derived in their turn from the contemplation of natural objects—as Wilde points out, the Impressionists did a good deal to put the beauty of mists and fogs and light effects 'in place' in the culture.[13] Monet thought that the fog gave London its 'marvellous breadth' because 'the regular massive blocks become grandiose in this mysterious cloak'.[14]

This recognizes the way in which our emotions, which seem to us so natural and instinctive, are at least partly culturally constructed.[15] But I also wish to emphasize the ways in which emotions change and become accessible over time, even at a basic perceptual level— Dickens as he looked out of a stagecoach was having a very different perceptual experience from Marinetti in his sports car; hence also the difference between the photographic likenesses in the paintings of Augustus Egg and the Muybridge effects of movement in a painting by a Futurist, also influenced by photography of a different kind.

My basic idea is that the emotions are the basis for our pleasure, as they interact with the processes of our understanding of the narrative situation projected by the work. As we understand different situations, we come to have different feelings, as I have tried to show for Hofmannsthal's three women. (And the same can be said for the three women and a young man of Kieslowski's *Red, White and Blue* trilogy.[16]) It is important to realize that our feelings aren't just added on to understanding—any more than our pity for the Marschallin is, however worked on, expanded, and empowered it may be by the musical accompaniment. Our emotions arise out of the mutually reinforcing combination of our understanding of her situation with the emotional effects of the music.

Emotions are not like free-floating clouds or tickles or cramps, though our *moods* can seem to be like this to us, precisely because we often can't detect the exact situation which is causing them . . . and this situation is at its worst in depression and neurosis. Emotions have more specific objects than moods, though the distinction is a matter of degree. A mood can develop into an emotion, as a general mood of anxiety becomes a specific fear, for example.[17] Emotions and moods therefore are the symptoms, and also the causes, of a great variety of speedy (and often enjoyably successful) cognitive processing. When we manage to 'tune in' to the joy of the concluding rondo of a Mozart piano concerto, the whole thing moves and comes into focus in the light of that mood. Of course we often fail to have the right or requisite emotion in a situation:

> And still I gaze—and with how blank an eye!
> And those thin clouds, above, in flakes and bars,
> That give away their motion to the stars;
> Those stars, that glide behind them or between,
> Now sparkling, now bedimmed, but always seen:
> Yon crescent moon, as fixed as if it grew
> In its own cloudless, starless lake of blue;
> I see them all so excellently fair,
> I see, not feel, how beautiful they are![18]

Emotions are ways of paying attention, they get us to notice things, and they are inextricably bound up with our beliefs about situations. If the music expresses suspense, we will worry about the hero going into a dark alley. And in sentimental art we can feel that our emotional responses have been manipulated or played upon, or irresponsibly flattered. Just as I cannot feel the pangs of remorse or regret without also believing that I have done something wrong, I cannot feel saddened by the Marschallin's situation unless I believe that it would indeed be sad to lose a young lover, in those circumstances.[19] If my beliefs change, then so do my emotional responses: I may come to feel (as Strauss himself may have done, and others certainly do) that his Trio is no more than sublime kitsch—perhaps because I have fallen out of sympathy with that kind of expression of character through music.

This cognitivist view of emotion also helps to put into question the view that reason is led astray by emotion, and it certainly involves the claim that our emotions may be more or less reasonable. Of course when we are angry we often go too far (as Goneril and Regan pointed out), but we can also see what caused Lear's anger and led him astray. There is good reason to believe that our emotions, particularly when aroused in the ordered conditions produced by art as analysed in Chapter I, can very usefully and adaptively guide and focus the cognitive, understanding component of our responses, and vice versa. When we pity Lear and are horrified by Goneril and Regan, it is because we have very complex attitudes towards them.

In doing this we can also adjust our cognitive frameworks; that is, the depth, or width of our focus. I can be totally absorbed in the emotional dynamic of *this* ball-by-ball conflict between batsman and bowler. Or I can focus on the larger context of the 'statistics' of this state of the match (it's 14 for 1, England are following on with 110 versus 360, Atherton is facing Alan Donald) and so I can consider the statistical likelihood of the success of either. Both these frameworks can be brought to bear on this (more or less specific) situation—and they carry different implications and emotions. The most intense (will he beat the bat again?) being at the most specific level, I think. (I try to get a larger and less intense perspective through the statistics: I reassure myself, by thinking that Atherton who has eight runs so far, also has an average of thirty-nine. He may do well.) Understanding and emotion are interdependent, in ways which have recently intrigued many cognitive scientists, philosophers, psychologists, and therapists, and it is the *interaction* between them which is the key to so many of our enjoyments in the arts.[20]

Empathy and Situation

The reader might well feel that in our discussion of emotions there is far too much about understanding and far too little about the idea, which is surely attached to the understanding of situations, that many of our pleasurable emotions must depend upon an empathic identification with others. For it is often supposed that we empathize or sympathize with the persons within works of art, and that this identification or feeling along with them is the chief source of our emotions. For many critics, however, sympathy is not so much a source of pleasure as a moral demand well met by literature: as George Eliot put it in her 'The Natural History of German Life', 'The greatest belief we owe to the artist, whether painter, poet or novelist is the extension of our sympathies' because 'Art is the nearest thing to life, it is a mode of amplifying experience and extending our contact with our fellow men beyond the bounds of our personal lot'.[21] These are entirely admirable Kantian considerations—which may lead to an emotionally informed respect for the autonomy of others, and an important understanding of its limitations. But this is really a reflective moral use of the work of art, which except in the obvious cases of moral admiration (for example as aroused by the heroic) often need not be particularly involved in our enjoyment of them. This is, I believe, far more concerned with our pleasure at an extension of our understanding, which may not be moral at all in any general sense, since it requires a consonance (or not) with our own dominant interests. This is not to say that we cannot learn plenty of new ones from works of art. And so I am inclined to argue that our pleasurable emotional responses are in general far more likely to be tied to the processes of understanding of a situation, than in our empathetic response to a person, as in our examples above.

This distinction is a necessary one, and is not just a matter of moral preference, because the emotions experienced by the protagonist, and those provoked in the observer, are very often not the same emotions. In cases of suspense, for example, we can care for the prospects of protagonists who are not even aware of the danger they are in, and the asymmetry here is obvious. The girl is enjoying her swim, and it is her insouciance which frightens us, because we know there is a shark about. (Or Sophie makes her protestations of love, and we are moved to think, 'How precarious and innocent she is'.) The audience's response here is rooted in our entertaining thoughts about characters, whereas the characters' own responses originate in their beliefs (including those which they don't express, but are attributed to them by an audience to rationalize the way they behave). Our emotional appraisal of situations is usually other-regarding and altruistic, so there is actually something a bit odd about those critics who insist on our identification with characters (though of course, depending on circumstances, there are plenty of fictitious persons with whom we can more or less easily identify—that is why professors can find the reading of the comic campus novel mildly embarrassing). On the other hand, we frequently respond emotionally to situations where there is no obvious connection to our own interests. This again suggests that we primarily assimilate the pragmatic *logic of actions in situations*, and have emotional responses to that, and only secondarily identify with protagonists. To do that, we do not need to empathize, but to have a sense of why the protagonist's response is appropriate, or not, to the situation.[22] (This reinforces my argument in Chapter 1 that our narrative understanding is primary.) Along with this, all sorts of sympathy or antipathy (most often mixed with moral judgement, including admiration) can link us to the character.

For example, Norman Bates in Hitchcock's *Psycho* is trying to dispose of the dead body of the woman he has murdered. Morally, we should hope that he would fail, so that he can be the more easily detected and punished for murder. But he is trying to dispose of a corpse, and of the car into which he has put it, and when the car seems to be failing to sink away with the body into a muddy pond, the audience feels anxiety and is relieved when it starts sinking again. We have cognitively identified with Bates's aims, and we are sympathetic to his purposes (largely, I suspect, because the girl we had previously followed is now dead, Bates is now at the centre of the narrative, and we wish the thriller-narrative to continue). As Grodal points out, in his analysis of this episode:

> The sceptical might object that the reason for identifying with such persons as criminals in visual narrative is the appeal to suppressed wishes; and in some cases this might be true. But it is not valid as a general explanation: we identify with Norman . . . because the film has cued us skilfully into reconstructing a situation in which the rational act is to avoid negative consequences. It is not subconscious and irrational drives which are set free, but, on the contrary, an individual rationality which is 'set free' from the rationality of social, supra-individual norms.[23]

What we most emphatically do not do here is 'identify' with Norman Bates's psychopathology (or those of Iago, Regan, or other evil or mentally deranged characters). For as Currie and Ravenscroft have argued, our imagined desires, i.e. those projected in works of art, which we can enjoy, are by and large the ones we can think of as morally defensible.[24] They say that when we are imagining, we often resist taking on the point of view of a character in cases in which the character does not believe that his aims are morally good (conversely, I would say, this allows us to enjoy with relish the excessively violent activities of James Bond, Rambo, and Arnold Schwarzenegger and others, as they save the world from destruction by even more evil men). Our problem is that we can reconstruct the *beliefs* of villains (that is why we are so satisfied when we grasp the psychoanalytic explanation of Norman Bates's behaviour at the end of *Psycho*), but 'We cannot easily construct for ourselves imaginative replicas of his wicked desires' (Currie and Ravenscroft's example at this point is Iago, but the argument holds for both men). 'Indeed the asymmetry between belief-like and desire-like imagining is striking'.[25] And they remark further that 'we tolerate lots of cruelty and suffering in fictions . . . so long as we are not asked to take on in imagination the desires of the character who brings about and delights in that suffering'.[26] From the point of view of our enjoyment, then, we can handle repellent desires if we think of them as alien beliefs, but not if we get involved with them as desires (beliefs and the appropriate emotions together). Most of us can understand the cultural argument which might lead to female infanticide, but not make an emotional investment in it.[27] The mixed and unpleasant feelings aroused by paedophile or sadomasochistic literature or images would be another example for many. Think of the contrast between understanding Humbert Humbert in Nabokov's *Lolita* and identifying with his desires. (Most men get round this—as do both of the film adaptations, directed by Stanley Kubrick and Adrian Lyne—by imagining and forming desires towards a much older girl, in Lolita's place.) But the explicitness of Nabokov's description in the novel should make this very difficult.[28]

The emotional provocation of works of art does indeed depend, secondarily, on our empathy, sympathy, and identification, on our ability to see matters from the other person's point of view, and no doubt on our having some of the emotions that go with that. But the force of our emotional *identification* with characters will obviously depend upon the degree of *their sympathetic consonance with our own experience*. And that can count a good deal for our pleasure and displeasure. It is never wrong for us to ask ourselves, when deeply moved, not just 'Who am I most like here?', but 'Whose interests here are most close to my own?' (Sophie, Octavian, or the Marschallin?). *Of course* the jealous man watching Othello *feels* the play differently from his more secure companion, partly because his mood or emotional state will selectively guide what he notices and what strikes him. And the same will apply to the paedophile reading *Lolita*. The poignancy of the Marschallin's situation is easily missed by the much less experienced young Octavians and Sophies in the audience. Furthermore, the result of all this more or less empathic understanding can be pleasurable or painful, because we are always going to be most moved by what is consonant with or conflicts with what we actually want, as an outcome to the narrative.

The distinction between appreciating and seeing the force of a belief, and sharing the desire and emotion that the belief can drive, is therefore vital for all that follows. It is perhaps most obvious to most of us in the interrelationship between homosexual and heterosexual desire, and sadistic and non-sadistic practices. To take some obvious examples, the person looking at Mapplethorpe's 'X-Portfolio' or Madonna's *Sex* will understand to some degree the practices the photographs imply, but will or will not be turned on by them, depending on the orientation of their desires (which may of course be bisexual: I am not suggesting that the differences between such orientations are at all clear-cut). And the same goes for all such differences of desire; it applies just as much to Augustus Gloop in *Charlie and the Chocolate Factory*, the central characters of *Sex in the City*, O in *L'Histoire d'O*, Voldemort in the Harry Potter books, and Hitler and Stalin in their biographies. We are circumscribed in our emotion and desiring responses by our development, our ability to imagine ourselves into other peoples' situations, and most particularly by our moral presuppositions. (Some of which may of course be repressing our 'true' desires.) Of course all of these can be changed, and the arts may well be a very deep and involving way of changing them. They certainly seem to teach many people about sex, and often in advance of their direct experience of it. But given the relative unmalleability of human beings in these respects, Currie and Ravenscroft's distinction between our beliefs and our desires (or rather, my adaptation of it) is worth bearing in mind. My examples in this book will not appeal equally to the desires of all my readers, though I hope that they appeal to everyone's understanding.

I will have more to say about our feelings of intimacy and solidarity with works of art and their protagonists in Chapter 6, but I wish to argue that here our emotional responses primarily depend on the arousal of a third-person *observer's appraisal of a situation*. It is our understanding of the narrative process of action that most affects our emotions and is the main focus of our interest and pleasure. Our curiosity about this—our drive to understanding—can override really unpleasant emotions, as in gruesome thrillers about serial killers.

Our theory so far seems to have a fairly clear application to literary works; that is, to poems, novels, and operas, where there is cognition through language, and which are expert in making a balance or tension between involving us in the illusions of first-person sympathy and third-person appraisal. The uncertainties of this have made many readers of Joyce's *Portrait* uncomfortable. (How ironic is the narrator to be seen as being in making his portrait of Stephen Dedalus?)

But the relationship of paintings to such matters as our understanding of plot and situation, and the emotional expressiveness of persons who are not 'characters' in the way that Marschallin is, can cause problems. We may get a sense of these if we compare two images, by Vermeer and by Picasso.

When we look at Vermeer's *The Love Letter* (Pl. 1) what we see through the doorway suggests the basics of a narrative. But the picture is full of incongruities, drawing attention to its own staginess and arbitrariness. The hanging curtain, the floor brush, the music sheet, and so on are all barriers to the amazing geometry of the inner scene. We seem to be invading the privacy of these women, as the eye is drawn to the light in a more or less disturbing act of voyeurism. But what have love letters and playing the lute to do with the laundry? And how can we respond to the persons involved? Is the seated woman really anxious, and 'uncertain' as Wheelock suggests? For him, 'the mistress' expression reveals the uncertainties of love that disrupt the serenity of a seemingly ordered existence, suggested here by the crystalline light flooding into her well-appointed interior'.[29] (This is a wholly unverifiable bit of narrative construction.) But the maid smiles. What should we know about mistress–servant relationships, or indeed love relationships, and the genre of the love-letter painting, *c.* 1669–70, to understand this? The foreground–background relationship produces an emotionally disturbing effect, as we attempt to grasp the situation in relationship to the geometry of the point of view. Our interpretation of what is going on, and so the way we may feel about it, may also depend on our reaction to objects which we may see as symbolic. (For example, Wheelock says that the calm sea in the picture behind the mistress, 'represents a good omen in love'.[30]) We have a kind of choice or balance to make here, between enjoying painting as still life, and as drama.[31]

Matters become even more complicated when we look at paintings which seem to lack this kind of contextual narrative support: for example, in Picasso's *Three Dancers* (1925) (Pl. 3).

Many paintings of dancers are celebratory. They can express social harmony, the release of physical movement, the joy of concord, and the stimulus of rhythm, all to be found for example in Matisse's *La Danse*. They can also, in more overtly symbolic modes, attempt to convey to us the mystical Platonism of the Three Graces, the sexual freedoms of an Arcadian or pre-Christian era, a dance to the music of time, and so on, depending on the associative depth of the image. In suggesting sexual union, marriage, communal celebration, folk expression, they image a sophisticated ordering of the body in movement, and so nearly always involve an extraordinarily achieved balance within the space of depiction, because the dance is disciplined by mastery in the arts of the ballet or the circus. (I mean that this learnt, artistic, disposition of the body has its corresponding formal balance within the image, as for example in the horseback rider in Seurat's *La Cirque*.)

Against this historical context, Picasso's *Three Dancers* (spring 1925; Tate Gallery) is deeply shocking. Its three figures are hand in hand, like the Three Graces, and their gestures indeed echo those of the ballet, and the primitive or folk dance. They are clearly in vigorous movement, and yet their expression and effect is disturbingly sad, or even painful. They seem to be in a room, dancing before a window. The sky beyond is blue, the wallpaper patterning at their sides is reminiscent of far happier paintings from Cézanne to Matisse, their arms are flung wide, and yet the effect of all this is muted and generally dark in tone. There is little grace or elegance here—or celebration of the body—indeed there is that potentially dangerous bodily mutilation which Picasso's caricatural disassembling methods for the human figure always threaten, after the *Demoiselles* and his Cubist period. The painting is a masterpiece, at the very least in the sense that it summarizes and competes with past tradition, and expresses so much of what Picasso was trying to do in the work of this period. It has an extraordinarily satisfying and complex monumentality. It is full of intricate interrelationships and ambiguities of line, to challenge our understanding, and these are all subdued to the basically simple composition of three figures entwined, which is so familiar to us from many other representations.

But a little further interpretation can bring the viewer to see why it might be felt that this is more a dance of mourning than of celebration. The central figure, elegant though she is, looks crucified, with her arms spread wide, as she stands in front of the firm vertical of the wall dividing the windows behind her. Once this is realized, another three-figure tradition in painting may come into view. I'm not sure how metaphorical or literal this 'into view' turn of phrase is. I believe that the different genres of painting, like a linguistic sequence, have different scripts and schemas, which we learn, that these help to organize what we see, and that (another metaphor perhaps) such schemas can indeed be (mentally) superimposed one on another, as in metaphor, in an ambiguous image like this. The painting, like the literature discussed earlier, gives us pleasure as we resolve such ambiguities and see how it is metaphorical, as Picasso here casts a 'Crucifixion framework' of association round the literal 'topic' of the dance as private expression.[32]

Our emotional response to this picture is therefore likely to be mixed, even contradictory and confused. Hilton sees 'a dervish-like frenzy, in which lamentation and celebration are inseparable'.[33] What could be interpreted as an ecstatically released, Bacchante-like abandon here may actually be the convulsive, clenched, and rigidifying expression of an agonized loss. Gowing says that the left-hand figure derives from the Maenad as Bacchante seen in Greek reliefs, and then taken up by Donatello when he grouped the three Marys at the foot of the cross.[34] For the informed, this will be another echo or leitmotif effect. Picasso also had an interest in the great Grünewald Crucifixion, which may have influenced this painting. Russell uses this figure of the Maenad to point to a tension or ambiguity in the image which reinforces my own interpretation—he says that she is used, with her tambourine crooked under her right arm, to 'epitomise the agonising incongruity between death and sensual life, which is the source of grief' (though I'm not sure that I accept the psychological law so blandly stated here).

I think, if it is possible to distinguish here within a sentence what cannot really be separated in experience, that many of the representational elements of the picture will allow for either interpretation, of release and of grief, but that its other elements, such as its colour tone, push us towards the darker emotions. John Russell believes that it 'speaks for a grief that is violent, destructive and disorderly', within an Expressionist tradition, which relies upon 'distortion in the interests of a greater intensity of feeling'.[35] It is perhaps near to hysteria (though the notion of hysteria in the early modernist period has all sorts of misogynistic connotations attached to it). If my interpretation so far is convincing, we have come to an understanding of the significance of the human behaviour within the image, its likely (narrative) situation, its likely generic presuppositions and connotations, and its metaphorical relationships of similarity and difference to some of its predecessor works. (This understanding parallels that outlined as pleasurable for literature in Chapter 1.)

But there is a problem. The women in Picasso's painting are (say) expressing their sadness, as appropriate to all sorts of sad situations, of crucifixion, of mourning dances, and so on. How is the sadness of such a situation communicated to us? How does the expression of sadness in the *Three Dancers* rhetorically provoke our emotional response?

We can 'read' and respond to sadness in others, more or less successfully, through their words, facial expression, gesture, clothing, and so on. We saw this in *Der Rosenkavalier*. But we can also see that within a visual image like Picasso's, even inanimate features, which cannot be the result of any conscious act of the persons depicted (like the flowing-down robes of the woman in a *pietà*), can also (by their very 'drooping', 'flowing down', etc.) express sadness for us (given the pathetic-fallacy associations we accept for such features within any given culture).[36] The emotions within our response therefore depend, not just on the relationship we feel we have to the persons represented and their situation (which involves our understanding of the human significances of mourning and grief, as we understand the human significances of the loss of a lover in *Der Rosenkavalier*), but also on our response to other modes of expression which are not attributable to the actions of the characters (and which correspond in some ways to the accompanying music of Strauss, as a kind of pathetic fallacy). Hence the emotional effects of the colour in Picasso's painting, and its jagged edges and twisted lines, and the essentially unrealistic distortions in the representation of the scene. These are certainly (to me) painful and unpleasing, and indeed I feel quite alarmed by the ugliness and anguished twisting about in this image. But do such features make us sad or anguished, in anything like the way in which we assume the women represented to be sad? Beyond our response to the situation, there are also these (inanimate) features of the painting from which we have learnt (in our culture, on our state of interpretative knowledge) to have emotional responses (as also to the orchestral accompaniment in Strauss's Trio). Their mood spreads from the protagonists to the whole, to their inanimate accompaniment. But how? Are the metaphorical correlations here just so well engrained that we not only make the appropriate connections (between for example 'dark' colours' and 'dark' emotions) but that the schemas they activate bring us to have the appropriate feelings? The conventions and emotional effects of all such Expressionist paintings are at issue here, with what Roger Cardinal calls their 'supercharged density of gestural energy'.[37]

Fig. 2 Munch, *The Scream* (lithograph, 1895).
How do we interpret the emotion here?
Can this be a picture of 'alienation'?

Compare the distortions from reality of Munch's *The Scream*, which are similarly expressive of emotion. (Munch also produced paintings entitled *Anxiety*, *Despair*, and *Melancholy* which raise the same questions.) There is an asymmetry or gap here between the extreme, shocked, expression of the protagonist and our imagination of a situation to 'rationalize' it—for what is the situation of the screamer coming across the bridge? The lack of a specified narrative situation tends to provoke interpretations of pictures which take their cue from inanimate expressive distortions, which lead us to see them, and to feel them, as expressing a generalized alienation and stress in modern urban life, in the case of Munch. But for all we know there might be a quite different rationalizing narrative—alienation is just the one 'in place' for us. (Suppose that the protagonist's little sister has just dropped into the water and been drowned. The expression could well be the same. But we know that in modernist Expressionism, the emotions are rarely to be rationalized in this complacent manner. Only angst will do.)

It is indeed the *absence* of the indications of a narrative situation which make the Picasso and the Munch and many other paintings modern and provocative in their vagueness of suggestion, and so dependent on an emotional response which we learn to have from formal conventions, which are only to be found in art, as opposed to a more 'photographic' recording of a socially intelligible reality.

The Paradox of Our Enjoying Unhappy Emotions

The pleasures we get from the drunken chorus of fellowship in *Die Fledermaus* and from the exultation of human brotherhood in the Choral Symphony are fairly obvious ones, although they arise from interestingly different (though not, to my mind, incompatible) beliefs about human solidarity. These are two of the sorts of things that many people obviously like to feel, and there are millions of others like them to be found in the arts, which can be erotically arousing, wildly exciting in coming to climaxes, hilariously funny, and so on and so on. But there seems to be something a bit odd about our saying that we enjoy the spectacle of the suffering of the Marschallin or of Picasso's three dancers, or Munch's screamer, let alone of Antigone or King Lear, Miss Julie, and Wozzeck. And yet (in a sense to be specified) we surely do.

I do not think we need to go so far as to say that we are enjoying the sad emotions caused by such works. If I am anywhere near right in my claim that such emotions are driven by the very same cognitive considerations as those we feel in our lives outside the enjoyment of art, then of course we really do feel uncomfortable and sad when Ophelia comes to her end, and we may or may not detest Hamlet for helping to bring it about. And we can at least understand the motives of the artist who overpainted the Hampton Court version of Bruegel's *Massacre of the Innocents* in an attempt to transform the children into farmyard animals.[38] No one could look at De Kooning's *Woman I* without some pain, disgust, or discomfort at her ugliness. As Sylvester puts it, she is 'shocking', 'hostile', 'a harridan' treated 'with violence'.[39]

De Kooning saw her as a 'vociferous and ferocious' idol.[40] Richard Wollheim has a much more Freudian explanation of my disgust:

De Kooning, then, crams his pictures with infantile experiences of sucking, touching, biting, excreting, retaining, snarling, sniffing, swallowing, gurgling, stroking, wetting. . . . They remind us that, in their earliest occurrence, these experiences invariably posed a threat. Heavily charged with excitation, they threatened to overwhelm the fragile barriers of the mind that contained them, and to swamp the immature, precarious self.[41]

She may indeed give some pleasure, to misogynists. (Such considerations also apply to much of the work, considered as representation, of Francis Bacon.)

The death of Tristan is not in itself something to be too happy about, either, even if Wagner can get us in a mood to endorse the

Fig. 3 Willem de Kooning, *Woman I* (1950–2).
Ugly? Disgusting? Regressive? Misogynist?

desire of Isolde to die (and to heart-rendingly moving music in the *Liebestod*) and to feel satisfied by the process (and certainly also by the long-delayed resolution of the dominant seventh in the music). Mahler's wonderful 'Abschied' final movement for his *Das Lied von der Erde* has the Liebestod as its ancestor. This farewell to life by one about to die moved Mahler to write to Bruno Walter: 'What do you think? Is that to be endured at all? Will not people do away with themselves after hearing it?'[42] The emotional responses of listeners to this movement are remarkable and they can give us some insight into the nature of the pleasure to be got from the contemplation even of painful matters; Richard Specht in 1911 saying that 'an almost unbearable quiet sorrowfulness speaks here in lofty, relinquishing mildness, very softly, entirely without pathos and without grand gestures; the peaceful voice of one who knows'.[43] For Benjamin Britten

It has the beauty of loneliness and of pain: of strength and freedom. The beauty of disappointment and never-satisfied love. The cruel beauty of nature, and everlasting beauty of monotony.

And there is nothing morbid about it . . . a serenity literally supernatural. I cannot understand it—it passes over me like a tidal wave—and that matters not a jot either, because it goes on forever, even if it is never performed again—that final chord is printed on the atmosphere[44]

We have genuinely painful emotions and anguished thoughts in response to such works of art, and there are plenty of people who simply cannot take the fictional violence displayed in the cinema and on TV, who weep copiously when moved by the story of others' sad predicaments, and so on. When I choose between a Johann Strauss waltz and Richard Strauss's exquisitely mourning *Metamorphosen* I know that the latter work is going to be tough for me in a way that the former certainly isn't (quite apart from the thoughts of the destruction of Munich and Dresden through Allied bombing that a historically aware listener might associate with this music). Ella Fitzgerald or the *Tritsch Tratsch Polka* will generally do better in lifting my mood. Nor can I doubt that many of the cruelties described in books and enacted in films have their exact counterparts outside fiction, as in the case of Roddy Doyle's harrowing description of a battered wife in his novel *The Woman Who Walked into Doors*.

And yet, and so, there seems to be something which *compensates* us for the unpleasant emotions and sad or revolting thoughts that many works of art can make us have, so that pleasure is *also* involved. Doyles's book was extraordinarily painful to read, but one of the many compensations here was the extraordinary heroism, dignity, humour, and resource of the woman narrator (which was no doubt partly illusorily lent to her by the non-suffering author).

There may be some kind of *combination* here that will resolve the tensions within the paradox of our enjoyment of the sad in artistic contexts. At least some of the pleasure we derive from such emotionally disturbing experiences seems to arise from their giving us the compensatory pleasure of an artistically ordered understanding. 'He tames his grief, who fetters it in verse.'[45]

In discussing the pleasure to be derived from the extreme case of tragedy, Tony Nuttall opts firmly for a version of the cognitivism that I am outlining here. In discussing *King Lear*, he dismisses, as I do, the explanation that we get pleasure because we know the play is merely a representation and not the reality.[46] The most we can say for this (and it is quite a bit, though it is a bit self-congratulatory) is that we indeed contemplate the play from a position of considerable safety, which differs from that of the characters, and that our pity can sometimes be made enjoyable by being morally self-indulgent. But Nuttall concludes that tragedy pleases 'because it show[s] the worst we can imagine ennobled by form, disposed in a stately progression, with that kind of intelligible sequence which is ultimately eloquent of control'.[47] I'm not too sure about the 'ennobling' or the 'stately progressions' here, but, as I have already tried to show, certain types of artistic sequence can indeed be reassuringly 'eloquent of control' and of those other features of understanding outlined earlier. The possible illusoriness of such feelings is not at issue here; it is the compensatory pleasure they offer which concerns me. For Nuttall, in tragedy 'the irresponsible pleasure of arousal is joined with bonds of iron to the responsibilities of probable knowledge and intellectual assent'.[48] But this kind of explanation is not sufficient alone; and indeed Nuttall reports Craig Raine as reminding him that 'all emotion is pleasurable'—and so he has to admit that sheer excitation or arousal may be pleasurable for us, however dreadful the stimulus, as in the blinding of Gloucester or in a different way, the storm at the beginning of Verdi's *Otello*. This irresponsible pleasure of arousal—and what is more, sometimes, at the intrinsically unpleasant and evil infliction of pain[49]—is indeed to be found, not just by those who gawp at traffic accidents, but also in many violent films, where it is more or less supposed to be controlled by authorial moral considerations. In Tarantino's *Reservoir Dogs*, for example, the relationship between the excitements of understanding, violence in the plot, and moral reflection is far from obvious to say the least. Maybe this is one of the differences between tragedy and popular melodrama, not that this merely generic distinction can do much to dissipate the conventional and often hypocritical relationship between the horrifying excitements of many violent films and the everyday morality and legality which is supposed to 'control' them.

We are supposed to find tension unpleasurable and its reduction pleasurable. But we like the arousal within these horrifying and suspense narratives. This seems to be a different system from the tension–reduction one. We don't just go for the final tension–reduction pay-off as the cavalry arrive (because we like the foreplay as well as the orgasm). Many people who go to horror movies like being grossed out by feelings of disgust, particularly if they are shared, audibly, with the rest of the audience. We have a 'means-oriented' telic system, and also one which Apter calls 'paratelic', which likes the arousal on the way to the end. So danger brings about telic avoidance, but also paratelic arousal, and so many people like the process of mountaineering, and not just the feeling of being at the top, or the warm bath afterwards, and so on.[50] The hope of a satisfactory conclusion remains dominant, however: compare the desperate irritation to be felt at the increasing 'arousal' of a preposterous comedy which is going nowhere, where energy and mugging is unredeemed by any intellectual control.

In suspense fiction we want relaxation of tension and explanation in the long run. Who is the serial killer? How is he going to be caught? We hope he will be, before the usually more sympathetic investigator (e.g. Clarice Starling) is harmed by the horrible villain (e.g. Hannibal Lecter). But in the shorter term, we also enjoy the frightening thought that she may be. And although we can cognitively label such narratives as mere fictions from which we can turn away, the hypothetical aspect is not actually necessary for our pleasure, as the mountaineering example shows.

We have to be very careful to distinguish the pleasures of understanding as control within the work of art here, from the further attempt to control or censor that understanding by moral principle. Plenty of gangster movies indeed use pragmatic considerations to give us an 'irresponsible' pleasure arousal. I indeed hope that Ray Winston in the film *Sexy Beast* will succeed in robbing a bank, basically because the ingenious process by which he is doing it is so suspenseful and thrilling, and without killing too many people, either too obviously (i.e. too explicitly within the genre) or too brutally. But I have these hopes most particularly for a quasi-moral reason; our gangster hero is being threatened with reprisals by another even more brutal gangster, if he doesn't cooperate. This provides a certain amount of moral relief of course (he is acting under duress). But not really enough for a strict moralist.[51]

If we look at some typical responses to sad work of a much more serious kind, we come to similar conclusions. For me Douglas Dunn's poem 'Second Opinion' is extraordinary for the way in which it focuses on the kind of deeply painful realization that can come to any one of us in beginning to confront the imminent death of someone we love. The poem is near the beginning of a magnificent narrative sequence, *Elegies* (1985). The speaker goes to a hospital in

Leeds for a second opinion. 'The minutes went by like a winter' and then he is called in. Here are the central stanzas of the poem:

> They called me in. What moment worse
> Than that young doctor trying to explain?
> 'It's large and growing.' 'What is?' 'Malignancy.'
> 'Why *there*? She's an artist!'
>
> He shrugged and said, 'Nobody knows.'
> He warned me it might spread. 'Spread?'
> My body ached to suffer like her twin
> And touch the cure with lips and healing sesames.
>
> No image, no straw to support me—nothing
> To hear or see. No leaves rustling in sunlight.
> Only the mind sliding against events
> And the antiseptic whiff of destiny.

'It's large and growing' says the doctor. So the speaker, and the poem too, and so we, try to come to terms with the unjust ('she's an artist') implications of what the 'young doctor' is trying to say. In its horrified, stoical struggle for understanding ('the mind sliding against events') the poem helps us to anticipate (or indeed to remember and compare) our own responses to such a situation. The emotional pain of our response and our sympathy and admiration for the clarity of mind of the speaker, and our fear for ourselves, can only be compensated for by the kind of understanding that the form and the juxtapositions and the disciplined movement of the poem can give us. The poem helps, but the anxiety it provokes is beyond that 'professional anxiety' of the doctor, saying goodbye, and ending the poem with what might seem to be the kind of irrelevant ordinary detail that might strike one in such moments; but is in fact a poignantly tactful reminder to the reader that the 'her' being spoken about is the speaker's wife, and that his marriage may well soon come to an end:

> Showing me to the door, a scent of soap,
> Medical fingers, and his wedding ring.[52]

I asked a number of students for their response, so far as it concerned their pleasure in this poem.[53] They certainly reinforce my general thesis that our pleasure mainly comes from (a sympathetic) understanding, but it also points to other factors. When asked what they enjoyed in the poem, the respondents frequently referred to the cognitive gain in reading it, from an (Aristotelian) enjoyment of 'representation as such' to the 'beauty' of the images of the poem, to an admiration of the author's control, and so learning from the poem how to express a painful emotion (a learning that might be useful in the future). Responses of this type included the assertion, in an echo of Freytag's 'joyful safety' theory, that the poem puts one's own life in perspective: 'it's selfish but reassuring to recognize that things could be worse'. The next most favoured type of response turned on a feeling of intimacy, sympathy, or solidarity—a sense of a common humanity, even an 'uplifting sensation' and a pride in being able to share such painful emotions with another person. Other responses praised the poem for sincerely getting to 'the core of an emotion' and for being able to change the reader's emotional state, even if the poem was 'not enjoyable in the sense of positive feeling'.

Real Emotions?

The account I have given so far involves 'real emotions': they are not just 'aesthetic' or 'pseudo-' or 'make-believe' ones. I have tried to show that works of art demand the very same kinds of cognitive strategy and emotional response as we bring to real-life situations. As Currie and Ravenscroft put it: 'If imaginings were not inferentially commensurate with beliefs, we could not draw on our beliefs to fill out what the story tells us, and story tellers would have to give us all the details explicitly.'[54]

The differences between emotions as aroused in our experience of everyday ongoing life and those as aroused in our experience of art are not such as to call into question the reality (or indeed the practical or moral consequences) of our emotional responses to art. The first difference is (often enough) that in relation to the artwork our experience is so often more ordered, less confusing than usual, and the second that our feelings and attitudes as evoked or provoked by the work of art obviously enough do not demand an immediate action from us in respect of the real world, since we are not usually in a context in which such actions are *immediately* demanded.

Both these characteristics help to make our experience of emotion in artistic contexts more pleasurable, since the one also involves the pleasures of understanding, and the other some protection from feeling obliged to exert ourselves immediately, in action. Though as Sartre unobligingly pointed out, if we really believe that a fiction is sufficiently like the real world, or true to it, then we are indeed morally obliged to act accordingly in the real world.[55] My attitude to wife-battering owes a great deal to Doyle. Indeed my beliefs and feelings about what characters did in the fictional text are just as rational and full of affect as they are for the people encountered in the newspapers, on TV, or in the history books. (That these demands exist, and probably should not be too long deferred, is presumably part of the point of Tolstoy's story of the woman deeply moved by a *comédie larmoyante* within a warm theatre, while her coachman freezes to death outside it. But that too is just a story.) Indeed it is quite obvious that the arts in general, however factual or imagined, can offer enough information for the beliefs we derive from them to be founded on considerations which are of the very same kind as those we have about the people around us in our everyday life. And conversely, when we interpret Othello's character, we use arguments from, and appeal to our experience of, real-life situations. It is therefore best to think of our understanding and emotional response to fictional narratives as *mediately* affecting the character of our actions in the world. We can have a more or less sincere emotional response to fictional waifs, and the test of *that* response is our subsequent behaviour towards real ones. Or, perhaps more scrupulously, towards waifs who are sufficiently like the fictional ones in the relevant respects for our compassion or concern to be aroused—this is what Dickens relied on in creating Jo the Crossing Sweeper in *Bleak House*. The fact that so many of Dickens's readers deplore the sentimentality of Jo's death scene, and so backslide from that and fail to support Dr Barnardo's, is beside my point, which is that the considerations and emotions aroused by fiction and by real life are of essentially the same kind.

Our acknowledgement of a significant artistic order in our emotional responses to art (the balance of regret followed by reconciliation in *Der Rosenkavalier*, our appreciation of the ambiguity of the relationship of vigorous exultation to convulsive grief in the *Three Dancers*) therefore does nothing to show that these emotional responses are not of the same kind that we have in our lives outside our interaction with works of art. But this is not of course to deny that it is more or less rational for us to have certain kinds of feelings, according to the *realism* of our beliefs about the world, and so also, according to the realism and phenomenological specificity of the works of art which arouse feeling in us.[56] Our emotions can be thought of as being brought about by stories on which it is reasonable to place more or less reliance, depending on the extent to which we judge that they are *realistic*. (For example, they will tend to cohere more or less with our other, settled beliefs about the world.)

My beliefs about the mental agonies of many who fought in the Vietnam war are very largely derived from those fictional sources which I think of as reliable (e.g. those by Tim Robbins), despite my having not a shred of direct experience of that combat, and very inchoate memories of documentaries and TV news about it. What we learn from the arts can help to constitute our most relied-upon beliefs, attitudes, and feelings. The same arguments as above apply to the much-discussed philosophical problem concerning the 'paradox' of our caring about fictional characters, who 'don't exist'. The history of religions shows that human beings have an amazing capacity for sustaining beliefs and emotions about non-existent objects. The nature of the gods can only ever be indirectly 'manifested', in what are (for the non-believer) no more than fictional narrative works of art, such as the Bible, epic poems, the pictures in churches, oratorios of a certain kind, and so on. Believers in such cases may attribute their responses to contact with a divine person. But for the non-believer, the real cause of the believer's emotions is a fictional narrative, communicated to them by an artist, as backed up by the interpretative truth claims and authority expressed in the supposed non-fiction, by theologians, priests, etc. What is at issue between the believer and the non-believer is the *rationality* and no doubt the value of the consequences of the beliefs which give rise to the emotions, not their existence. The same relationship should govern our attitudes to the claims of fictions and of non-fictions. Fictions are of course more rational than theology in that they don't try to populate the *real* universe with types of entity that don't exist. Characters in fiction are only meant to be very like the human beings outside it. Gods who are anything like those described by theologians are much harder to find outside the (fictional) narratives which describe them.

The Sentimental

It is a sense of unreliability in this respect which has led many critics to attack the emotional responses which they categorize as sentimental. I. A. Richards and others say that they involve an overload of emotion, something which 'goes too far' because it relies upon an unjustifiable mimetic simplification. The emotions which so many of his contemporaries felt when confronted by brass bands, school reunions, processions, and so on were for Richards simply 'too great for the occasion', and not justified by the facts.[57] One of his more obvious examples is that of men who proclaim that their schooldays were the 'best of their lives'—when they were actually wretched.[58] My guess is that a few just lied and the rest exaggerated, but for Richards, such sentimental responses are a kind of conceptual mistake, because the emotion involved is in some way not rationally justifiable by reference to its cause (as if it were rather like the excessive emotion of a neurotic individual who fears spiders).[59]

But what are the standards of justification to be here? Of course art often simplifies and exaggerates. That is what we often like it for. The early education of Lionel Bart's *Oliver* is even less plausible than the one invented for him by Dickens. We may of course be misled by this. But is there anything wrong with the pleasures such works arouse? Richards and his successors are particularly distrustful of the popular arts in this respect. But how do those who are deeply moved by cottages covered in roses, charging elephants, little girls naively dressed up for parties, or by TV soaps, sloppy pop songs, plasticized pin-ups, and fluffy kittens, fall short? It is indeed true to say, as I have already argued, that if they were having different, more 'appropriate', and more truthful thoughts about all these subjects, they would be having different and perhaps morally better feelings.

Richards and others may also be pressing on the painful judgement that people who enjoy such things tend to be relatively ill-educated and ill-informed, and so 'we' at least would not like to be like 'them'. They are making a moral demand for a certain level of sophistication in the ways in which, they think, we ought to represent and therefore understand the world. Sentimental representations within the culture involve the selective blotting-out of disagreeable information, the desire to fantasize something naive but 'unreal' about life, and a wallowing in the emotions thus aroused for their own sakes. It is a kind of culpable ignorance.

This wallowing is an encouragement to have 'bad' emotions, which are maudlin, mushy, pathetic, or kitsch; or to have melodramatic and violent emotions, and so sensational, lurid, gruesome, and shocking; or crudely negative aggressive ones, which are crass, raw, and primitive.[60] So they can be; and moral judgements here are easy to make, and I do not dispute them. But I am concerned with the ways in which exaggerated feelings can be pleasurable. For these sorts of judgements often fail to take a closer look at the pleasures which are actually involved in 'the better kind of sentimental work', by which I mean those which do not attract an obviously adverse moral judgement. These are not so much those to be found in the kitsch of the mass market, as in the work by Dickens, Renoir, Tchaikovsky, or Puccini, and many contemporary film makers, who are working for a relatively well-educated public—and indeed for one which is conscious that it ought to be well informed—and are on the whole aware of the usual moral constraints and considerations.

Consider the blatant emotionalism of the first meeting of Rodolfo and Mimì, in Act I of *La Bohème*, or Mimì's death in Act IV (with its harking back to the themes of 'che gelida manina'), as her hands grow cold for the last time.[61] Or the romantic outburst of Rodolfo when he sees Mimì 'as if wrapped in a halo' of moonlight (according to the stage direction).

> O soave fianciulla!
> O dolce viso
> di mite confuso alba lunar,
> in te, ravviso
> il sogno ch'io vorrei sempre sognar!
> (O gentle maiden!
> O sweet visage
> bathed in a soft lunar dawn,
> in you, I recognize
> the dream I would like to dream for ever!)

Bellaigue, a contemporary critic, attempted to describe his response to this sort of thing in 1898:

in the last act, listen to how one of Rodolfo's phrases expands. Listen to the violins singing with full bows, the tenor with full heart, and the music rising, always rising up to those trembling, seemingly bewildered notes, from the instruments and the voice. However much you may try to protest, perhaps in the depths of yourself, against your too easy and too physical pleasure, your pleasure will be the stronger. Do not be ashamed, because these accents go far, further than the situations, feelings or characters. And they also come from afar: from the old, illustrious land where melody is born, where, fallen and impoverished though it may be, it still survives and does battle. Loved for itself, for itself alone, Italian melody remains the sign or memory, enfeebled but still affecting, of something great, almost sacred.[62]

Maybe he is right to look to the past: the opera is full of nostalgia (for many, a suspect emotion, but a high-ranking source of pleasure) for a mythical bohemian Paris, and for the carefree youth of the artist, no less idealized here than the mere privations of Richards's British schoolboy in his private school. This elimination of all but melodramatically satisfying disagreeables, and emphasis on a stereotypical, clichéd view of romantic love, is part of a long tradition (which extends far beyond the Paris of *La Bohème* to American musical comedies, like Lerner and Lowe's *Gigi*).

There are many such works in the canon whose combination of fantasy and strong feeling make them sentimental in this way: from the Romantic movement to the ballets of Tchaikovsky, the films written by Marcel Pagnol, the painting of the Pre-Raphaelites, and many more.

Compare Munch's *The Scream* with, for example, Millais's *The Blind Girl*. She is intended to arouse intense pity. The sky beyond her has not one rainbow but two—her sister turns and presumably exclaims with delight at the sight, and 'to rub it in, Millais has the blind girl's right hand plucking at a wild flower, a harebell, while a beautiful butterfly lodges on her right shoulder. In case there might still have been a dry eye in the house, Millais depicts the blind girl as having a concertina on her knees'. There is even a sign round her neck reminding us to 'Pity the Blind'.[63] Victorian narrative painting, such as Robert Braithwaite Martineau's *The Last Day in the Old Home* (1861) or Holman Hunt's *The Awakening Conscience* (1853) or pictures of eviction by cruel landlords, or death scenes, looks for an emotional response which is positively demanded by what we infer about a melodramatic situation, and by the conventions of emotional involvement, often an eroticized pity, for certain types of person, such as fallen women, beggars, and sick children, as in Luke Fildes's *The Doctor* (1891), or admiration for the cult of the home and for the mother as in Charles West Cope's *A Life Well Spent* (1862).

The pleasure of the sentimental responses we have to such works indeed depends upon a fantasized simplification and idealization in

Fig. 4 Millais, *The Blind Girl* (1854–6). A feel-good picture about someone feeling bad and asking for pity.

which we are released from the fatigue of too much reality-testing. Although *too much of this* may really be as bad for us as any other terrible diet, and would be particularly bad if it actually came to form our world view, there is nothing much that I can see wrong with the actual *pleasure* of such responses, at least to these middlebrow works. And so we need to distinguish carefully between different kinds or levels or intensities of sentimentality, and between the experience of it and its moral consequences for some persons rather than others. Indeed 'sophisticated' people might relax a good deal and even in some morally improving ways, by cultivating them. Our ability to have such strong emotional responses lies within a moral and cultural tradition of sentiment and sensibility, of which in an age when a sceptical understanding is dominant, we need to remain aware.[64] Does not sentimentality often manifest a moral generosity?[65]

From our point of view, a work of art which is cognitively inadequate is not *ipso facto* a poor cause of certain kinds of *pleasure*. Although our pleasurable emotional responses can indeed occur at different levels of complexity of understanding, very many works of art would be open to the accusation that they do not produce or imply a fully articulated, morally acceptable philosophy of life. (They are not all as 'mature' or serious, for example, as Dr Leavis tended to demand, and that is why he wrongly thought Dickens a mere entertainer.) But a thoroughgoing demand that the situations in literature or the arts which arouse our emotional responses should always be fully reasonable and comprehensively accurate with respect to the nature of the world (and in whose view? Plato's?) would do away with most of the arts, and certainly all of my examples so far. Think of Strauss's admission about the kitschy quality of his Trio. The arts often simplify or exaggerate, from Beethoven through Schubert to Gershwin, in favour of a strong and pleasurable emotional response, and a release from complex cognitive demands is often also the point for the consumers of many such pleasures.

The 'Standard' popular songs of the period from the 1920s to the 1950s, for example, give life to quite simple clichés, which thereby snag in the mind along with an emotional pull. These were much attacked in the 1920s and 1930s for their 'Jewish sentimentality'.[66] The cliché in such songs isn't just a verbal tic; it is more like idiom expanded into archetype.[67] 'I can't get started—with you', 'How long has this been going on?', 'Just one of those things', etc.[68] The Gershwins take commonplaces—such as 'the way you hold your knife' so that 'These foolish things remind me of you'—and aim at a basic if simplifying consolatory truth—'they can't take that away from me'. These songs can be obviously sentimental and clichéd as in 'You are the promised kiss of springtime | that makes the lonely winter seem long' (from Kern's 'All the things you are'), or ingenious and humorous as in the long list of virtues in Cole Porter's 'You're the top' (1934) which typically contrasts a witty detachment with gross sentimentality. In many excellent instances (particularly in Hart and Porter) standards fix their message by the rhyming conventions of light verse, and a kind of anti-romanticism, which puts the song in tension with its clichéd sentimental origins. Indeed, Richard Rodgers said the secret of his best songs was the clash between (his) 'sentimental melody and unsentimental lyrics' (provided by Hart)—punctuated by caustic rhymes[69] (for example, in 'Mountain Greenery', 'Thou Swell', and 'Blue Moon' which is deliberately full of cliché rhymes).

Of course many of us cannot get pleasure out of really cringe-making sentimentality—tear-jerking human-interest programmes are not for all, although they are for many, and it is difficult to deny that there would be some losses to general human benevolence if Oprah Winfrey, Esther Rantzen, et al. were to be put out of business. It is easy to feel conned and manipulated by Hollywood movies and TV soaps, as they crawl towards the climactic—'I love you son', 'I love you too dad'—exchange within their minimalist dialogue. The rhetoric here is straining to get us to have the 'right' feelings, including an excessively wound-up amount of temporary concern and sympathy. And we are right, surely, to distrust the self-conscious and self-congratulatory aspects of such responses, especially when the selective editing of the world as we know it is so crude and so obvious. Films like *Forrest Gump* and *Life is Beautiful* delight some and revolt or appal others in just this way. As Milan Kundera puts it,

Kitsch causes two tears to flow in quick succession. The first tear says: how nice to see children running on the grass!
The second tear says: How nice to be moved, together with all mankind, by children running on the grass!
It is the second tear that makes kitsch kitsch.[70]

We have conflicting moral intuitions in this area, and they can apply just as much to rabble-rousing politics as they do to sentimental philanthropy. These intuitions concern our tolerance of the kind or degree of simplification habitual to those emotions of which we morally approve.[71] But it is possible to distinguish here. We mustn't judge all sentimental works by the criteria we may bring to Little Nell or pictures of fluffy kittens or the more dreadfully religiose of Country and Western songs. *La Bohème* is not exactly of this kind—of course students don't burn manuscripts to keep warm, but they can be terribly, even excessively moved by jealousy and loss, and so can we. Some of us. And so I am inclined to say that the pleasures of many sentimental works are often enough the pleasures of a (defensible) idealization.

The interpretation of Harriet Beecher Stowe's *Uncle Tom's Cabin* has shown up some interesting dividing lines in this area. As Jane Tompkins points out, it is not so much that emotionalism and tears are self-indulgent, maudlin, and ineffective, as that we have in our obsession with the background political and economic conditions for evil failed to see the importance for the nineteenth century, and indeed for our own, of the 'change of heart'.[72] It is our strongly felt and even sentimental attitudes to others which can be the real agents for political change, driven by a moral-emotional commitment, most particularly for those in the nineteenth century who had a Christian redemptive view of the universe, but also I would say for anyone who can grasp that a change in our emotional attitude towards persecuted or disadvantaged individuals, and even a sentimental bond with them, will change our behaviour. It is an ethic connected to what may be distinctively feminine, and to some degree domestic, values. This is what the sentimental episode such as Eva's death in *Uncle Tom's Cabin*, aims at, and it powers the still popular classic sentimental melodramas such as Frank Capra's *It's a Wonderful Life* (1946) which so movingly dramatizes the emotional and caring, rather than principled, or political, or even justice-oriented, interdependence of the individual and an admittedly idealized small-town community.[73]

The pleasures of the sentimental are allied then to those of all art which idealizes, from the neoclassical to the wildly utopian, to the childish fantasy shared by adults, of which the Harry Potter books are an outstanding example.[74] They include the obviously sexy, all ideologized representations of human beings (from the Soviet heroic worker to *The Triumph of the Will*) and even those Monet paintings of Argenteuil and elsewhere which put in the boats and leave out the factories.[75] This cleaning up is obviously pleasurable for us, and it is difficult to see what is wrong with it. As we shall see later, moralists and politicians like to dictate what should or should not be included in art; but this leaves the pleasures of idealization exactly where they were. Sentimental art is obviously more coercive and controlling than more fully speculative works; the sentimental comes on strong and the idealizing tendency is to disguise or eliminate imperfection. But Richards and his allies are merely condescending in assuming that audiences for sentimental or idealized work are so easily gulled—and even if they are, it is not likely to be the nature of an artwork that is to blame. Armstrong is right to argue that idealization doesn't deserve the pejorative charge that it carries in modern usage.[76] And nor does its ally, sentiment. Both qualities really stand and fall together, so far as the demands we may want to make about accuracy and truthfulness in mimesis are concerned. And I suspect that, apart from some obvious differences—David and Ingres appeal to a rather different class of people than Greuze or Millais or Augustus Egg—

that the emotional appeal is essentially the same for both types of art.[77]

In both cases 'reality' is cleaned up for us, and an ideal presented, which may inspire, awe, or console.[78] There is an appeal to the exercise of moral sentiment, and the artwork can be redeemed from mere moral or political exhortation by the pleasure (and the inspiration) it can give us through its very process of idealization and emotional simplification.[79] Indeed there is a strong case for saying that many great works in fact depend upon a sophisticated elaboration of some quite basic, and in lesser works, obviously sentimental situations. The great artist can take a cliché and make it into great art. The plot of *Pride and Prejudice* is at one with those of the many Mills and Boon romances which Austen no doubt influenced: a young woman encounters an apparently hostile gentleman, slowly, after mistakes, appreciates his 'true nature', and falls in love with him (and his property). And marries him. This graded sequence of suspense causing setbacks, the recognition of virtue, the marriage ending of comedy is pure cliché.

Of course there is plenty of cold and repellent neoclassical Fascist art, and plenty of impossibly gooey and melodramatic sentimental art, from the dramatization of *East Lynne* to the daily soaps. But the pleasures of these seem to me not to merit the condescension they so often endure. The sentimental contemplation of acts of kindness (in TV programmes designed to raise money for charity), quite apart from its use of emotive responses as strong motivators (strong enough to get you to the telephone before you cool off), hardly fails to emphasize the moral importance of charity for its recipients, any more than the heroic postures of David's *Horatii* fail in their way to emphasize the importance of even a dissentient civic duty, of the value of taking up arms for a good cause, and so on. Nor are we 'reasonable people' usually as much deceived by the idealization involved in such appeals as Marxist critics from Barthes on have claimed. Indeed as John Armstrong points out,

Ideal images don't, as a rule, seek to pretend that they are presentations of how the world is or ought to be; the expectation is that the spectator will recognise this. In fact the very notion of an ideal is contrastive. The pernicious force of idealisation comes, precisely, when this contrastive sense is lost and the ideal is taken to be a description of how things are.[80]

It's getting into the Abbey of Theleme (or a Mediterranean yacht) in real life, without bringing about injustices, that is the problem. Utopian fictions are not to be rejected. We should be able to love the ideal, and the idealized work of art, without cynicism.

But there are further problems ahead. My basic model, of an emotional relationship aroused by our understanding of persons in situations, is not always so easy to find in some kinds of music and painting. 'Music alone' lacks the words through which persons most intelligibly express their emotions, and although it is a complexly ordered sequence, it is not (or not at all obviously) a sequence for which we may be aroused by the interests and desires of a literary narrative. Much painting is of scenes and objects whose relationship to the concerns of human beings is not always obvious, and abstract paintings needn't have any persons or everyday objects of use in them at all. Our emotional responses here, and the pleasures we get from them, therefore need an explanation which goes beyond that offered so far.

Notes

1. Hofmannsthal, cited in Alan Jefferson, *Richard Strauss: Der Rosenkavalier* (Cambridge: CUP, 1985), 8.
2. Peter Conrad points out that *Der Rosenkavalier* is a peculiar combination of *Le nozze di Figaro* and *Tristan und Isolde* (Conrad, *The Song of Love and Death* (London: Hogarth, 1989), 209–10).
3. Norman Del Mar, repr. in Jefferson, *Rosenkavalier*, 23.
4. I follow here the Decca Record Company translation.
5. The main theme of this Trio, which is introduced by the love theme from Act II, Scene i, strangely enough turns out to be based entirely on a transformation of

the waltz 'Nein, nein, I trink kein Wein' which comes from the supper music which had accompanied Ochs's attempts to seduce the disguised Octavian. It continues 'the symphonic scheme of recapitulation [here] without regard to the original significance of the material employed' (Norman Del Mar, repr. in Jefferson, *Rosenkavalier*, 75). The Finale of the opera as a whole is a symphonic coda using themes and material from the waltz material, from the Presentation of the Rose, and so on. The depth and allusion and aptness of this is reinforced by the use of leitmotif, so that at this point we also hear themes which had been associated earlier on with the Marschallin and Octavian's resolution as her lover.

6. Roger Scruton, *The Aesthetics of Music* (Oxford: OUP, 1997), 135–6.

7. There is an orchestral version of this trio recorded by Antal Dorati.

8. Cf. the standard example of the different musical accompaniments to the same film clip of a woman walking downstairs—'suspense music' here will suggest that something is going to happen, and melodramatic music will let us know that something has already happened. Cf. Noël Carroll, 'Notes on Movie Music', in his *Theorizing the Moving Image* (Cambridge: CUP, 1996), 139–45.

9. Nor is it easy to enumerate the 'basic' emotions. Michael Power and Tom Dalgleish in *Cognition and Emotion* (Hove: Psychology Press, 1997), 68, opt for anger, sadness, fear, disgust, and happiness, along with Johnson-Laird and Oatley (cf. ibid. 94). But Lazarus wants more: Anger, anxiety, fright, guilt, shame, sadness, envy, jealousy, disgust, happiness, pride, relief, hope, love, and compassion (cited ibid. 90). A summary table of the candidate lists (ibid. 103) include— as well as, mainly, those above—surprise, interest, expectancy, wonder, joy, subjection, tender emotion, anticipation, love, contempt, shame, and anxiety. Against the 'basic list' idea are Ortony, Turner, Russell: 'It is not meaningful to distinguish emotions from the appraisal component'—by which they mean an interpretation of the situation which causes them (ibid. 100). I agree, on the basis of my analysis of narrative above, that the typology of emotions will always arise from the basic appraisal scenarios in human experience, particularly 'those which underlie and shape emotional development' in any given culture (ibid. 101).

10. Ibid. 266.

11. Niall MacMonagle (ed.), *Lifelines*, i. 18, 34.

12. And the same goes just as much for our culturally induced apprehension of the elevated 'significance' of Beethoven's last quartets, as it does for our enjoyment of the tradition of the nude (though many feminists might argue that what is actually in place for men in that case shouldn't be).

13. Hence Oscar Wilde's question, through his Vivian in 'The Decay of Lying' (1891), which could well apply to all the wonderful Monet pictures of London Bridge and the Houses of Parliament, as well as it does to Whistler: 'Where, if not from the Impressionists, do we get these wonderful brown fogs that come

creeping down our streets, blurring the gas-lamps and changing the houses into monstrous shadows? To whom, if not to them and their master, do we owe the broad silver mists that brood over our river, and turn to faint forms of fading grace curved bridge and swaying barge? The extraordinary change that has taken place in the climate of London during the last ten years is entirely due to particular school or Art.' *The Complete Works of Oscar Wilde* (London and Glasgow: Collins, 1966), 986. Wilde is a bit of a post-structuralist, who sees the world as created by our cultural assumptions: he goes on: 'For what is Nature? Nature is not a great mother who has borne us. She is our creation' (ibid. 986).

14. John House, in Paul Hayes Tucker et al. (eds.), *Monet in the Twentieth Century*, exh. cat. (New Haven and London: Yale UP, 1998), 9, citing René Gimpel, *Journal d'un collectionneur* (Paris: Calmann-Levy, 1963), 88.

15. Cf. Peter Goldie, *The Emotions: A Philosophical Explanation* (Oxford: OUP, 2000), ch 4, pp. 84–122.

16. Cf. Scott Andrew, *The Three Colours Trilogy* (London: BFI, 1998).

17. Cf. Peter Goldie, *Emotions*, 17–18 and 143–7 (using the work of Musil as an example).

18. From Coleridge's *Dejection: An Ode*, in Coleridge, *The Major Works*, ed. H. T. Jackson (Oxford: OUP, 2000), 114–15.

19. The typical 'belief emotions' are fear, anger, jealousy, pride, pity, grief, indignation, remorse, regret, gratitude, etc. But are all emotions belief-dependent? Could I have a lovely feeling about a sunset without having any beliefs about it? The 'sublime' is thought to be problematic precisely because we are none too clear about the relationship of beliefs about the object, to the emotion evoked. The same obviously goes for 'neurotic' emotions, like an excessive fear of spiders.

20. It is this changing of the cognitive frameworks for emotions that underlies much successful therapy: cf. e.g. Gillian Butler and Tony Hope, *Manage Your Mind* (Oxford: OUP, 1995), 11 and *passim*, and concerning depression, 245 ff.

21. George Eliot, in *Selected Critical Writings*, ed. Rosemary Ashton (Oxford: OUP, 1992), 263.

22. Cf. Noël Carroll, *The Philosophy of Horror* (London: Routlege, 1990), 91–2 and 95.

23. Grodal, *Moving Pictures*, 95.

24. Gregory Currie and Ian Ravenscroft, *Recreative Minds* (Oxford: OUP, 2002), 33–4.

25. Ibid. 34.

26. Ibid. 35.

27. Cf ibid. 36.

28. There is also plenty of confirming evidence for the view sketched above from the study of responses to violence—e.g. as reported in Jeffery Goldstein (ed.), *Why We Watch: The Attractions of Violent Entertainment* (New York: OUP, 1998), which shows that we are amazingly willing to approve of 'righteous violence'

(cf. 207 ff.), but that we are strongly unlikely to identify with the perpetrators of it (cf. ibid. 199 ff.). Nevertheless 'the best evidence is that the audience is disturbed and disgusted by scenes of violence but continues to watch it anyway' (ibid. 215).

29. Arthur Wheelock Jr., in *Johannes Vermeer*, exh. cat. (New Haven and London: Yale UP, 1995), 182.

30. Ibid.

31. Of course the combination of human 'character' (real or mythological) and historical situation can be immensely more complicated than this. Hence the challenges to our understanding and emotional response, made by the intellectual tradition behind paintings like Raphael's Stanza della Segnatura and its *School of Athens* (cf. Marcia Allen (ed.), Raphael's *School of Athens* (Cambridge: CUP, 1997)), the theologies and Neoplatonism behind Leonardo's *Last Supper* and Botticelli's *Primavera*, and the history behind Gericault's *Raft of the Medusa*, let alone the horrors of Picasso's *Guernica* (1937). All of these are as indebted to external literary and other written materials as any poem or novel, and offer complexities for our understanding of as great a magnitude.

32. We can rationalize this emotional response (or try to decide what kind of response would be 'appropriate') if we track Picasso's likely intentions in making the picture. It was prompted by the death of a Spanish friend of Picasso's (Ramon Pichot) whose profile can be seen under the left arm of the central figure. (This is according to John Russell, *The Meaning of Modern Art* (London: Thames and Hudson, 1981), 270; but Tim Hilton says in his *Picasso* (London: Thames and Hudson, 1975), 150, that Pichot had married Germaine, the lover of Picasso's dead friend Casegamas, and that it is her profile we can see.)

33. Hilton, *Picasso*, 149.

34. Reported in Russell, *Modern Art*, 270.

35. Ibid.

36. Such effects are indeed also to be found e.g. in Rogier Van der Weyden's *Descent from the Cross* in what Kenneth Clark called the 'restless articulation' and the 'clashes and struggles' of the drapery (Clark, *Looking at Pictures* (London: John Murray, 1960), 50).

37. Roger Cardinal, *Expressionism* (London: Paladin, 1985), 97.

38. Walter S. Gibson, *Bruegel* (London: Thames and Hudson, 1997), 144.

39. David Sylvester, *About Modern Art: Critical Essays 1948–97* (London: Pimlico, 1997), 358.

40. Ibid. 368.

41. Richard Wollheim, *Painting as an Art* (London: Thames and Hudson, 1987), 348. Cf. the discussion of this kind of explanation of our response in Ch. 6, below.

42. Cited in Stephen Hefling, *Mahler: Das Lied von der Erde* (Cambridge: CUP, 2000), 56.
43. Cited ibid. 73.
44. Cited ibid. 116.
45. And 'The interest that we take in the deaths of Hamlet, Gertrude, Claudius, et al. is not sadistic, but is an interest that the plot has engendered in how certain forces, once put in motion, will work themselves out. Pleasure derives from having our interest in the outcome of such questions satisfied.' Noël Carroll, *Philosophy of Horror*, 179.
46. A. D Nuttall, *Why Does Tragedy Give Pleasure?* (Oxford: OUP, 1996), 83.
47. Ibid. 99 (cf. Aristotle's *Poetics* 1448^b 13 ff.). This theory thinks of tragedy as 'an exercise in understanding in advance the real horrors we may meet and the psychic violence they may cause', ibid. 104.
48. Ibid. 104.
49. In his study of 'The Evil Character' in his *Ethics, Evil, and Fiction* (Oxford: OUP, 1997), 61 ff., Colin McGinn considers those who desire to cause others pain, when it is not directed to any further end, such as just punishment, or to gain notoriety, or in the desire to dominate, and so on. These evil persons like causing pain, 'for its own sake' (ibid. 75). They do not simply wish to reduce other persons to their bodies—since that could be done, for example, by sexual pleasure. One of the problems that McGinn sees here is this—what is it exactly that makes the pain of others pleasurable? (Ibid. 76 ff.) He notes that De Sade approves of the exceptionally arousing property of pain, but thinks that the sadist will not choose pain simply because it is more powerful. He offers an answer by pointing out that 'pleasure only increases one's attachment to life'— whereas the sadist will try to make the sufferer give up all his or her values, to the point that 'the sufferer ceases to value his life'. Even in less severe pain 'one values one's life less when it is a life of pain'. So the infliction of pain has caused his victim to give up 'his attachment to life itself'. Indeed 'he no longer values his life above all else, but is prepared to lose it for the cessation of pain. So the inflicter of the pain has caused his victim to give up one of his deepest values; he has disrupted in a fundamental way the value-structure of the victim' (ibid. 77). And should the sadist wish to compare his own wellbeing to the situation of his victim, 'envy makes its unholy alliance with cruelty. The sadist's project can act as an antidote to deep existential envy' (ibid. 79).
50. Cf. Grodal, *Moving Pictures*, 101, who cites Apter.
51. Cf. the discussion of Hitchcock's *Psycho*, above, p. 41.
52. Douglas Dunn, *Elegies* (London: Faber and Faber, 1985), 12.
53. I make no claim at all for the representativeness or statistical significance of these responses: I merely report them as a check on some of the kinds of responses I have been analysing above, and as some indication of the different ways in which

they might be expressed by intelligent students of English (in ignorance, I should add, of my own theory).

54. Currie and Ravenscroft, *Recreative Minds*, 13. Some say that it may be a kind of 'aesthetic sadness' which is only like 'real' sadness. But how? Are we really subject to such 'shadow' emotions? More technically, can we make sense of such a two-species theory of emotion, so that we experience 'real' ones and 'aesthetic' or 'make-believe' ones?

Nor can 'aesthetic' emotions or beliefs be saved by invoking anything like the 'willing suspension of disbelief'. This just doesn't happen, as Carroll points out, for readers cannot recall having made it, and we cannot in fact will what we believe, *Philosophy of Horror*, 656. We can hypothesize and imagine, but that is different.

55. Cf. Jean-Paul Sartre, *What is Literature?*, tr. Bernard Frechtman (London and New York: Routledge, 2001), 15.

56. Kendall Walton offers an excellent example of this specifity in his thought experiment concerning a person who gets progressively more stuck in a cave while he is spelunking. It is the phenomenological richness of the description that counts here, not just the bare belief that you are trapped in a confined space; e.g. 'eventually, the ceiling gets too low even for crawling; you wriggle on your belly. Even so, there isn't room for the pack on your back. You slip it off, reach back, and tie it to your foot; then continue, dragging the pack behind you' and so, unbearably, on. (Kendall Walton, 'Spelunking, Simulations and Slime', in Mette Hjort and Sue Lane (eds.), *Emotion and the Arts* (Oxford and New York: OUP, 1997, 39). This passage should, incidentally, also evoke quite a bit of motor imagery.

57. I. A. Richards, *Practical Criticism* (1929; repr. London: Routledge and Kean Paul, 1964), 255 ff.

58. Ibid. 261.

59. Richards therefore tends to demand that the situation within a work of art be concretely and coherently enough presented to justify the emotional response it provokes, ibid. 264. Not a bad idea, for reasons stated above.

60. Quite how these types of emotional response, all of which are quite obviously enjoyed by many, relate to one another, is uncertain. Many commentators would give the responses I have mentioned a socially pejorative characterization, as 'uncouth', 'unrefined', 'vulgar', 'common', etc. Their consumers are adolescent, consumerist, nostalgic, corny, tasteless, and stupid. I am not concerned here with such judgements.

61. Cf. Arthur Groos and Roger Parker, *Giacomo Puccini: La Bohème* (Cambridge: CUP, 1986), 54, who note that this point is ironically(?) marked by a skull and crossbones in the autograph score. They discuss the death of Mimì, ibid. 74 ff.

62. Bellaigue, cited ibid. 137.

63. William Lyons, in Hjort and Lane (eds.), *Emotion and the Arts*, 146. Millais's painting is brilliantly discussed in relation to discourse about blindness, by Kate Flint in her *The Victorians and the Visual Imagination* (Cambridge: CUP, 2000), 64–92.

64. Cf. Michael Bell's study, *Sentimentalism, Ethics and the Culture of Feeling* (Basingstoke: Palgrave, 2000).

65. Solomon, in Hjort and Lane (eds.), *Emotion and the Arts*, 234, says that the sentimental is open to four main objections, as involving the 'tender' emotions, as weak or excessive, as self-indulgent, and as false or fake. But he wants to defend sentimentality in terms of the first consideration, and this links with my idea about generosity, above.

66. Cf. David Schiff, *Gershwin: Rhapsody in Blue* (Cambridge: CUP, 1997), 88 ff., and the explicitly anti-Semitic account given by Constant Lambert in his *Music Ho!* (1934; repr. London: Faber and Faber, 1966), 184–6.

67. With a pretty standard structure too—a simple 32-bar chorus of 4 times 8, usually going aaba, making three repetitions of a melody with one variation. 'I love you' in 32 bars, according to Philip Furia, *The Poets of Tin Pan Alley* (New York: OUP, 1990), 13, 14.

68. This is an effect of art of no small consequence, as Christopher Ricks has shown in looking at clichés (as revived by Beckett) and at common idiom in Bob Dylan. Christopher Ricks, *The Force of Poetry* (Oxford: OUP, 1984), 356–9, and his *Beckett's Dying Words* (Oxford: OUP, 1993), 62–85.

69. So Furia reports, *Tin Pan Alley*, 91.

70. Milan Kundera, *The Unbearable Lightness of Being* (London: Faber and Faber, 1985), 251.

71. This, Solomon points out, is often the 'self-indulgent' charge, that sentimental art makes us feel better about ourselves. But he says, what is wrong with this, in contrast e.g. to the self-righteousness that accompanies doing one's moral duty or moralizing? (Hjort and Lane (eds.), *Emotion and the Arts*, 237.) Michael Tanner, citing Solomon, ibid. 238, says that 'to be sentimental is to be shallow', and that sentimental people don't follow up on their feelings. But how does he know!! He clearly hasn't met Ida Arnold in Greene's *Brighton Rock*. And think also of contemporary responses to Dickens.

72. Jane Tompkins, *Sensational Designs: The Cultural Work of American Fiction 1790–1860* (New York: OUP, 1985), 122–46.

73. I owe this distinction between an ethic of caring devoted to the needs of individuals, and one of fairness, devoted to rules of justice, to the work of Carol Gilligan, most particularly her *In a Different Voice* (Cambridge, Mass.: Harvard UP, 1993), and also to Will Kymlicka's discussion in his *Contemporary Political Philosophy* (Oxford: OUP, 1989), 262 ff. The different ethics involved are particularly associated with the differing moral assumptions

of men and women in our culture. It is reasonable to believe that an interaction between the two attitudes could be managed, so that men come to see more clearly the advantages of an ethic of care, and indeed of the emotions involved in it.

74. Janice Radway's study *Reading the Romance* (Chapel Hill, NC: University of North Carolina Press, 1984), tends to suggest that women readers of romance are well aware of the literary conventions involved.

75. Cf. Paul Hayes Tucker, *Monet at Argenteuil* (New Haven and London: Yale UP, 1982), *passim*. This is a fascinating and detailed study of the relationship of art to historical reality.

76. John Armstrong, *An Intimate Philosophy of Art* (London: Allen Lane, Penguin Press, 2000), 128.

77. Anthony Savile is peculiarly severe here: 'a sentimental mode of thought is typically one that idealises its object under the guidance of a desire for gratification and reassurance' (*The Test of Time* (Oxford: OUP, 1982), 241). Why not?

78. Buildings can attempt this too: cf. Armstrong, *Philosophy of Art*, 128 ff., on the Royal College of Physicians in Edinburgh.

79. In any particular case, the degree of complexity, intensity, and order present may increase or diminish the pleasurable value of the work of art to us, but the *pleasurable* response to the process of simplification—to the point of fantasy—seems to retain its quality if not always its magnitude.

80. Armstrong, *Philosophy of Art*, 131.

3 | $\mathscr{B}$eyond Words: Sensation

Pleasure and the Verbal

I have introduced some of my main arguments concerning our pleasure in the understanding of narrative, and the relationship between emotional response and judgement. I now wish to build up again towards a more complex level, by looking at those elements in our pleasure in the arts which are far less accessible to language—these are imagery and sensation, abstraction from 'reality', and the ordering effects of 'form'.

The role of sensation in pleasurable response raises a general issue, which as we shall see, is particularly important for our appreciation of music without text and painting without (obvious) representation.

We are often tempted to believe that our understanding of the world is fundamentally linguistic, and so the tendency to feel that important emotional experiences must have a verbal expression or correlate is perennial.[1] Chorley, for example, argues in 1834 that we cannot listen to Beethoven, Mozart, Haydn 'without having their sentiment—nay, when we are in a fanciful humour—their *story*, as clearly impressed upon our minds as if it had been told in words'.[2] And for Wagner and many of his followers, the cosmic implications of the instrumental movements of the Choral Symphony just had to be supplemented by their fanciful text: 'The instruments represent the rudimentary organs of Creation and nature [*shades of Disney's Fantasia here!*] and what they express can never be defined or put into words.' These are 'feelings which issue from the chaos of the first Creation'. Words on the other hand make things 'definite and clear' and the text is finally united with the instruments in this symphony because 'the musical poem is urging toward a crisis, a crisis only to be voiced in human speech'.[3] In such an interpretation the early movements of the symphony are already 'musical forms' which are seen as 'poems'—they have had a narrative imposed upon them. The 'creation myths' of these movements then seem to 'need' a final divine or human pronouncement, to have a moral to them. But it is simply not true, that all our significant or emotionally arousing or pleasurable experience is or needs to be verbalizable in this way.

We can't say that an infant (non-speaking) child happily at play isn't *thinking*. In the same way, a batsman is certainly thinking about how to play fast bowling, all the time—but the most vital bit of thinking he does as the ball approaches is hardly verbal, while he may all the same be experiencing all sorts of emotional states. (There probably wouldn't be time for it—any more than there is for the virtuoso pianist to think about the next note.) No more was Monet or any other painter always accompanying his brushstrokes with a verbal commentary. On such occasions, and on many others, such as making love, we have at times to let the sensations and intuitions of our (well-trained) bodies (including the relevant parts of the brain) do our thinking for us. The mental processes of appraisal and of deciding whether an image looks right or wrong, or of getting a musical paragraph to flow in performance, need not depend on a verbal analysis. And if I know what you look like and have to meet you at Paddington station, I am not looking for someone who satisfies a verbal description. (Though I may well help myself, by reminding myself of a verbal description, if I'm meeting someone whom I don't know, and the batsman too may occasionally have been afflicted by some kind of golfer's doubt, and remind himself, as the bowler approaches, to be sure to move his feet.)

Audiovisual communication isn't always a matter of 'signs' on the model of linguistic signs. In a film (or a Larson cartoon), say, there is the (analogue) representation of a dog, and a communicative intent, which is surrounded by language, because it is executed by human beings. But the analogue representation can't be *reduced* to the verbalized communicative intent of the cartoon or film, despite much pressure in contemporary theory to think it so. Even the dog who listens to His Master's Voice doesn't just signify something else, he simply is exactly the way he is (if he is indeed a he). A huge amount of our experience, and certainly of our pleasurable experience, therefore depends upon our capacity for perceptive, intelligent, and sensitive responses that are not verbalized—however concerned we may also be, in some verbalized way, about the context in which such experiences occur, and for its effects, notably including 'I won!' and the dreadful 'How was it for you?'. If I like the way you look, or a Renoir looks, or a bottle of wine tastes, I don't like your or its *description*, I like the way you and it look, or the taste of the wine. Of course this behaviour is, as a functioning part of human institutions, *indirectly* dependent on all sorts of verbal understandings and interpretations, for of course all these likings take place, for *Homo sapiens* at least, within the *context* of our linguistic verbal behaviour: and they can be inspired by, and motivated by, verbally expressed beliefs. And of course, as we shall see in Chapter 6, our likings give rise to a huge amount of verbal interpretation, which can certainly affect our feelings about the work of art. Love letters do the same kind of job. But our pleasurable, sensational experience of people and works of art need not be accompanied by words. Even your conversation, when it includes the rhythms of your speech, your gestures, and the way you look, is not just a verbal experience, although it may depend on the most minute discrimination. The same goes for my motivations for looking at you or a Rembrandt in the first place, although they may depend upon a whole series of (iffy, ideologized, snobbish, etc.) verbalizable beliefs, which may give me reasons for my desires, or guide my eyes. Such beliefs can be quite irrelevant to the actual experience of enjoying the kinds of physical sensations they help to secure for us, with all their orchestration and organization, as I shall be describing them in what follows. The discrimination of our sensational responses is a large part of our pleasure in art, as in much else, and the development of this kind of sensitivity is part of our understanding of its nature.[4]

Works of art obviously evoke sense-experience, as we imagine Cummings's 'busted' statues, the tactile qualities of Picasso's goat's udders, delight in the particular blend of voices in a performance of Strauss's Trio, or react to the carefully graded pianissimos of Mahler's setting of the word 'ewig' or try to magine the kind of painting that Lily Briscoe is making. But the ways in which the arts appeal to them are distinctive (as earlier writers on aesthetics, with a sense of its Greek meaning, knew). For it has long been a question whether art-works are somehow to be defined as 'proportioned to sense' for us in advance (e.g. by formal organization) so that our sight, hearing, touch are peculiarly pleasured by them—an obvious example is the Pythagorean mathematical approach to musical harmonies. *Per contra*, that which is not so helpfully proportioned (e.g. those objects thought to be 'sublime' in the eighteenth century, or the many pro-liferating contradictions of the 'postmodern sublime') will cause a problem, because they somehow exceed our senses and hence our understanding. They were thought to be too 'big' for us—awesome, frightening, and so on—and so there are problems about our simply enjoying them.

Literature too can be literally 'sensational' in arousing those physi-cal states (of racing pulses and so on) which are associated with emotion, and even more obviously so when that is reinforced by musical accompaniment. Nietzsche reported the effects of *Tristan* on him, as 'irregular breathing, disturbance of circulation, extreme irri-tability with sudden coma'.[5] Works of art can be *intellectually sensa-tional,* because we are literally physically aroused and excited by our own mental processes in understanding them. Pornography is just the most obvious example. The having of many emotions involves the pleasant or unpleasant experience of bodily states. Such responses include, for example when we are horrified by *Carrie, The Shining,* or something like that, those of muscular tension, cringing, shrieking, shuddering, recoiling, tingling, frozenness, chilling, paralysis, trembling, nausea, apprehension, and a heightened alertness (which may lead to involuntary screaming at sudden events), and so on.[6]

Wine

A very fundamental example of the transition from sensation to pleasurable response is to be found in wine-tasting, where we work up from our sensations of smell and tastes in the mouth to a complex experience. This can lead to a feeling of acceptance, the perception of a harmonious balance, as the taste evolves from initial sensation to final impression. But it is difficult, and it is a reason for my concerning myself with it, to *specify* our cognitive responses here; that is, to find the language to describe the sensations we feel.

If we look at this process in a little detail, we find that wine tasters start by making generic and classificatory discriminations: they learn to tell apart the typical taste characteristics of different grape varieties. These most powerfully define the taster's expectations, and are the most obvious sensory features for the novice. The Sauvignon Blanc grape, for example, would lead us to expect something 'floral, musky, smoky with a slightly raw herbaceousness suggesting bruised leaves, in keeping with its derivation from the French *sauvage*'[7], and be crisp, or grassy. In a Loire wine, such as Sancerre, Sauvignon can be described as having a 'dazzling aroma of blackcurrant leaves'. The Chardonnay grape has notoriously many different styles in different parts of the world, and it varies even in France, where it produces champagne, Chablis and white burgundy. On the Côte-d'Or in Burgundy for example, it can range from toasty and nutty (as in Meursault) to butterscotch. A Corton Charlemagne may have 'a characteristic bouquet of truffles and toast'. In Champagne it can be 'biscuity'. And outside France, in the Napa valley, it can 'offer lots of pear, vanilla, spice and nutmeg shadings that turn supple and fruity on the finish'. In South Africa it may have a 'toffee and biscuit nose with a touch of grapefruit and flowers, and a quite complex, honey and toffee palate'; in Australia, Chardonnay may have a herby sustained peachy taste. And so on for the other grape varieties. The reader will have noticed the large number of references to smell in the above: this is because, as Michael Shuster puts it, 'Smell is a cerebral prelude to the palate's carnal gratification, conjuring up intensely vivid memories of people, places, occasions and emotions. It is, by a long way, the most important of our senses for both wine-tasting and wine-drinking. Most of what we describe as "taste" is in reality "smell" '.[8]

All these characterizations are intended to help to define the taste of a wine, by giving approximations to the sensational effects on us of other things, which are more easily identifiable as individual objects within the world than are sips of wine, and whose smell and taste is *like* that of the grape in the glass. (This move to objects in the world is a typical one, as we shall see in discussing painterly abstraction.) But what the taster will actually learn to discriminate, by a combination of these smell and taste approximations, is the characteristics of particular wine types. In the end white Meursault and Corton Charlemagne should smell like (prototype examples of) Meursault and Corton Charlemagne, and nothing else, and successive years of those wines by the same maker should have a close family resemblance. The aim is to aid recognition and connoisseurship by giving us labels for our sensations in tasting. These show how different wines have different artistic identities, as they are put together by the wine maker. The problem for the wine taster is then to decide what combination of characteristics the grape types used in this particular bottle have, and to evaluate them. At a slightly higher level, the taster is looking for a combination and succession of sensational elements—from the colour of the wine, through its smell, to its taste in the mouth. The transition from smell to taste is of particular importance, because taste always involves a continuing element of smell.[9]

But what are we going to *like* in all this?[10] At this point we make the awkward transition to language discussed earlier.[11] Nearly all writers rely on two of the most central pleasure metaphors—those of 'balance' and 'harmony'.[12] Indeed such metaphors are very likely to be the best we can do in describing sensation relationships of taste and colour blended, and be as basic to our apprehension as the spatial metaphor of movement is, when applied to a rhythmically organized sequence of pitches. They express our basic background beliefs: the models and presuppositions that we bring to experience. It is how we make sense of things—from a 'harmony' of tastes or colours or sounds to (as we shall see) describing our moods in terms of the weather. For 'human rationality is imaginative through and through, in so far as it involves image-schematic structures that can be metaphorically projected from concrete to more abstract domains of understanding'.[13] In wine, smell and taste, with all their discriminable components, are expected to come together in some kind of 'harmony', so that in coming to appreciate wine, one is learning what things go together, to the best effect. It is like asking 'Do these colours go together?' or 'Is one of them, e.g., the taste of vanilla, arising from the use of oak, too prominent, so that it masks the taste of the fruit, or is it just there to cover or compensate for an unpleasing underlying acidity?' We can learn to discriminate these elements separately, and indeed to a certain extent we can thereby enjoy them separately, but they are most pleasurable when they come together *over time* in a harmonized, non-verbal experience. This basic 'structure' of a good white wine will help us to discern a pleasing balance, for example between sweetness and acidity, through a temporal process. The elements here, and the order of our apprehension of them, according to Peynaud, include:

(a) Sweetness, which is at its maximum after 2 secs then disappears after c.10 secs. (The alcohol in a wine tastes sweet, and feels warm.)

(b) Saltiness and acidity, which are rapidly perceived, but persist longer.

(c) Bitterness, which lingers longest, but it is most variably perceived. And then

(d) A complex aftertaste which is a combination of taste and smell, perceived after swallowing (which constitutes the desirable 'length' of the wine).[14]

This very roughly gives the succession of the sensations involved in tasting a wine. They are conventionally described as the three phases of 'attack', 'evolution', and 'finish'. This order arises in the sequence above, as the tongue 'perceives' tastes, from the tip to the back. It is this physiology which underwrites a typical note on a very cheap Côtes du Rhône Blanc: 'It is pale yellow, with a gooseberry nose, and a fresh crisp taste of similar character, but ending on a softer note tending towards pineapple.' The sequence here may be fixed by inexorable physiological laws, but its timbres or colours can vary infinitely.

There is a cognitive element here when we taste wine and *judge* it to be 'structured' or 'balanced', or 'harmonious' or 'centred'. This should happen when all the sensation-giving properties of the wine, such as its acid, alcohol, and individuating flavours, are perceived to be in appropriate and pleasing proportions. When they go wrong, we may judge the wine to be 'hollow' (something missing between first and last impression) or 'lean' (with a lack of mouthfilling flavours) or 'light' (lacking in alcohol and body) or 'rough' (because its acid or tannins are too dominant and coarse).

This vocabulary used by tasters for the evaluation of a wine is not very precise. The typical enjoyer of wine is likely to say that it is 'attractive', or 'charming' (patronizing), or 'crisp', or has 'depth' (it fills the mouth with developing flavours as if it had an extra dimension); or is easy, or elegant (when strength, flavour, aroma, attack, middle and finish textures all come together in a not overblown or too assertive manner), or 'fat' (with lots of finish and length), or appealingly fresh (i.e. fruity with good acidity); when it is fruity, a wine has body, richness, a perceived ripeness of its grapes; and it can be 'supple'.[15] But these are judgements which *supervene* upon the sensation-experience analysed earlier. They make a reflection on different types of harmony and balance—some are better than others—as the 'elegant' Margaux goes far beyond an 'easy'-to-drink, but far less complex, country wine. And the greatest wines have an inner sweetness and intensity of long-lasting flavours. They are bigger than their followers.

This simple example from wine-tasting raises a basic question for our analysis of all kinds of appreciative enjoyment involving sensation—to put it crudely, given that your perceptions back up all these descriptions, do you *also* enjoy the fact that the wine merits the description?

For we can pay a conscious, verbalized attention to our sensations—so that they become a particular kind of perception-under-a-description. There is a verbal–non-verbal dialectic here. As Kenneth Clark once put it with reference to painting: his 'senses will probably begin to tire' so that he must 'fortify' himself 'with nips of information'. This helps to keep his 'attention fixed' while his 'senses get a second wind'.[16] We are learning to discriminate what is there, and our cognitive judgement oscillates back and forth to our sensations. This also helps it to facilitate (depending upon the reliability of our memories[17]) the comparison of one wine, or painting, with another. Our growing awareness amplifies our enjoyment through comparison.

There is indeed a sense in which we can enjoy the description of the wine, in a more or less intimate relationship to our physical sensations. Compare this to the rather different thrill of knowing at the same time that you are drinking a frightfully expensive Château Margaux 1961. I am inclined to say, however, that this judgemental–sensational interaction can only pay off in the long run if the taste-sensation of the wine types we are discriminating between really does give us a harmonious, coherent, balanced, and above all intense and complex sensual pleasure. And there is by now a good deal of agreement about their ranking.

There is a quite general problem here and it applies as well to all our non-verbal, sensational satisfactions in the arts. We can to some degree distinguish our physical responses, to a hot bath, orgasm, or massage from our emotional or attitudinal responses to them. This may produce a tension within us between the two modes of pleasure; shall we identify it with the sensation itself (the 'raw feel') or with our own more complex contextual attitudes, of liking or enjoyment? This apparent dichotomy, which is really a combination between 'immediate experience' and 'belief and attitude', will confront us again and again. I like the way you tickle me, and also the fact that it is you who is doing it. The sensational effect of your performances, certainly in the longer run, when variations are taken into account, may be inseparable from my attitude to you as a personality. And the same can be true of my attitude to a great wine maker, great lover, painter, composer, or poet. I will attempt to face up to the full consequences of this tension in discussing appreciation and interpretation in Chapter 6.

Music is a particularly clear yet very much disputed art in arousing this tension between 'pure sensation' and 'emotional attitude'. It can put us through a very similar pleasurable process to that described for wine, as we discriminate the colours of timbre, tone, and their succession. As Kivy points out, there are features to perceive even in a single well-executed note on the violin or trumpet, particularly from performers like Arthur Grumiaux or Miles Davis, who can make it *interesting*.[18] Music is almost pure aural sensation, of tone plus pitch and harmony, so that the timbre and the balancing of chords (and indeed the harmonic articulation) in a single piano piece by Debussy is demonstrably very different, and differently enjoyable, as it is played by Gieseking, Pollini, Michelangeli, Uchida, Zimerman, Arrau, and others. (And the same would go for their Beethoven or Chopin.) All this happens, because of the extraordinarily varied possibilities that great composers offer us at this 'sensational' level.[19]

Our pleasure in painting similarly depends on our sensitivity to light in a picture—its saturation and intensity of colour—and their interrelationships.[20] Our enjoyment of the visual sensation to be derived from the relationships between colours is very frequently compared to the process of hearing a musical chord, most notably by

Kandinsky,[21] but it is also like the taste sensation in discriminating the flavours within a good wine. We tend to like, or dislike, certain ranges of colour, the balance of warm and cool, as we like balances between acidity and fruit, or the timbre and contrast of the suspended chords in Debussy. Vermeer is cool (more blue) and De Hooch more warm (more ochre).[22]

How, let alone why, we like this kind of thing, as many people do, is not something we can talk about with nearly as much confidence as wine tasters, for whom such sensory discriminations are of such commercial importance that a vocabulary has grown up to make them, if not completely precise, at least negotiable. But equally clearly we *learn to have* all these sorts of feelings and likings, in all the media, as we move on from the illustrated books of childhood to the colouristic worlds of the painter. We similarly come to get to know and enjoy the 'palette' of orchestral or sound worlds, from Monteverdi, through Rameau, Debussy, Ravel, and Richard Strauss, to Arvo Pärt and Ligeti, and through the infinitely variable ways in which these colours can be realized in performance.

The vocabulary in which we report such sensations is usually well out of the way of our everyday object-related vocabulary, and so there are difficulties of identification. Of course it would not be impossible for us to attach a vocabulary to our discrimination of sensations, for music and painting. The eskimos were (and falsely) supposed to make highly articulated discrimination of different types of snow through a wide technical vocabulary[23] but they did, and we could, evolve a diction and turn of phrase which follow our *pragmatic needs* for such distinctions. Such a lexicon, once developed, would be an achievement of description just like any other, and would have to appeal to the advantages felt by the group of its users for its confirmation.

I realize that the examples cited above, which I believe to be enjoyable, can contrast with others in ranges of colour (for me, Monet's very purple haystacks or Renoir's very orange or pink nudes) that I don't like very much, even though Monet and Renoir, who should know, obviously did like them for one reason or another. And I am sure that everyone else makes this kind of variable judgement (or no one would wear Hawaiian shirts). In music one might equally take exception to the overloaded harmonies of Skriabin (or Schoenberg), the violent atonalism of Berg, or the dull pounding neoclassic drive of many thickly orchestrated bits of Hindemith. In such less enjoyable cases we can often see the technical or mimetic or symbolic *point* of doing it in this way, but we just don't enjoy the sensations which result. (Mark Twain was not wrong to say that he had been told that Wagner's music was much better than it sounded.) Of course we can change our minds and come to like such things, as in the obvious case of those initially disturbing but later accepted dissonances in music, both over history (so often appealed to to justify the 'progressive' introduction of what sounds like discord) and over the history of our own listening. The same might apply to much 'harshly' expressionist painting, from Van Gogh to Nolde and others.

This account of some of the non-verbal pleasurable sensations to be derived from art is on one level quite obvious. But many critics and theorists have found it very disturbing to think that works of art (and particularly works of art which also represent aspects of the real world) should be experienced in this way. As Zuckerman points out for a notorious example: 'The listener to the music of *Tristan* . . . must surrender to the experience of being uncomfortably involved in its excitement. *Tristan* is intentionally over-effective. The listener is supposed to be overwhelmed. Wagner's harmonic lushness is not merely productive of aesthetic delight, it is pathogenic, and the disease is hyperaesthesia.'[24] To take the sensationalist view seems to be 'merely hedonistic', to leave something out which is usually, for those who object, some kind of morally constraining response, or some kind of knowledge which it would be virtue to acquire. That is why Wordsworth's account of his reliance upon sensation and his pleasure in landscape from *Tintern Abbey* on is so revolutionary. He moves from 'animalism' (sensation) via 'Passion' and 'appetite' to

> A feeling and a love,
> That had no need of a remoter charm,
> By thought supplied, nor any interest
> Unborrowed from the eye

But he has a narrative and metaphysical and moral end in view. He is

> Well pleased to recognise
> In nature and the language of the sense
> The anchor of my purest thoughts, the nurse,
> The guide, the guardian of my heart, and soul
> Of all my moral being.

Childhood was for Wordsworth the age of sensation[25] which can be trained for acute perceptions in later life, and recalled as part of the consolations of memory.[26] This psychology, even if originally derived from a Hartleian associationism, led to a poetry which remains, particularly in *The Prelude*, quite independent of its philosophical or pantheistic implications, because it is amazingly attentive to immediate sensational experience of all kinds, and gives it a function in our human, rather than our merely aesthetic development, of the greatest importance.

This leads to a historical battle between sensuous appeal and moral claims, which notoriously confronted Pater, but what he is basically asking for seems to me to be defensible. His conclusion to *The Renaissance* (1873) is a *locus classicus*, not so much for the irresponsible and subjectivist, as for an anti-linguistic view of nature and art. Pater endorses the Arnoldian criterion that the aim of criticism or appreciation is 'To see the object as in itself it really is'. But he further defines this as the need to 'know ones own impression [of the object] as it really is, to discriminate it, to realise it distinctly'. He wants to ask 'What effect does it really produce on me? Does it give me pleasure? and if so, what sort or degree of pleasure?'[27] For Pater, pleasure seems to involve an emotional response unassisted by verbal reflection. His conclusion argues that we should dwell on our experience of the work, not as of a solid object 'in the solidity with which language invests them' but as giving us impressions, which may be 'unstable, flickering, inconsistent, [and] which burn and are extinguished without our consciousness of them'. Beautiful objects (in the world and the arts) should 'rouse' and 'startle' the 'human spirit' into 'sharp and eager observation', for

> Every moment some form grows perfect in hand or face; some tone on the hills or the sea is choicer than the rest; some mood of passion or insight or intellectual excitement is irresistibly real and attractive for us,—for that moment only. Not the fruit of experience, but the experience itself, is the end. A counted number of pulses only is given to us of a variegated, dramatic life. How may we see in them all that is to be seen in them by the finest senses? How shall we pass most swiftly from point to point, and be present always at the focus where the greatest number of vital forces unite in their purest energy?[28]

Form, tone, mood, pulse, focusing, and vital energy are what interests Pater (and Turner, and Ruskin, in different ways) and they are all sensational qualities which are to be found in painting and in music of this period.[29] Indeed it is discrimination of sensations, for example the discrimination of different kinds of skin tone or the relationship of skin to underlying muscle in painting, or the different kinds of timbre possible in the performance of early music on 'authentic' instruments, or in the performance of the work of Debussy, or our appreciation of the relationship of sound to rhythm in virtually any poem of distinction, let alone any Wordsworthian sensitivity to states of the weather (to be seen in the English watercolour tradition, and the work of Constable, Turner, and others, leading to Impressionism), which needs to be learnt and made the focus of our attention, very much as the tradition from Wordsworth to Pater through Hopkins demands. (And of course there are similar traditions in other countries, hence the extraordinary influence of France on aesthetic movements everywhere.)

This approach to sensation-oriented work (abstracted from any obvious human, situational drama) dominates in the late paintings of

Monet, who maintained indeed that he painted his sensations.[30] As Virginia Spate says, he aims at the representation of aspects of the visible world at a particular moment, one which seems to have 'no past and no future', directed at nature alone, and cut off from emotional identification with the (human) subject. It transforms the world, into 'a place of sensual plenitude, an ideal protective closure against the losses brought by time'. It is 'a self-contained world where the loveliness of flowers, foliage, sunlight and water offers an alternative to the manufactured world'.[31] But his methods, with their claims to a scientific accuracy in capturing light, atmosphere, and so on, aim at a strict realism, as he makes 'a lasting image of the transient intersection of multiple perceptions'.[32]

As Pisarro put it: 'The Impressionists have truth on their side, it's a healthy art based on sensations, and it's honest'.[33] All the same, his colours could never exactly be those 'of nature': his paintings had to endure the artificialities of pigment, and beyond these technical limitations and opportunities, there was always room for a further 'harmonic adjustment', often in the studio, of the colour relationships within the painting, and these are a matter of art. We can often be sure that these adjustments were intended to make the image in some way more satisfying, as a decorative object, to the viewer.[34] Indeed the effect of colours in a painting primarily depends upon the contrastive and complementary relationships between them within the painting.[35]

The ways in which painting can aim at such ends, and provoke variations of mood and emotion through the depiction of the colour— and for the Impressionists, the light—in 'nature' as the painter sees it, are wonderfully demonstrated by Monet's series paintings, for example those of the early morning on the Seine (Pls. 4 and 5). As Tucker tells us, he made this sequence from 1896 to 1897, sometimes rising at 3.30 a.m. to be on the river at dawn. They were made in an inlet, and they do not depict the main body of the river. There are twenty-one paintings in the series, mostly from 1897. They are nearly all almost square—with the branches of trees and their reflections running vertically, and the water rising towards the middle horizontally, being set off by the curves of the vegetation. The backlighting flattens the forms, and so dematerializes them. They were painted from a flat-bottomed boat and they were worked on in sequence, as the light changed.[36]

Spate describes the series as dreamy, meditative, evanescent, almost precious in colour scheme, characterized by 'cool harmonies of green, blue, lavender, mauve and silvery whites' and 'Only occasionally are they warmed by hazes or patches of rose and gold or sharpened by an orange-pink dawn sky or the brilliant blue of a daylight sky just freed from mist'.[37] Their refined veils of thin paint, with little impasto and relatively few discrete brushstrokes, are a technical departure for Monet. His work has an extraordinary tension in it, between what we may take as a fanatical truth to appearances, with all that that implies for the enjoyable emotional effects on us of such objects in the 'real world', and a non-mimetic, pleasurable sense of the mood that such harmonies amongst painted colours can create for us.

This extraordinary poetry was much appreciated by Monet's contemporaries. For Guillemot the Seine series was 'a marvel of contagious emotion [and] of intense poetry', and for Arsène Alexandre it gave 'the impression of light, refined joy . . . [and] well being that one can find, these days, only in the paintings of Corot'.[38]

In 1891, the critic Désiré Louis offered an extraordinary range of literary and musical models and metaphors, in attempting to evoke for the reader the effects of such paintings:

We must recognise him as a subtle artist and a powerful poet of nature. His skies, whether pure or cloudy, gay or melancholic, resonate with the mysterious sounds of the universe. He forces the spirit to think and to soar above these magisterial representations . . . of reality . . . In front of this seductive painting, you have the impression of a full and benevolent life which makes you recall the intoxication one feels with the dawning of a new day'.[39]

In order to convey the effects of visual sensation, Louis, like the wine taster, turns to metaphor. These *models* for pleasure abound. These representations also resonate *like music in harmony with the universe*, and so some colours go with others in a satisfyingly 'harmonic' way.[40] (They 'fit' with perception, they are beautifully and surprisingly unifed.) They make his spirit soar to some kind of Platonic realm. Louis's images are indeed idealizing ones—but this is not all. Here down below, he thinks, we are to be 'seduced' by such painting, given the impression that life is good (full and benevolent) and indeed 'intoxicated' by it, as we behold the 'dawning of a new day' literally to be enjoyed in the paintings we have just looked at. And so the dominant pleasure metaphors of sex, alcohol, and musical harmony are brought into play. The example of Monet also reveals a small part of the abundant evidence which shows that we perpetually see landscape and its weather as a literal transform of mood and emotion, and vice versa.

The reader may well be wondering whether it is possible to give as sensationalist an account of literature as of wine, music, and painting. In the case of literature, it is very difficult to be clear about any similar basis for our enjoyment of the art in sensation, beyond the fact that much literature is heard, many poems are or descend from songs, and so on. For it is obvious that the effects of metrics, rhythm, and sound in poetry are vital parts of an organized, sensation-based, process of communication, by which poetry when spoken indeed approximates to music. All this is extremely obvious in the work of many poets and very self-consciously so in Gerard Manley Hopkins. It is part of what Eliot meant by the 'auditory imagination', as 'the feeling for syllable and rhythm, penetrating far below the conscious levels of thought and feeling, invigorating every word'.[41]

Think of different versions of a Hamlet soliloquy by various actors—they vary the sense, but they always vary the music too (if they are sensitive to it), and the semantic motivations for this do not always have to be obvious. This is a neglected but essential aspect of literary performance which links poetry and song, and which is much more clearly subject to sensation-based performance variation.[42]

The *music of verse* is most obviously and dramatically grasped if we think in this way about the contrasts between our reading a poem aloud, with all its metrics and phonics controlling conventions, and our thinking what it means to us in the ordinary prose of our heads, or of a poem in a foreign language and the prose translation at the foot of the page, or the evolution from prose draft to finished work.[43]

Sensation effects are also a matter of imagistic evocation. Nevertheless natural languages are 'signifier systems which rely heavily for their semantic components on perceptual and motor modules' so that when we see or read about someone drinking coffee, we may 'mentally simulate taste, heat and motor sensations as well as the visual appearance of the cup'.[44] This relationship has been much studied by linguists, who are impressed by the way in which language shows our bodily experience in the world.

In Auden's 'On this Island', for example, the 'musical' pleasuring properties of the poem[45] beautifully reinforce semantic considerations, but just like the instrumental accompaniment to the singer, they have melodic sensational pleasures to offer of their own:

> Look, stranger, on this island now
> The leaping light for your delight discovers,
> Stand stable here
> And silent be,
> That through the channels of the ear
> May wander like a river
> The swaying sound of the sea.

In the opening lines the imperative 'look' leads to a complex internal rhyme and assonance which seems to be an equivalent for the recurrent things seen in the 'light' as well as in what 'The leaping light for your delight discovers', the discovering being a kind of pathetic fallacy but also inspiring a trust in nature to show us rather than us searching. This internal music leads naturally to a direct concentration on sound in the 'The swaying sound of the sea' which is to be found in the (punning) 'channels' of the ear. And in the second stanza, the appeal to our sense of rhythm and sound is even more overt:

> Here at the small field's ending pause
> When the chalk wall falls to the foam and its tall ledges
> Oppose the pluck
> And knock of the tide,
> And the shingle scrambles after the suck-
> ing surf,
> And the gull lodges
> A moment on its sheer side.

This is enjoyable in itself as an imagist picture, and its subdued echoes of the Dover scene of *King Lear* reinforce the sense that the poem is about visual auditory perception within the mind as much as anything else, and so about the ways in which memory and past visual imagery can interact within the poem, as

> Far off like floating seeds the ships
> Diverge on urgent voluntary errands,
> And the full view
> Indeed may enter
> And move in memory as now these clouds do,
> That pass the harbour mirror
> And all the summer through the water saunter.

This is a reassuring, fantasizing view of memory as sensation, where (in England!) the clouds 'all the summer through the water saunter' (which is an internal rhyme and a pleasure-oriented verb). All our past summers seem sunny, in this impressionist seascape.

However, this sketch of an Auden poem should not lead us to believe that the experience of a musically organized and pleasurably vivid sense-imagery need always accompany reading. It seems to be triggered by a certain kind of difficulty, when that imagery is needed to contribute to comprehension. I can just tell you that an elephant is bigger than a mouse, but if I am asked whether a mouse or a hamster is the larger I may well have to consult some mental

imagery. In general we get by on pretty bare propositional information, and so it seems likely that the flow of words through a novel
is not attended by much imagery, for most people. 'Consciousness
is not a picture gallery', and imagery is not always an essential part
of the reader's experience. We do not necessarily 'see' characters
in fiction. It is a special pleasure to have imagery, as in the Auden
poem.[46]

There is much more, if unfashionably, to be said for the ways
in which imagery in literature can appeal to the sense modes in arousing memories of pleasurable visual (or tactile) sensations—for
example the appeal to the visual in much of the work of Charles
Tomlinson. This is to be found as much in prose fiction like that
of Proust and Woolf, as it is in the obvious example of written
pornography, the pleasurable test of which is that it secures some of
those feelings of arousal which are usually caused by visual and tactile
experience.

Notes

1. This view has been encouraged by much recent critical theory, particularly that
   which suggests that we are all caught within a culturally transmitted linguistic
   web, which we use to interpret *all* our experience. But cf. e.g. Stephen Pinker on
   'mentalese', *The Language Instinct* (London: Allen Lane, the Penguin Press, 1994),
   ch. 3.
2. Cited in Jim Samson, *Chopin Ballades* (Cambridge: CUP, 1992), 11.
3. This is Wagner's fictional account, which is put by him into Beethoven's own
   mouth, and is cited in Nicholas Cook, *Beethoven: Ninth Symphony* (Cambridge:
   CUP, 1993), 72.
4. For an account of the relationships between our various sense modes and the
   world, see Diane Ackerman's *A Natural History of the Senses* (London: Phoenix,
   1996). Her account of synaesthesia, pp. 287–99, is particularly interesting,
   because as we shall see, the pleasurable non-verbal often has to be described in
   cross-modal terms—the 'balance' of a wine, the 'harmony' of colours, and so
   on.
5. Nietzsche in his *Der Fall Wagner*, ch. 5, as cited in Elliott Zuckerman, *The First
   Hundred Years of Wagner's Tristan* (New York and London: Columbia UP, 1964),
   80.

6. Cf. Noël Carroll, *Philosophy of Horror*, 24, though I am not sure that one needs to go as far as Carroll does, in asserting that 'In order to be in an emotional state, one must undergo some concomitant physical agitation, registered as a sensation. You could not be said to be angry unless your negative evaluation of the man standing on your foot were accompanied by some physical state, like being "hot under the collar" ', ibid. 25. It is not surprising then that many emotion expressions carry quite accurate implications for our bodily experience—the basic metaphor here is that of a vessel filled with liquid—as we 'burst with joy' or 'explode with anger' and so on. Cf. the evidence cited in Mark Johnson, *The Body in the Mind* (Chicago: Chicago UP, 1987).

7. Émile Peynaud, *The Taste of Wine*, tr. Michael Shuster (London: Macdonald Orbis, 1987), 57.

8. Michael Shuster, *Essential Winetasting* (London: Mitchell Beazley, 2000), 12. This is the best practical guide to the actual tasting of wine I have found, in a number of years of buying and selling it.

9. Peynaud classifies smells as falling into animal, balsamic, woody, chemical, spicy, empyreumatic, etherish, floral, fruity and vegetal groups, *Taste of Wine*, 190–1. If this goes wrong, then there is, for white grapes, 'a lack of clarity, a faint stink, like garlic in character and sometimes suggesting sweat'; or there may be the effects of oxidization when a 'smell of apples, quince, then almond and nut entirely replaces the primary and secondary aromas' or the wine can seem to be 'fatigued, cooked, or burnt or with the smell of stale oil or butter' (ibid. 64).

10. Peynaud tells us that 'Sweetness is the only taste that we really like and other tastes are only pleasant when they are softened', ibid. 173.

11. Cf. Shuster on wine and language, *Essential Winetasting*, 24–8.

12. For an interesting discussion of balance as a central image schema, which runs across the sense modes, see Johnson, *The Body in the Mind* (Chicago: Chicago UP, 1987), 73–100, esp. 87 re complex notions like 'balance of power' or 'balanced personalities' which derive from basic bodily notions. Many of his ideas (as at 73 ff.) are dependent on Arnheim's views on visual structure in his *Art and Visual Peception* (1974).

13. Johnson, *Body in the Mind*, 194.

14. Cf. Peynaud, *Taste of Wine*, 69, and 72 ff.

15. These descriptions broadly follow the vocabulary popularized by Hugh Johnson, whose yearly handbooks to wine are immensely influential.

16. Kenneth Clark, *Looking at Pictures* (London: John Murray, 1960), 16–17.

17. Though experience here can become more and more useless—and may have to be filled in by the imagination of what ought to be there. There is a decrease in sensitivity of taste with age, along with a reduction in number of the taste buds from age 50, which speeds up after 60. The young have an average of 245 taste

buds per papilla. The average for those between 70 and 85 is only 88 (Peynaud, *Taste of Wine*, 107). But the old have the supposed advantage of being able to make more comparisons.

18. Kivy, *Philosophies of the Arts*, 88.

19. Hence the apprehension of Debussy's 'impressionistic harmony' as non-functional. He produces a chord or series of chords which seem to be thought up for the pleasure of the moment, for the fleeting impression granted the listener, a harmonic colour for its own sake. (This seems to be Trezise's paraphrase of the thoughts of the Belgian composer Gilson in Simon Trezise, *Debussy: La Mer* (Cambridge: CUP, 1994), 36.)

20. And maybe painters can suggest other sensory modes so that Courbet can in painting flowers 'create the effect of their velvety softness and fragility by the shapes of the areas of colour and tone and by an extraordinary degree of simplification and a sensible delight in their tactile qualities'. Mary Acton, *Learning to Look at Paintings* (London and New York: Routledge, 1997), 61.

21. For a brief account see Christopher Butler, *Early Modernism* (Oxford: OUP, 1994), 37–46, and Paul Overy, *Kandinsky: The Langiage of the Eye* (London: Elek, 1969), 80–104.

22. It is some of the sensation-giving and sensation-suggesting effects of art I am concerned with here. But the latter are always restricted to the insides of our heads. Some things the arts can only point at: they have to be *experienced* inside your skin—or skin to skin. No poem, no picture can actually provide the raw feel of interpersonal sex, any more than Monet on the beach can give you the feel of sunlight. Is it just these 'raw feels' that art must lack, even as it provokes desire for them by its significations?

23. Cf. Pinker, *Language Instinct*, 64.

24. Zuckerman, *Wagner's Tristan*, 21.

25. Cf. Melvin Rader, *Wordsworth: A Philosophical Approach* (Oxford: OUP, 1967), citing esp. *The Prelude* (1805), ii. 237–80.

26. Cf. the classic passage at *The Prelude*, I (1805), i. 581–62.

27. Walter Pater, *The Renaissance* (1873), introd. I follow Pater's text here (p. 14) and for the conclusion as repr. in Graham Hough and Eric Warner, *Strangeness and Beauty* (Cambridge: CUP, 1983), ii. 14. There is an edition by Adam Phillips (Oxford: Oxford World's Classics, 1986), and the conclusion is on p. 150 ff. But it has the changes made for the reprint in a later edn.

28. *Renaissance*, as repr. in Hough and Warner, *Strangeness and Beauty*, 31, 32.

29. And so it is not surprising, given this description of a visual experience, that Pater also thought that 'all art aspires to the condition of music'.

30. Cf. John House, *Monet: Nature into Art* (New Haven and London: Yale UP, 1986), 40, 90, 133, and esp. 218.

31. Virginia Spate, *The Colour of Time: Claude Monet* (London: Thames and Hudson, 1992), 7–8.
32. Ibid. 10.
33. Cited ibid. 216. Spate later adds (217) that 'In all the thousands of words of his letters, Monet never hinted at any emotional projection of himself into the "moods" of nature, even though his perceptions were coloured by his subjective being.'
34. On Monet coming back to the motif in the studio and seeking out these harmonies, cf. ibid. 207, 208. Monet's friend Whistler also aimed at colour harmony. Cf. ibid. 221, where Spate also discusses notions of the decorative, acceptable to the avant-garde.
35. For a magisterial historical study of colour, including contrast and complementarity and much else, see John Gage, *Colour and Culture* (London: Thames and Hudson, 1993), *passim*.
36. Here is another contemporary response: 'Each object is *visibly* bathed by the air which endows it with mystery, envelops it with all the colorations which it has borne before arriving at it. . . . The drama is created scientifically, the harmony of forms accords with the laws of the atmosphere, with the precise and regular procession of terrestrial and celestial phenomena', Octave Mirbeau, cited ibid. 206.
37. Ibid. 238.
38. There is indeed a strong influence of Corot on the *Morning on the Seine* series which is in part a tribute to the silvered harmonies of Corot's paintings of trees reflected in still water Cf. Paul Hayes Tucker, *Monet in the '90s*, exh. cat. (New Haven and London: Yale UP, 1989), 238, 246. The influence of Corot is discussed in detail, ibid. 246 ff.
39. Désiré Louis in *L'Évenement* on 19 May 1891, cited in Tucker, *Monet in the '90s*, 3–4.
40. Louis's parallel of landscape to music can go the other way. In the following passages Kannes develops a sublime landscape metaphor for Beethoven's Choral Symphony (wholly irresponsibly, to my mind, but cf. below, p. 112): 'Like a volcano, Beethoven's power of imagination tears the earth asunder when it tries to check his fiery progress; with marvellous persistence, it develops figures which at first sight seem almost bizarre but which the master, through his skill, transforms into a stream of graceful elaborations that refuse to end, swinging upward, step by step, to ever more brilliant heights. With inexhaustible creative power, the master places new obstacles in the path of his upward rushing stream of fire. He impedes it with tied figures that cut across one another . . . He inverts his phrases, forcing them down into terrrifying depths, and then uniting them in a ray that stands out against the clouds and disappears high up in an entirely unexpected unison . . . He gives the eye no rest! . . . [He] transforms the entire

mass of his figures into a transfigured, blue fire, like a scene painter' (cited in Nicholas Cook, *Ninth Symphony*, 27).

41. T. S. Eliot, *The Use of Poetry and the Use of Criticism* (London: Faber and Faber, 1964), 118–19. Cf the analysis of Eliot's music, particularly including the metric of *Four Quartets*, in Harvey Gross, *Sound and Form in Modern Poetry* (Ann Arbor: University of Michigan Press, 1964), 169 ff., 204 ff. Such factors tend to be pointed to, not so much for their own sakes, as when they reinforce an interpretation: e.g. when 'A needless alexandrine ends the song, | That like a wounded snake, drags its slow length along', in Pope's *An Essay on Criticism* (1711), 356 ff., cf. Christopher Butler and Alastair Fowler, *Topics in Criticism* (London: Longman, 1971), 'Sound and Sense' 312–37, and 'Metrical Structure', 338–66. But the music of verse can be enjoyed without interpretation, just like Mozart.

42. Exceptions to this neglect include Charles Bernstein (ed.), *Close Listen UP* (Oxford: OUP, 1998), esp. Peter Huddeston, 'The Contemporary Poetry Reading', 262–99. Cf. also Betsy Bowden's study of Bob Dylan's treatments of his own texts in performance in her *Performed Literature: Words and Music by Bob Dylan* (Bloomington, Ind.: Indiana UP, 1982).

43. For a remarkable example, see the evolution of Yeats's 'Speech after long silence' as analysed in Booth, *The Company We Keep*, 110–11.

44. Grodal, *Moving Pictures*, 22. He is following Antonio and Anna Damasio ('Brain and Language', in *Mind and Brain: Readings from Scientific American* (New York: W. H. Freeman, 1993), 54–65) here, who argue that 'the semantic components of natural languages rely heavily on the non arbitrary sensory-motor component of the mind'.

45. Printed as 'Look, stranger', in *W. H. Auden: Collected Poems*, ed. Edward Mendelson (London: Faber and Faber 1976), 112. It is given the title 'Seascape' in the score for Britten's song cycle, *On this island*.

46. cf. Nell, *Lost in a Book*, 216, 219. Peter Kivy, *Philosophies of the Arts*, 57 ff. takes a similar view. We don't see characters and settings in the novel the way we see a mountain in Cézanne's picture. The objections to the inner-cinema idea are two: that people don't report that their experience is like that, and that in any case it has the wrong model of language. Of course there will intermittently be some images in most reading, and more or less for different readers. Nevertheless 'Vast stretches of novels are not *visualised* but *comprehended*' (Kivy, *Philosophies of the Arts*, 59), and words do not in general cause images to pop into our heads.

But poetry and novels don't just convey information in the narrative sense. They can inspire painters. Millais's *Mariana* is clearly not 'the' Mariana, (what could be) but a version of her which elaborates on some of the relevant information in the poem. Why shouldn't the reader of the poem, if a good visualizer, get a similar pleasure from some parts of such an imaging exercise?

In general, Kivy is right: we read (primarily) for information that will help us with the logic of narrative. That is our pleasurable drive to understanding. But there can be more to it than this.

4 | *B*eyond Words: Enjoying Abstractions

I now want to consider some relationships between sensation and emotion that may seem to be far removed from controlling narrative associations. Pleasures indeed that may be as non-verbal as those of enjoying wine. They principally occur in our looking at abstract art, and in our enjoyment of 'absolute' music; that is, music which is independent of the setting of any text. I will follow Peter Kivy in calling this 'music alone'. For with the rise in the later eighteenth century of 'pure' instrumental music, art as formal expression took over from art as representation as a critical concern. Music had till then been firmly associated with text, and so the new instrumental idiom was 'the avant garde of the age of Enlightenment', because it did not rely on representation.[1]

A similar crisis occurred with the later rise of non-representational abstract designs in painting. Clive Bell was one of many to see the connexion between the two developments:

At moments I do appreciate music as a pure musical form, as sounds combined according to the laws of a mysterious necessity, as pure art with a tremendous significance of its own and no relation whatever to the significance of life; and in those moments I lose myself in that infinitely sublime state of mind to which pure visual form transports me.[2]

Abstract work, in the sense I am investigating here, can seem to free us from such practical everyday concerns, and so totally absorb us in its own. As Kivy puts it:

It is the blessing of absolute music that it frees our thought to wander in worlds that are completely self-sufficient: worlds where all is resolved, so to speak, with no loose ends, worlds that when they are grasped satisfactorily, give us that to think about which, for the duration of the experience, completely frees us from, so to speak, the failure of thought and gives us thought processes that, if the composer is up to it, can only succeed, can only resolve to a satisfactory conclusion.[3]

Most of the Western music with which we are acquainted is an artfully structured, formal process of events, which is designed to give us satisfaction. It can do this largely because in the tonal era at least, it incorporates a tension and release model (inherent in the harmonic procedures of the period) and this model can be used to account for the feelings of pleasure we can get from the dialectic between order and disorder in music, and the satisfaction we get from the feeling that its elements move towards a resolution. For example, when I listen to a familiar work like Brahms's *Second Symphony*, I have the impression of a 'perfect order' in which every note counts. Nothing it seems could be added, nothing taken away. And only *this* Brahms symphony can do this for me—'Only this one will do'. As the first movement of the work grows from its opening motif, Brahms's use of harmonic conventions sets up expectations; it delays, diverts, and satisfies them.

And for most commentators specific emotions seem to be involved too: a typical analysis of the work by Antony Hopkins characterizes this movement in general as 'lyrical, sunny, and full of a quality of serenity which at times warms to a positive radiance'. He also shows how the music of the first pages of the score which may seem to be no more than a 'disarming melody' is really 'a series of fragments' so that each part or phrase of the melody is full of potential for separate development later.[4] The analysis here looks at the underlying growth of a process which, once we are reasonably literate in the harmonic procedures of Western music (as we all are, willy-nilly, through the various media), can produce feelings of interest in outcome, resolution, and satisfaction, even for a listener who doesn't listen 'analytically'. And so 'the first bar provides us with a three note motive on the cellos' (from which so much is to grow); and then horns and wood-wind 'carry on their untroubled course' until the violins enter, in a 'descending chain [which] seems to dissolve as it does down to a single muttered drum-roll'. After this, 'trombones brood quietly while the woodwind periodically reminds us of [the three-note motif of] bar 1 again'. 'Then, in the forty-fourth bar, the sun comes out and these tentative suggestions of melody flower at last in a lyrical out-burst from the strings' where the opening three-note pattern is still of considerable importance.[5]

This is a typical attempt to characterize some of the musical events in a symphonic movement, by seeing them as expressions of psycho-logical states, where moods are again very like the weather—as 'untroubled', 'dissolving', 'brooding', 'flowering', then 'suggesting' and 'bursting out'. It also emphasizes continuity and development, by encouraging an awareness of thematic processes and transforma-tions. This seems to involve an appeal to a kind of narrative under-standing, which lends to the music a causality which is perceived as very like that of dramatic events. Hopkins thus indicates some of the ways in which we can get pleasure from our sense that music makes progress of a psychologically interesting kind, as the melody 'flower[s] at last'.[6]

A good performance of this type of symphonic movement will bring out in various ways for the listener the possible implications of this formal structure, as the performer of a poem will articulate its syntax in particularly expressive ways. (It articulates for us the per-former's version of its provocative rhetoric.[7]) When a great per-former sets the metre and rhythm for the exposition of a great work, we are 'taken along'. Bruno Walter, Toscanini, and Furtwängler all begin Brahms's Second Symphony in rather different ways.[8] We can therefore enjoy musical performances as rhetorical variations on a known thing (e.g. for what it reveals 'of the score', in the way that Gielgud reveals something 'of the text' in Shakespeare) and as a vari-ation on our memories of previous performances. This is a peculiarly reliable pleasure—because our past experiences of works of art tend to be more reassuringly satisfactory than those of risotto, blondes, or men with moustaches. For example, I may trust this performer to give the whole the kind of rhythmic articulation and 'drive' that will ensure that I feel in the end as complete a sense as possible of satisfaction. Part of the pleasure we derive from music in performance seems paradoxically to depend on the refreshing of our sense of its apparently inevitably going 'this way', when we also know that this is a performance which varies in many respects from previous ones.[9]

When I listen for example to a performance of the second movement of Mozart's Twenty-first Piano Concerto, I know that I will get a great pleasure from the poise of the melodic line in the piano above its orchestral accompaniment. As in the enjoyment of dramatic speech, much depends here on an apparent spontaneity (not arch, not self-conscious, etc.) in interaction with the implied discipline of the form (as the Shakespearian actor plays off the conversational style against the underlying iambic pentameter rhythm).[10] Some pianists manage a sublimely confident continuity of the melody over a kind of void, with each note beautifully placed as the next step, as if the piano really could sing (when it can't). This assured yet tentative simplicity (the note or word has to appear as if from the background of thought, not be strung out on a line) is quite different from an obvious virtuosity. The provocative rhetoric within the structure of the music can be given an intensely human (because song-like) articulation.[11]

What we have analysed so far is just part of our pleasure in the understanding of music and it is, I hope, consistent with what we said earlier about coherence and order. Along with the sensational pleasures referred to above (the limpid caressive tone of Perahia, the more solemn weighting of Brendel), we understand musical performance through a quasi-narrative completion and order. We arrive at satisfying ends through routes which are partly expected (because relatively conventional) and partly unexpected (because they are relatively unconventional or new to us, and in any case are varied and made spontaneous in successive performances of the same work). In the

Pl. 1 (*above*) Vermeer, *The Love Letter* (c.1669–70). Speaking looks amid symbolic furniture; what narrative do we project onto this glimpse?

Pl. 2 (*right*) Sargent, *Mrs Hugh Hammersley* (1893). The glamour of the brush-stroke.

Pl. 3 (*above*) Picasso, *The Three Dancers* (1925). A linear
ambiguity which reinforces mixed emotions: fear, celebration,
and mourning together.

Pls. 4–5 (*facing*) We often use the weather to express our
moods; and here are two of Monet's twenty-one versions of
Morning on the Seine (*above*: Hiroshima Museum of Art;
below: Art Institute of Chicago), painted in the period 1896–7.

Pls. 6–7 Rothko's *Untitled (Violet, Black, Orange, Yellow on White and Red)* (1949), and, to the right, *Blue Penumbra* (1957). Can simple colour move us? Need we interpret abstractions as hidden representations?

Pl. 8 Bonnard, *The Breakfast Room* (1930–1). Denied our usual clarity of vision, we have to pay attention to the play and colour of the surface.

Pl. 9 *(for right)* Bonnard, *The Bathroom* (1908). Not just a beautiful nude; a subtle balance and rhyming of forms.

Pl. 10 Vermeer, *View of Delft* (*c*.1660–1). How does our pleasure in the painterly surface relate to our interpretation of depth?

Pl. 11 (*facing above*) Chardin, *A Lady Taking Tea* (1735
A tactile intimac

Pl. 12 (*facing*) Rembrandt, *Self-Portrait* (1659
A minute attention to the signs for ag
expresses and demands a compassiona
understandin

Pl. 13 Manet, *A Bar at the Folies-Bergère* (1881–2). Are we allowed to admire this attractive young woman, or should 'critique' intervene to inhibit us?

Pl. 14 Howard Hodgkin, *Dinner in Palazzo Albrizzi* (1984–8). A painting to be enjoyed, not so much for the words we might associate with it, but for its wonderful use of colour.

process tension is aroused and satisfied, more or less. We so often want something to happen in music—the climax to be good and loud, the tension being built up to be released, the crash of the chord to fall with the exact element of surprise!!—as after the drop to pianissimo on the bassoon in the first movement of the *Pathétique* just before the great outburst at bar 160. These pleasures indeed also arise from our desire for certain kinds of bodily sensation—obviously so, when (paradoxically enough) we want what we expect to strike us as *surprising*.

A central feature of my account of musical pleasure so far (with its corresponding commitment to the values of continuity and resolution, order and unity) is that it is a formal (or 'syntactical') account directed towards our understanding. But music means much more to us than this, as my account of emotional effects in the works cited here and in Chapter 2 shows. One question is—what are these tensions and pleasurable emotions *about*? If music or painting of this kind is sad, or 'triumphant', or makes me feel sad or triumphant, untroubled or sunny, what is it that the work of art and I are sad or triumphant about? Without a text, which articulates the kinds of cognitively justifying situation we saw in *Der Rosenkavalier*, the *Three Dancers*, and other works, can I really be sad? We know already that we can enjoy sensations without any verbal association, but can I have the pleasure or grief of the emotions without any beliefs about the situations which cause them? What kinds of pleasure are there in the emotions which are caused by more or less 'abstract' works of art? Or are they, indeed, just states of mind brought about by complex states of sensation?

Fauré's Élégie *for Cello and Orchestra*

It may help if we do as before, and look at a fairly informal account of an example: Fauré's *Élégie*. I find a kind of pleasing melancholy sadness here, rather than a mourning one (as in the funeral march in the *Eroica Symphony* or Elgar's Second Symphony).[12] The title of course gives us a clue, but let's suppose that we (or the listener) don't know the title—we just come across it on the radio in the car.

Can I find ways of characterizing the music that by *metaphorical extension* could also be thought to apply to an experience of a sad event? I think this gets us a good part of the way; we could point to its kinetic properties, of being drooping, stumbling, slow, hesitant, low voiced, quietish, and not vigorously assertive. (Our implied characterization is getting quite depressed here.[13]) And as we identify with or get into the music (as we play it through within us) we too might have our version of these kinetic sensations and feelings. And to use another set of—vocal—metaphors, the music is dark-toned not bright, ruminative rather than assertive (here I am characterizing the melody of the cello line as if it were indeed a kind of linguistic expression). And maybe it concludes with some very 'bare' rather than 'rich' harmonic chords to show desolation and emptiness.[14] I am on the whole convinced by my descriptions, but I don't know which way they go. If we already accept that the music is sad, and wish to characterize it as such, we will indeed look for metaphorical attributes to describe it that will go with that, and I have found them.[15] But does the *music alone* really cause us to come up with the sad thoughts and feelings of the kinds I have mentioned? Certainly the music gets us to *feel something*, but can it really be specified this way? Is the language of description misleading us? Or does it have the status of our metaphors for wine?

It may help to remember that there are limitations on the range of the emotions which music can be taken to express.[16] The many subtle variations of emotion as caused by situations can't be expressed by it, without text. Even if the tentative rising movement of the *Tristan* prelude 'yearns', it cannot on its own clearly yearn for any particular Isolde about to appear, for a particular woman, or indeed any woman at all, though it may seem to us to be yearning in a particularly sad and indeed erotic manner because we know this is Wagner's *Tristan*. The emotions which music alone expresses will be generalized ones. I can't hope for music to express for me exactly the way I feel when the one I love brings me a cup of tea in bed, but I can listen to the opening orchestral music of *Der Rosenkavalier* and not feel wholly deceived or let down, when the curtain goes up on two lovers discovered in bed in the morning, because I realize or infer that the music I have just been listening to in the prelude is turning into an accompaniment to the verbal expression of a previous sexual excitement and satisfaction. I can then well imagine that this has been expressed in the orchestral prelude.[17]

Music and Narrative

The main argument against music's expressing such emotions and so pleasurably arousing them in us turns on the assertion that music (without text, or by extension, without specific conceptual associations) cannot depict or create those narrative *situations* which, as we have seen, are usually criterial for the nature of our emotions. On this view, if music is sad, that's odd, because there ought to be something that the music is sad *about*. (If I am sad at the thought of my friend Harold, I know who I am sad about, and why, usually. He is seriously ill. Being saddened by Faure's *Élégie* isn't at all like being saddened by someone for such a good reason.)

We have to try to decide whether music can be sad in and of itself, or if we can only really be saddened by it if we can contribute to it some appropriate thoughts about appropriate things; that is, come to associate some kind of verbally expressed narrative with it.[18]

Composers have developed over the centuries all sorts of *conventional forms of association* between music and pleasurable emotions, including sad ones. And we can do it for ourselves too: an obvious example of this type of association is our superimposition of melancholy nostalgic memories on music, so that it becomes, so to speak, the accompaniment to a film scene in our lives. (Hence the biographically inclined staple of *Desert Island Discs*.) And in programme music, like Tchaikovsky's *Romeo and Juliet* Overture, we can be *told* that the differently characterized sections of the music are *intended* to correspond to 'moonlight on the garden' (harp chords), to the battle of Montagues versus Capulets (cymbal crashes), to the love of Romeo and Juliet (big soppy horn theme and strings), to Friar Laurence's benediction (solemn choral music)—and so on, to the death of the lovers. And in Dukas's *L'Apprenti sorcier* we can learn to perceive the musical equivalents for the intoning of spells, the rising of the water, the division of the brooms, and so on (even without memories of Disney's *Fantasia* to guide us). All these associations can indeed affect our emotional response to the music, which can pleasurably provoke emotions, with the help of narrative associations. And musical sequences can be helped to resemble narrative. All of these activities are more or less intelligible 'going concerns'—and the correlation of music as heard to some kind of imagined narrative has no doubt given pleasure to many and made listening to music easier for not a few. But it is far from clear how emotional associations of this kind can be brought about by the general run of classical sonatas, quartets, and symphonic movements, although they nevertheless attract all sorts of interpretations of this kind.[19] Take as an example some of the wildly conflicting emotional characterizations given by critics to the dramatic beginning of the recapitulation of the first movement of Beethoven's Choral Symphony.[20] Grove saw this as the triumphant assertion of a purpose accomplished, a 'mission fulfilled'. Edward Evans thought it expressed 'courage, ardour, hopefulness, fortitude'. But Tovey saw it as a 'catastrophic return' with 'the heavens on fire'. 'There is something very terrible about this triumphant major tonic', he says. Antony Hopkins keeps up the eschatology by saying that 'It is awe inspiring in the same way that a vision of the avenging angel would be'. So his emotional response is one of 'Terror'. Treitler says we have the shock of catastrophe here, because we now have fortissimo where before we had pianissimo: it is 'the shock of being pulled into the opening with great force, instead of having it wash over us'. But the feelings of terror, catastrophe, optimism, and triumph are very different emotional responses to attribute to the same passage, let alone to find the sexual allegory found in it by Susan McClary: for her this is 'one of the most horrifying moments in music, as the carefully prepared cadence is frustrated, damming up energy which finally explodes in the throttling, murderous rage of a rapist incapable of attaining release'.[21]

Nevertheless, such intrusions of the verbal to make an emotional characterization, of one kind or another, are undoubtedly part of the response of serious musicians to great works. Alfred Brendel interprets the third movement of Beethoven's Op. 110 as 'Passion music—a complex of baroque forms in which ariosi and fugues are interwoven.' One of Beethoven's own instructions for expression here is 'wearily lamenting'.

The first part of the fugue tries to counteract the 'lamenting song'—which, it has been noted, bears a resemblance to the aria 'It is finished' from the St John Passion. There is no immediate healing effect: the second arioso shows this not only by its abrupt semitone drop but also by the way in which the melodic line becomes porous, expressing, with its continual sighs and pauses for breath, the reduced resistance of the sufferer. [22]

By listening associatively, an immensely distinguished performer can come to feel the music in a certain narrative way, and to feel that it expresses the emotions he specifies, and presumably, attempt to play it that way. Whether, by some weaker standard of general musical literacy, we can all feel such emotions without any conscious awareness of the Bach and other associations when hearing Op. 110, is doubtful. But this movement, for such a generally literate listener, will certainly *resemble* some other sad music he or she has heard. It will indeed, in some broad way, be sad. And so a problem arises for our enjoyment of sad music, because it is sad without any compensation through cognition or insight of the kind one can get from a sad poem.

What then is it for a (non-text-supported) piece of music to (please us) by being, obviously enough to many of us, sad or triumphant or exhilarating or erotically arousing? The reality of the emotional effects here mustn't be doubted or obscured by any failure on our part to find or to agree upon a conventional *name* or precise description of the responses involved. Indeed as Sparshott points out, 'Feelings don't all have names and *a fortiori* the feeling expressed by a piece of music might have no name'.[23] Accordingly, Zuckerman reminds us with reference to *Tristan* and the *Ring* that these psychological states have proved 'unlabelable by a century of argument among writers of thematic guides'.[24]

Hanslick argued that such music can only really express the dynamic properties of feelings—their strength, speed, slowness, increasing, and decreasing intensity, and so on. And so I hear Faure's *Élégie* as hesitant, low-voiced, etc. and Brendel hears sighs and pauses for breath in Op. 110. Chabrier's *Marche joyeuse* is joyous, because it is animated, syncopated, bright, brash, bouncy, and so on.[25] This kinetic approach depends upon a possibly largely metaphorical association between emotions and bodily movement. Adjectives such as 'forceful', 'weak', 'languid', 'agitated', 'restless', 'calm', 'excited', 'quiet', 'indecisive', 'vacillating', 'graceful', 'awkward', 'clumsy', 'tripping', 'rhythmic', and 'fluent' are movement words which can also be used to characterize aspects of the way we feel. The movement of music can be asserted to have these characteristics too, and so performed alla marcia, animato, or con forza. One might compare this to the (not particularly accurate) thought that confidence and good spirits at least sometimes equate with rapid and decisive movements, agitation with spasmodic movements, dejection and death with drooping, slowing up, and collapse, as say, at the end of Strauss's *Don Juan*.[26] These kinetic qualities can arouse our emotional responses, according to Gurney and others.[27]

But such theories still cannot show how music alone can reliably present us with the beliefs that motivate emotion, and so cannot show how it represents any very definite feeling or emotion. This lack of a specific object would not matter, if some emotions or moods are states of mind which can be directly accessed by music, without needing to be directed to a 'real world' or situational object. We would then only have to justify our general characterization of such moods, in terms of the kinetic and other features of the music.

We might then be able to adapt a weak version of the Cooke thesis. We learn (through our 'acculturation') a number of standard characterizations of types of music alone—often by imagining some broadly appropriate situations for them (funeral march, happy dance music, etc). Subsequently we feel similarly about other pieces which are alike in the relevant respects. Then the general characterization of a piece as joyful, triumphant, or mournful can be more or less correct or incorrect, just via family resemblance. And cultural convention will get you a fair part of the way—via such generic characteristics— (as it does for the generally 'joyful' New Year's Concert in Vienna). But whether the music will provoke such a characterisable feeling in any particular listener may depend directly upon the individual's response to the kinetics of the music. I know, by such convention, that Shostakovich's *Festival Overture* is *meant* to be happy and celebratory, but to me, it's just a noisy explosion of energy without that emotional tone at all—it sounds more like 'frantic' than joyous to me. (But maybe that's just the tone of celebration in Russia.)

Music and Character

This anecdotal appeal to 'the kind of person who would behave like that' leads me to another, complementary way of describing our relationship to the emotional qualities we discern in music—and this stems directly from the *expressive* (performance-like) qualities we associate with the dynamics of kinesis. For the expressions of feeling I have appealed to are seen as the characteristic and indeed characterizing properties of persons. And so it may be worth asking whether music alone can be thought of as engaging us by the emotional expression of a personality.[28] You might well think that if music alone can't really have a narrative, then it can't have characters in it either, because persons have surely got to be capable of doing something of a narrative kind, in order to reveal their character. If music can't have, refer to, or clearly depict objects, which after all include people, how then can it portray characters? And yet many works purport to be character studies, with more or less (textual) narrative support—*Ein Heldenleben*, *Falstaff*, *Kreisleriana*, and all the Don Juans through Liszt to Richard Strauss.

Elgar's *Enigma Variations* is a central work from this point of view—without a single hidden narrative, and not really designed as a symphonic poem, but with a good deal of textual support for its attempts at characterization. Francis Sparshott's analysis of this work is exemplary for the claim that orchestral music like this can express character.[29] Since the work is dedicated to 'my friends pictured within', the listener 'is . . . invited to speculate what sort of person in what sort of aspect is being portrayed' (*IM*, 232) but without of course having any way of knowing if it is a true likeness, or some kind of caricaturing. Characters in *Enigma Variations* are portrayed through imitations of their speaking voices, and rhythmic equivalents to the way they converse, and we are also supposed to hear them laughing and whistling and stammering. (For W. M. Baker, Elgar tells us that we hear an occasion when he '*forcibly* read out the arrangements for the day and hurriedly left the music room with an inadvertent bang of the door' after which his guests (the woodwinds) discuss him.)[30] We are also supposed to hear the way they move, dancing or bustling (*IM*, 235). It's plausible to think of this kind of music as *emotional portraiture*, such as of the 'Gentleness and nobility' of character which Elgar tried to impart to his music in relation for example to his portrait of Jaeger as 'Nimrod'. Elgar wrote to him, 'What a jolly fine tune your variation is: . . . it's just like you—you solemn, wholesome, hearty old dear [!!]' (*IM*, 238). The music of this variation is often heard as 'solemn'—but as 'wholesome and hearty'? When Frederic Ashton devised choreography for his ballet to the Enigma Variations he had to go further in this direction and devise a more or less plausible narrative that would indeed express character and go with all the dance movements which he had specified, as appropriate to the music of the piece.

Interpretations which attempt to attribute a character to a piece of music, as to a person expressing their emotions, as many composers have assumed, are difficult to assess. In the case of music and dance there do seem to be criteria of appropriacy running through kinesis, and bodily movement, to expression of emotion, in a more or less specified narrative context, as we can see from the ballet. But it would be a step beyond this to accept Budd's account of his emotional responses to Elgar's *Violin Concerto*. He asserts that it has 'features of mind, character and feeling' that are 'are integral to the value the music has for us'—they are emotional turbulence, exquisite tenderness, mounting excitement, ecstatic release, passionate regret, sincerity, and wistfulness.[31] I feel something like these emotions, all of which are enjoyable, when I hear this music too; and I suppose that it is not merely by analogy or equivocation that we can say that the Concerto has a 'character' which can bring such emotions together, if we identify in this way with the provocative rhetoric of the performance.

If we enter a 'world of feeling' within a work, we may indeed believe that those feelings cohere within a 'character' and enjoy the music as expressing one. The music of Delius, of late Stravinsky, and the heartless clatter of early Prokofiev are all very different in these respects. But what sort of character do they express? What is meant by the 'femininity' of Chopin or Fauré, the volatility and/or camp detachment of Poulenc, the persistent, steady, rock-like integrity of Bruckner, the emotional conflicts in the 'neurosis' of Mahler? These are qualities from biography that many listeners claim to hear 'in' their music, and in differing performances of it. The whole issue of the emotional tone in much of Shostakovich's music is controversial, after the publication of his purported *Testimony*. We are told for example that the *Fifth Symphony*'s Finale, which official Soviet culture endorsed as a 'celebratory return to the major' and full of 'optimism', is now to be seen, according to some, as actually 'forced'—an 'ironic' and brutally destructive fascistic march.[32]

Attacks on the quality of the feelings such works provoke are difficult to sustain, without slipping sideways or away from the nature of the feeling to a moral judgement. Is 'optimism' better than 'brutality' from the pleasurable point of view? I have heard the March from Tchaikovsky's *Pathétique* played both ways. We certainly seem to be asked to take on an attitude. The emotional stance of Tchaikovsky in the first movement of the *Pathétique* is obviously temperamentally very different from that of Sibelius in the first movement of his Fourth Symphony. Scruton thinks that the sentimentality of the last movement of Tchaikovsky's *Pathétique* Symphony is 'overdoing its display of grief'. And by overdoing it, is it not really doing it at all? This question of sincerity, so to speak, separates the author from the musical substance.[33] 'The forced climax, the sentimental cadence, the sugary harmony—these are defects in the *musical* nature of a composition, and at the same time faults of character, which turn us away (or ought to turn us away) from the thing that possesses them.' He goes on to judge that 'the musical process is also a moral process'. This is because Scruton is of the school of Kundera (discussed in Chapter 2, above) in seeing sentimentalism as a form of self-congratulatory pretence: it is 'no different from sentimentality in life. The sentimental work invokes a "great emotion", not in order to feel it, but in order to claim the credit of feeling it, without the cost of really doing so'.[34]

Performances of this movement of Tchaikovsky's symphony, by Mravinsky, Bernstein, Stokowski, Cantelli, Klemperer, Karajan, and so on, are amazingly different from one another in the effects produced by these alliances between powerful personalities and the music. And so when we come to consider the complex activity of following a musical sequence and deriving from it an emotional response, it does seems plausible to find an interaction between musical performance and a sense of character. For pleasure we would need to approve of this or at least admire it, for example the granitic integrity of Klemperer, as opposed to the witty inflections of Beecham, in Beethoven's *Seventh Symphony*. There is nothing wrong of course in our enjoying both—in their different ways. Such characterizations would encourage us to enjoy even music without text, by liking it as we like at least two persons, as they express themselves, more or less in alliance: composer and performer (this will be discussed in Chapter 6, below).

Abstraction in Painting

From the point of view of the viewer trying to get pleasure from what is manifestly present in an image, abstraction in art can be characterized in largely non-historical terms.[35]

First of all there is our satisfaction or frustration in the resolution of a *tension* between abstraction and representation. An extreme instance would be our making out the subject of a Cubist guitar or portrait, but there are many other less radical types of abstraction which by simplification or some other means can tease and satisfy the viewer by their relationship to some real-world subject matter. Matisse's sketchy lines in his depictions of the nude articulate a rhythmical abstraction at the same time as they direct our attention to a 'real-life' musculature. Kandinsky's evolution from representation to abstraction is a classic historical instance: and those who have analysed his work have often attempted to interpret the more and more hidden objects within his paintings (that is, an apocalyptic imagery of castles, towers, horses, boats, spears, trumpets, and so on). Mondrian's *Composition No 10 in Black and White*, formerly subtitled *Pier and Ocean*, of 1915, maps out a relationship between its two putative objects, so that the wave-like field of crosses (only some of the 'pier') may seem to flash as waves do, though in a very metaphorical kind of a way.

This gives John Golding (who discusses the image under its earlier title) 'a feeling of perfect equilibrium', and he also finds in this image a 'pulse and shimmer' of interaction between horizontal and vertical lines, so that 'their pulse, their rhythm have become the pictorial image'. Beyond this 'a Blavatskyan cosmogony' would see water as 'the base and cause of all material existence'.[36] This is hardly visible in the image—though the notions of vitalism and energy are often central to modernist work like this. It is nevertheless typical of much

Fig. 5 Are abstract works poetically suggestive, or
do they just play with our visual responses to their
formal aspects? This is Mondrian's *Composition 10 in
Black and White 1915* (oil on canvas, 85 × 108 cm.)

abstract art to gesture at such poetic, metaphysical, and theological universals. Jackson Pollock also claimed (by very different means) to be concerned with 'the rhythms of nature. The way the ocean moves'.[37] There is no doubt that the rhythms for the eye of many of his works, like the great *Autumn Rhythm* and *Blue Poles,* are an impressive part of their impact on the viewer.

Beyond this there is an attempt to free oneself more or less completely from the objects of the material world by producing images which depend on relationships of shape, design, and colour rather than on any obvious allegiance to representation. This is a form of 'absolute' abstraction akin to absolute, textless music. Delaunay's *Sun and Moon* (1913) resembles the sun and moon, but it might, just as well, be seen as an arrangement of coloured disks. The basic distinction here seems to be between paintings which look more or less 'geometric' (in relationship to mathematically more or less regular shapes, with perhaps a hidden harmony, as in Purism) and those which look more or less 'biomorphic' to viewers (where the forms seem to be more organic than anything else, as in Kandinsky, before he turns to geometric abstraction). Both categories can seem to be more or less representational. The geometric abstract may seem to tend towards the static, the biomorphic maybe leaves room for more dynamism, but the Futurist painters and many others quickly managed to make geometric abstractions that were to be seen as having within them, like the Mondrian, dynamic tendencies and energies (such as Balla's *Abstract Speed + Sound,* 1913) so that the relationship between 'geometric' abstraction and the world is often ambiguous.[38]

For both such modes, colour has its own supposed emotional effects upon the beholder.[39] Kandinsky thinks of colours as having distinct emotional characteristics, as a keyboard which plays divine music which causes 'vibrations in the soul'. For Mondrian red is earthbound and sensual, for Pollock it connotes life, danger, war, and sorcery.[40] This claim for the metaphorical correlation between musical chord and colour chord is almost universal, and many modernist painters take music as a metaphorical model for their work. Klee is perhaps one of the most explicit of these.[41]

Colours which are more or less 'pure', and abstract shapes, which are more or less related to well-known geometric figures, lead to a formalist 'absolute' abstraction in which the work is thought to be 'autonomous', in so far as it draws attention to nothing but itself, is non-representational, and so lacks any obvious allegiance to the external world. It is entirely itself, not a copy of anything, and it aims at a pleasure for us which is cut off from the everyday concerns which things like Chardin's jugs, Turner's storms, and De Hooch's domestic scenes imply, although the pictures of all three of these artists have wonderful 'abstract' qualities. The relationship of abstract painting to the political order has therefore been an uncomfortable one, and to religion too often one full of mystical portentousness.

In this respect abstract painting is indeed like the 'absolute music' of the previous century in that it claims to obey its own internal laws, and can make similar claims to emotional expressiveness. Hence Kandinsky's ideas of the 'inner necessity' of feeling, or the claims to affect made for the abstract expressionism of the New York School. Abstract paintings were taken to express all sorts of psychological conditions—such as existentialist angst—within the artist, not easily to be transmitted to the viewer, but certainly supposed to be understood as part of the 'meaning' of the work. Wols and Pollock are obvious examples.

Much of the turn from representation to abstraction in the history of painting therefore depends on our learning to derive a pleasurable emotional response from what becomes simple geometric or irregular shape or 'pure colour' in many later painters. But how can such non-representational elements and their colour combinations alone cause within us emotions which give us pleasure? They do not engage us in a drama; they are not representations of objects or situations (like Monet's landscapes) which give us pleasure outside art. Nor do they often or obviously or directly suggest pleasurable physical sensations to be derived from our contact with the world—as the

Impressionists did for light. It looks as though a further step has been taken along the path towards a pure sensation, in the immediate experience of the painter's colour, uncontaminated by any notion of its being used to represent a natural 'object', any more than the taste of wine does. For abstraction in art, which has worked at many different distances from representation, by definition plays with and denies our wish to rationalize our responses by naming and analysing situations and natural objects.

All these aspects of abstract art give rise to problems for our pleasurable response, which in some ways parallel those which we found for music above. We can see this if we look at responses to the later work of Mark Rothko (from about 1950 on). I have chosen Rothko as an extended example, partly because his atmospheric painting makes a step beyond the abstraction of Monet (Pls. 4 and 5). Here the rectangle of the canvas is a one-colour ground visible along the edge of, and occasionally through, an opening between three or four horizontal blocks of colour with brushed surfaces and furry borders (Pls. 6 and 7). These shapes are bled into their ground, fusing both into a single plane. In a series of works like this, it is not so much the geometry as the *emotional content or effect* of the work which most varies. Rothko's oblongs of colour, which are immaterial, cloudy, and atmospheric (weather metaphors seem inevitable once again), tend to darken, towards a reddish brown, towards the end of his career. The consensus seems to be that these later canvases are therefore 'sadder' than their lighter predecessors, and even 'tragic'. Rothko's earlier paintings in general are seen as calm, passive, recessive, and even self-effacing; the later as more disturbed. Whereas a Pollock tends to be in perpetual, often agitated movement, a Rothko can give an impression of stillness which, enhanced by the very large scale on which he works, has given to many viewers a sense of unanalysable sublimity in his images. In series, the colour relations of his canvases seem to be part of a recurrent attempt to define something mysterious, which is purely internal to itself. They have no obvious mimetic or instrumental relationship with the external world. If they facilitate a withdrawal into a contemplative or even a mystical state, then so much the better. One might think that Rothko is searching for a pure 'chord' of feeling between the base colours of his paintings.

This parallel of abstract art to music is frequently made by Rothko's interpreters—and yet Rothko is emphatic that his emotional effects are meant to go beyond a mere quasi-musical pleasure:

I am interested only in expressing the basic humane motions—tragedy, ecstasy, doom and so on—and the fact that lots of people break down and cry when confronted with my pictures shows that I *communicate* with these basic humane motions. The people who weep before my pictures have the same religious experience I had when I painted them. And if you, as you say are moved only by their colour relationships, then you miss the point![42]

It is as doubtful that a Rothko painting can present anything like a 'tragic' situation, as it is that the recapitulation of the first movement of the Choral Symphony can be concerned with biblical 'apocalypse'. But some of Rothko's interpreters nevertheless try to indicate a hidden cause for these grander emotions, and they typically do this by suggesting that they are partly brought about by a perhaps subliminal reaction to an indirectly represented object, which can then carry its usual cultural import. But this move is as controversial as the imagining of a situation for music alone, and for similar reasons.

Stephen Polcari thus argues that Rothko was influenced by and reproduced in his early work classical images, of columns, of sacrifice, and of entombment. He suggests that such images still lie behind the later more abstract work, which is in 'ideographic form—part figure, part architecture, part nature, part past, part present, part future, part entombment, part subconscious, and part emotion'. This is quite a mixture: so that 'The totemic form or abstract thought-complex [of the later work] ultimately alludes to the more specific early forms—[to] the rectilinear architectural fragments, the Greek column figures, the stratigraphic zones, the tiered figures, the entombment composition'.[43] This means that an image like *Number 11* of 1949 resembles the segmentation of earlier column figures. Polcari also finds an entombment in Untitled (*Violet, Black, Orange Yellow on White and Red*) (1949), arguing that

A symbolic black line with the thinnest trace of a black 'head' at the left resides between a vertical colour figure with two upraised red 'arms', as in a combination of the Virgin Mary with Christ on her lap and a Greek wailing figure.

Orange Gold and black (1955) is another entombment composition 'with a slash of black across its middle for Christ' but alternatively, he observes that it may be, 'more simply, a column figure with abacus'.[44]

Robert Rosenblum has a different underlying model to release our response. He sees in images of this kind 'the annihilation of matter and a precise yet mystical content'. Their horizontal divisions evoke the primordial division of earth or sea from cloud or sky in 'luminous fields of dense, but quietly lambent colour' that seem to generate the primal energies of natural light. He thus appeals to a romantic tradition, which extracts supernatural mysteries out of the phenomena of landscape, but nonetheless wonders if Rothko's abstractions are not just 'aesthetic objects . . . Where an epicurean sensibility to colour and formal paradoxes of the fixed versus the amorphous may be savoured'.[45] There is certainly some tension between these two approaches and the responses they seem to imply. Of course a pleasure in abstract painting might be more or less enhanced or aggrandized by some awareness of the importance or 'sublimity' of a disguised subject matter, just as absolute music might be helped along by some associated narrative.

So there are two types of pleasurable response being argued for here: our being pleasured by pure colour and colour relationships, and the ambiguity of forms, fixed and amorphous, and the enhancement or direction of this response through symbolic, theological, theoretical, or emotional *associations* between the abstract image and some object or situation. (The appeal to the sublime, so often made also for the work of Barnett Newman, also rationalizes for us some 'appropriate' emotions, as if the Rothko were an unfathomable landscape.)

It is as difficult to explain how an 'epicurean sensibility to colour', to visual or aural sensations (which undoubtedly do give us pleasure), can arouse emotions, as it was to specify an emotion for a good bottle of Puligny Montrachet. Despite the speculations of Kandinsky and Plato and many others, there doesn't seem to be much that is certain that we can say about the correlation of particular colours (or musical modes or harmonies) to particular emotions.

Where mimesis occurs, by association or otherwise, the colours may bring the nature of the pleasurable object to us more vividly or intensely (so that the mystery may then become, 'Why should any one *like* looking at the mists on the river in the morning?' or 'Why enjoy military marches?'). But it surely is the case (when we see a Monet or a Rothko) that although a picture may cause in us pleasurable and even nostalgic reminiscences of our own experience, there is also something in the harmonic relationships of colours and shapes alone which gives us pleasure. These (sensational) pleasures, of colour and tone, etc., go along with our tendency to have emotional responses or at least mood-responses to them which need not (*pace* Polcari and Rosenblum) be mediated by our experience of natural objects. Some of these responses are culturally reinforced and so relative (and not necessarily the more reliable for that). Hence the mood associations we may have for colour (in our case, say yellow = happy, black = sad) but they do not go far to help us to *discriminate* the subtlety and variation between canvases by Rothko and Monet, or painters like Mondrian and Ellsworth Kelly.[46]

Maybe Waldemar Januscak is right to remind us of the sensational basis here (with some metaphorical intensifiers that remind us of Louis on Monet): he says that a Rothko is

a terribly simple thing, an immediate visual thrill—comparable say, to coming across a field of rape in bloom—followed by a kind of psychological immersion in the colours themselves . . . Your thoughts soak and relax in the pictures like a tired commuter coming home to a hot bath. A beautiful Rothko does to the eyes what beautiful food does to the taste buds.[47]

Notes

1. Cf. Kivy, *Philosophies of the Arts*, 6, pointing to the importance here of Kant and Hegel. Cf. also Carl Dahlhaus, *The Idea of Absolute Music* (Chicago: Chicago UP, 1989).
2. Clive Bell, *Art* (1914; repr. Oxford: OUP, 1987), 31.
3. Kivy, *Philosophies of the Arts*, 209: he goes on to say that the same may apply to non-representational visual art, or mathematics. And as Scruton points out, 'One reason for denying that music is a representational art is that it provides our paradigms of pure abstraction; of forms and organizations that seem interesting in themselves, regardless of any "fictional world" which this or that listener may try to attach to them' (Scruton, *Aesthetics of Music*, 122).
4. Antony Hopkins, *Talking about Symphonies* (London: Heinemann, 1961), 109. These technical thoughts about the way in which the music is put together need not be present to consciousness during a performance, even for musically trained listeners. But they do help to explain the grounds for our sense of background unity and coherence in the work.
5. Ibid. 110.
6. For further psychological confirmation of the expectation model adapted here, cf. M Aschmuckler, 'Expectation in Music: Investigation of Melodic and Harmonic Processes', *Music Perception* 7/2 (1989), 109–50; also W.W. Gaver and G. Mandler, 'Play it again Sam: On Liking Music', *Cognition and Emotion*, 1/3 (1987), 259–82. On the thematic transformations and coherence of the opening movement of the Second Symphony see also Leonard Meyer, *Explaining Music* (Chicago: Chicago UP, 1973), 59–63, 70–2.
7. Cf. e.g. Trezise, *Debussy: La Mer*, 27 ff., esp. 29 ff., comparing ten recorded performances. The files of the *Gramophone* magazine provide thousands of examples of the analysis and comparison of performances.
8. Or compare the powerful measured tread of the *Eroica Symphony* under Klemperer or Giulini, to the faster rhythms of Karajan or Norrington or Rattle, or the innumerable possible ways of playing the simple repeated chords at the beginning of Beethoven's Waldstein Sonata.
9. It is thus hardly surprising that Schopenhauer and others saw music as an especially revealing expression of the will; and also that in so many obvious cases (*Tristan*, the opening of *Der Rosenkavalier*, the duet in *La Bohème*, Act I) our emotional involvement in musical forms has more or less explicit erotic analogues.

10. Compare, as a thought experiment, Fischer-Dieskau with Gérard Souzay, singing Fauré.

11. On expectation and tones leaning towards 'wanting' one another compared to the words in a sentence, cf. Scruton, *Aesthetics*, 52 and ff. He argues also that they follow from one another 'like bodily movements' and this also sounds to us like 'rational agency' as a tone is heard as a response to its predecessor (in a Kantian 'causality of reason', one of intention, cf. ibid. 76).

12. In this last case the march is so much 'in place' as part of a (military) mourning human activity that it may well connote mourning just by being a march with certain conventional musical features, such as 'sad' or sighing appoggiaturas and a dragging rhythm.

13. Can we say that a human being who was also a cellist would play that way if he was sad? Then the music, through the implied persona of the creator or performer or both, would be spontaneously expressing her sadness. I think this one won't quite run, because if we tried to say what we would expect to hear in such a case, I suspect we would just run through our repertoire of already-recognized-to-be-sad music, and play something like that. The cellist would so to speak be saying the right conventional thing, and the established genre would carry the main burden of expressing sadness.

14. Cf. the extraordinary chording in the sad depiction of landscape-by-association in Sibelius's *Tapiola*.

15. The words here should mean what they mean in ordinary speech and in central cases—so that 'sad' when applied to music is not used in a special sense. You couldn't learn what sadness was just by listening to sad music, because the centre of its meaning is found elsewhere, as an emotional response to agreed-to-be-saddening situations.

16. And by 'expression' here, I mean an aspect of a work of art or its performance that is understood to be the indicating or evidencing of mental states. Cf. Jerrold Levinson, *The Pleasures of Aesthetics* (Ithaca, NY: Cornell UP, 1996), 101–2.

17. But how could the first-time listener tell that the tension in the music is *sexual*, as opposed, say, to expressing the excitement one might feel at a football match? We haven't yet learnt to associate those thrusting assertive horn themes with a text which affirms Octavian's masculinity. By the second hearing, there's a conventional association established, if one is informed enough and alert enough to look out for it. But how is the horn appropriate to Octavian's sexuality? Directly or just metaphorically? Thrusting?

18. But what about moods, which can be pretty non-specific in their narrative demands and focus on objects? When we have them (for one reason or another) we can spread them around to all we come into contact with. We paint it black, see things darkly, droopily, or however. Indeed we often look for music to play which will match or counteract our moods. But hearing music as sad (just as a

projection of our pre-existent moods on it) won't work to show that the music is sad music.

19. Deryck Cooke tried to find a way around this, in his *The Language of Music* (1959; repr. Oxford: OUP, 1989) by bringing back a subliminal text, in arguing that non-textual music could rely on the previous, text-based, establishment of such emotional associations, which still carry their effect. This argument is implausible, for although the sophisticated listener may indeed be able to build up a workable lexicon of such emotional associations (as Cooke himself quite obviously did), the 'hard cases', such as the Beethoven symphonic movements, or the separate movements of Bach's keyboard partitas, still remain difficult to explain convincingly in these terms, for example when Cooke himself analyses Mozart's Fortieth Symphony, ibid. 232 ff.

20. At bar 301. I quote the responses as reported by Nicholas Cook, *Ninth Symphony*, 65–6.

21. Susan McClary, 'Getting Down off the Beanstalk', *Minnesota Composers Forum Newsletter* (Jan. 1987), cited in Nadine Strossen, *Defending Pornography* (New York: New York UP, 2000), 96. I will discuss this kind of sexual reductivism in Ch 6, below.

22. Alfred Brendel, *Music Sounded Out* (London: Robson, 1995), 70.

23. Francis Sparshott, *The Theory of the Arts* (Princeton: Princeton, UP, 1982), 88. Note that this affects the question of the way in which important feelings may fail to become part of a interpretation and critique. Cf. our enjoying colours and flowers without being able to name the emotion they cause. It may therefore be just a matter of 'the feeling I get when I hear X'.

24. Zuckerman, *Wagner's Tristan*, 12.

25. Maybe such music gives pleasure, and we say, 'This pleasure I am feeling must be an emotion'. Because pleasure goes with emotion. But suppose it is actually just a complicated kinetic sensation of arousal? (I feel it this way.) My description above suggests that both elements are involved.

26. Cf. Malcolm Budd, *Music and the Emotions* (London: Routledge, 1992), 65.

27. Scruton says that 'Light is cast upon the expressive character of music if we see the response of the listener as a kind of latent dancing—a sublimated desire to "move with" the music, and so to focus on its moving forms.' *Aesthetics*, 357.

28. I shall be arguing later that one of the pleasures of the arts arises from our intimacy with another person, see p. 174ff., below.

29. Francis Sparshott, on 'Portraits in Music: A Case Study of Elgar's Enigma Variations', in Michael Krausz (ed.), *The Interpretation of Music* (Oxford: Clarendon, 1993), 231 ff., hereafter *IM*. Further references are given in the text.

30. Just before no. 13 in the score, cf. *IM*, 236. 'One 'sitter' is evoked by way of the sounds and movements his dog makes' (*IM*, 236). In var. 11, G. S. Sinclair's bulldog Dan falls into a river, paddles up and down, and barks (*IM*, 239).

31. Budd, *Music and the Emotions*, 149–50. No one more tender here than the 16-year-old Yehudi Menuhin. But what can we imagine him being tender about?
32. Cf. Ian Macdonald, *The New Shostakovitch* (Oxford: OUP, 1990), 120–34. How can we decide who is right here? Can the music be performed in different ways to reflect this difference?
33. Scruton, 'Notes on the Meaning of Music', in *IM*, 193 ff. Scruton points out that if philosophers think that such states of mind are merely analogous to what is expressed by a musical work, that makes it hardly credible that we 'should take the kind of intense moral interest that leads to such a judgment of Tchaikovsky's work'. But this is a circular argument.
34. Ibid. 197–8. But how does he know?
35. For our present purposes it is sufficient to describe 'manifest content' as that content which, if you didn't see it, would suggest to a reasonable observer that you were illiterate so far as those conventions of representation were concerned—i.e. you would be expected to see a goat, a woman and her servant, clouds, dancing women, trees and a river, and so on, in some of the images discussed so far.
36. John Golding, *Paths to the Absolute* (London: Thames and Hudson, 2000), 26.
37. Pollock, cited ibid. 13.
38. Kandinsky explained at the Bauhaus (most implausibly) that the apparent movement of an element to the left is 'adventurous' and 'liberating' whereas to the right it is 'familiar' and 'reassuring'. See Frank Whitford, *Bauhaus* (London: Thames and Hudson, 1984), 112.
39. This is partly because colour theory in the 19th cent. paved the way for a treatment of colour as an independently expressive emotion-arousing element in painting.
40. Cf. Golding, *Paths*, 36, 120.
41. Cf. Andrew Kagan, *Paul Klee: Art and Music* (Ithaca, NY and London: Cornell UP, 1983), e.g. on *Alter Klang* (1925) where each rectangle of colour is a 'note', pp. 68–74, or on *Polyphonic Setting for White* (1930), ibid. 79 ff., and *Ad Parnassum* (1932), ibid. 85–93.
42. Cited in Robert Rosenblum, *Modernist Painting and the Northern Romantic Tradition* (London: Thames and Hudson, 1975), 215. But how does even the Rothko Chapel in Houston (1965–6) convey a 'religious' experience? It is discussed at some length, ibid. 215–18.
43. Stephen Polcari, *Abstract Expressionism and the Modern Experience* (Cambridge: CUP, 1991), 130–1, 140.
44. Ibid. 141. However this may be, Polcari also wishes to argue something more abstract, that Rothko's nuances of brushwork 'create sensations of *immanence, of indwelling vitalist emotion and radiant spirit more sensed than perceived*' so that 'Rothko was able to transform physical matter or nature—the pigment and

vehicle of paint—and the concreteness of sensations directly into emotional and spiritual effect without the intermediaries of recognisable outer forms and symbols' (ibid. 144). This is very like Kandinsky.

45. Rosenblum, *Modernist Painting*, 213, 214, 215.

46. There is so far as I know no certain correlation between music and painting or between the physiology of chord perception and that of colour combinations to ground this analogy, despite the undoubted fact that some synaesthetic musicians, notoriously Messiaen, firmly associate particular chords with particular colours.

47. From an article by Waldemar Janusczak in the *Guardian*, Sat. 20 June 1987, p. 11.

5 | *B*eyond Words: Appreciation, Technique, and Form

Our enjoyments can be relatively thoughtless, and not much concerned with improvement by any very complex understanding. We can say that we know enough to 'just enjoy' the kiss, the tickle, or the ice cream, or to familiarly dream our way through a Liszt étude, a Shakespeare sonnet, or a lovely Corot landscape, because the context of understanding by which we enjoy such things, however minimal, is established beforehand. But we never *really* just do this, because as long as we are attending to such objects, we can be shown to be enjoying them under *some* description or another. Thus Kivy describes Mrs Munt at the famous performance of Beethoven's Fifth Symphony in Forster's *Howards End*:

Mrs Munt need no more be able to describe music in music-theoretic terms, to be said to understand it, in her fashion, than she needs to be able to think about it in those terms, to be said to perceive and enjoy it, in her fashion. All we require is that Mrs Munt be able to describe the music in the terms under which she perceives it.

Tibby might be able to give a technical, i.e. 'Music-theoretic' description of the music they are both hearing, in terms of its keys and intervals, but Mrs Munt will also be able to give (in my terms) a 'phenomenological' account—she can perhaps tell us what in the music made her tap her foot. And both of them, as Kivy notes, 'will be describing the same *sonic* event'.[1]

By the same token, even for our most thoughtless pleasures, we are usually able to come up with some kind of description and often even to make some sort of a comparative evaluation. Everyone has their preferences, even amongst brands of baked beans and hamburgers (even if they don't go to the comparative studies reported in magazines like *Which?* to articulate or reinforce them). We may not need to think much about the nature of many of our enjoyments, and we can get on with them as we are. We are more concerned with ensuring that we are going to have some. But on other occasions, we may be inclined to test or extend the way we have been primed by our understanding, in order to get more, even out of a familiar work, or notoriously, out of sex—hence the sex manual.[2] Or we may wish to try to extend the range of the things we enjoy. Then we are on the way to wanting to learn, in order to appreciate.

We all approach experience with such beliefs and expectations.[3] Our pleasure in art involves a complicated dynamic interplay, between our *anticipation* of the experience (for example our sense of what makes a good colour harmony, our generic expectations about musical climax, or the function of our desires within narrative, when we hope for or fear what might happen), our *recognition* of what is currently going on in it, and our *retrospection* concerning the interaction between the two.

The complicated question I want to ask in this chapter is: 'What holds this dynamic process together, not (just) from the point of view of comprehension, and so for example of our maintaining a certain conceptual tension and coherence (which, as I have already argued, counts for pleasure, and can involve us in its own dialectic, of established order versus the threatened disorder of the unexpected, and the bringing of the two through the work of art into an intellectually satifying coherence of understanding), but from the point of view of *appreciation*, that is of *maintaining our pleasurable response* to the experience, by paying attention in a particular way?

In approaching this topic I am going to rely on examples which exemplify the metaphorical model of *oscillation* and *amplification*. According to this model there are 'oscillatory' cognitions which can 'amplify' our pleasure, which lie at the centre of the temporal and dynamic process of our experience of the work of art. It is this dynamic process of understanding, in which *sensation, emotion, and cognition are mutually enhancing*, which constitutes appreciation.

Focusing, Surface, and Depth

In painting, for example, this oscillation can involve an alternation between our perception of surface and depth. A strongly realistic image, such as Vermeer's great *View of Delft* (*c.*1660) (Pl. 10), has an extraordinary physical presence, because of its emphasis through the medium of paint on the materiality of the city—its rough stone, its separate roof tiles, etc. We oscillate from attention to the medium to our imaginative reconstruction of the represented object. Some of the techniques for achieving these textures are described by Wheelock—for example the use of an under-layer of sand for the roof tiles at the left, the sculpting of the central tower of the Nieuwe Kirk, and so on.[4] And so we can see a tile, *also* as a clever combination of brushstrokes. The pleasure of the oscillation between the two lies in our exercising a highly adaptive visual skill.[5]

There are plenty of other things to marvel at, in a rather naive way, in an illusion-producing painting of this kind—the representation of reflections on the water, the overpowering lowering sky and its cloud ahead of the light, the sheer followability of the interrelated buildings, and their differing textures and feel.[6] I am impressed by the economy of the use of blue roof and red tile, and their mysterious balance and harmony, the subtle angling of buildings in relation to the angles of the boats, and the sense of what you can't see behind the main façade. People talk, relatively isolated on the bank in the foreground—but the city itself offers no human figure. It's a painting about the man-made in nature, made up of masonry, sky, and water, all depicted with amazing virtuosity.[7] (It is one of only two extant paintings by Vermeer not concerned with the domestic scene.) Above all it can be seen as a study in light, and in calling it a 'study' I immediately raise once again the sense of our enjoyment of works of art as performances, as displays of technique, of our sense of the hand putting on the paint. This is particularly striking when Vermeer paints something that someone else has painted—from the white-washed wall of *The Little Street* (c.1657–8) to the elaborate decorations of the virginal in *A Lady Seated at the Virginal* (c.1675).

This display of virtuosity, leading to an appreciation of 'the way the paint goes on', is overt in some of the paintings of Sargent, as Elizabeth Prettejohn eloquently demonstrates. For example in the aprons of *The Daughters of Edward Darley* (1882), or the way in which the rhythm of the diagonal folds in the skirt in the portrait of *Mrs Hugh Hammersley* (Pl. 2) gives a 'sense of movement' where each diagonal 'is one supremely confident stroke of the brush, surprisingly large in scale and indeed difficult to read unless the viewer stands back from the picture'.[8] And in Sargent's *A Morning Walk* and *Paul Helleu Sketching*, 'The pictures depend on a state of tension between the vivid illusionism of the portrait likenesses and the extravagant artificiality of the paint, where both "are constantly in play with one another" and this "interplay" is also central to the solid psychological dimensions of the portraits'.[9]

Similarly, in the work of Monet which we discussed, and in many other such cases, there is a pleasure in understanding the relationship between what we take to be a *representation* (of trees in the morning mist or lilies on a pond) and our visual sensations of colour, as they are defined by Monet's different kinds of brushstrokes. Monet's paintings of water and the reflections on it in his later images of ponds and lilies are astonishing studies in surface and depth—in the real world and in the painting, as for example the surface impasto of the lilies over their watery ground stands in for and mimics the weight of the vegetation suspended in the water.

Our appreciation of this relationship, between our thoughts about 'states of paint' and what we see as 'states of the world', between sensational surface and representational or conceptual depth, is a pleasurable and curiosity-satisfying activity. It can oscillate between our looking 'through' the image to its subject or object—'so this is one way to represent morning mist'—and our awareness of the harmonies and textures of the paint which achieves this illusion, which requires a conscious relationship to the literal body of the work. (The oscillation here is similar to the metaphor and ambiguity we looked at in Chapter 1.) Our understanding—of the relationships of representation to the world, and of the representation to its own means— is flattered. There is a kind of interpretative reflexivity here.

These relationships of surface and depth all depend on a play with focal length, as the distance from the picture surface at which it can produce the most complete illusion of reality. Come a bit inside that focal length and you are paying attention to the surface (with varying rewards). John Elderfield points to an interesting subversion of these conventions in Bonnard, who disrupts the convention that the picture plane should all be in pretty good focus for the moving eye, so that

painting, rather than seeking to represent the varying distinctness of foveal, parafoveal and peripheral vision, should, in Baxandall's words, 'instead register the field of vision offered within the frame with equal distinctness so that the eye can operate in its normal scanning way.[10]

In Bonnard's pictures, on the other hand, the canvas overall looks 'muzzy', particularly at the edges, as if they are part of our peripheral, less sharp vision. (Our optical acuity is only at its greatest at the centre of the gaze where the image is 'foveated'; it is quite good for twenty degrees either side of that ('parafoveal'), then it deteriorates in peripheral vision.) The 'fuzziness' of the visual sensation offered by Bonnard's paintings arises from the fact that they are 'a continuous membrane . . . nothing is scrupulously detailed as if seen close up. Therefore, no part of the surface seems veridical when foveated . . . any part of a Bonnard will only be veridical when it is *not* foveated, that is to say, when it is seen in parafoveal or peripheral vision, or at a distance.' (see Pl. 8)[11]

Elderfield justifies this apparently frustrating procedure by arguing that it helps us to 'savour the diversity of the paint handling', partly through these focusing effects, which 'keep the beholder on his toes by teasing him between one point of fixation and another'.[12] Bonnard's techniques thus promote the pleasure of an artfully delayed understanding, through

visual *masking*, the reduction of visibility relative to the ground, such as occurs with the peripherally hidden images in Bonnard's paintings. It may be thought to confirm the Chardin element in Bonnard, the placidly utopian element, in so far as the hiding merely delays the finding, and leads to the pleasurable shock of surprise that marks the moment of detection: The beholder can learn from this how to use Bonnard's painting imaginatively to represent the anticipation of a simultaneity between pleasure and surprise, which is to say, to represent a hedonism that rescues pleasure from every surprise.[13]

Bonnard, in drawing our attention to the handling of the surface of his painting (as also does Monet), takes us back through the process of perception to an 'earlier' stage from which we have consciously to move forward again to a (mimetic) understanding. For as Grodal points out, this drawing of attention to the surface, and hence to a perceptual recoding, is a typical process for much modernist and later art, which moves 'upstream' from the usual (realism-inducing) modes of understanding. They go 'against the grain' of the usual modes of vision, and disrupt the usual systems of comprehended 'meaning' in favour of what Grodal calls 'intensities'. We normally live in a 'mid sized world' in which 'the prototypical level of meaning is one at which we have objects, and agents, and acts and preferences relating agents to objects'. But this can be short-circuited in art which 'gives salience to pre-meaning intensities' such as 'the non-figurative, texture dominated level' we find in much modern painting. Abstract expressionists, and Impressionists who 'highlight phenomena of local intensities' like Bonnard, bring us back to an attention to basic sensory processes. The usual narrative (or 'midworld') structures are short-circuited, partly because 'to tell a story or make mimetic representations is not felt in the twentieth century to be quite the central "aesthetic" endeavour that working with basic perceptual phenomena is'.[14]

'Significant form'

Our satisfaction in the formal arrangement of the image—which tends to pleasure through an (often deceptive or not immediately apparent) integration or unity of the design—depends upon our paying attention to the canvas at the other end of the focal range; but Bonnard exemplifies this as well, as we can see from what Whitfield has to say about *The Bathroom* (1908) (Pl. 9):

the figure is placed at the centre of the picture, her body weighing down the soft ripples of the curtains and the divan and balancing the verticals of the window and walls. The rounded curves of her head, breast and buttocks echo the three round forms receding into the picture—the tub, the basin and the chair which carry the eye back to the nude in her mirrored image.[15]

This balancing, echoing, and leading of the eye is, I believe, part of what Fry and others meant by our pleasure in what he called 'significant form'. This aspect of painting is discussed in all sorts of ways by many critics since Fry, in the gestaltist work of such as Arnheim and Gombrich, and in the more overtly formalist tradition, from Greenberg to Fried. I am not concerned here with formal*ist* views (as disguised recommendations for the ways in which painting ought to go, or as a way of analysing the twentieth-century development of abstraction). I am thinking of significant form simply as an idea which facilitated appreciation, by pointing to some of the ways in which we can enjoy the organization or design of a painting. 'Significant form' in this sense isn't necessarily important for the interpretation of the 'meaning' or situation of the image (though of course formal analysis perpetually shows how such formal arrangements can reinforce such significance), but in the way in which it can bring about the enjoyment of a special sort of balance or dynamic equilibrium within the work, which is appreciated in a contemplative rather than an inquiring state.

Fry's account of Cézanne[16] turns on such essentially pleasurable responses of satisfaction, by pattern-finding ('correspondences'), the perception of hidden unity ('planning'), and the appreciation of subtlety and harmony:

> His composition at first sight looks accidental, as though he had sat down before any odd corner of nature and portrayed it; and yet the longer one looks the more satisfactory are the correspondences one discovers, the more carefully felt beneath its subtlety, is the architectural plan; the more absolute, in spite of their astounding novelty, do we find the colour harmonies.[17]

Fry, like Lily Briscoe, is interested in the imposition of order or design upon vision. For him the post-Impressionists go back to 'ideas of formal design' in painting. With Cézanne, 'the whole structure of Impressionist design broke down, and a new world of significant and expressive form became apparent. It is that discovery of Cézanne's that has recovered for modern art a whole lost language of form and colour.'[18] He has a view of the phenomenology which underlies such judgements, since he believes for example that '[pictorial] unity is due to a balancing of the attractions of the eye about the central line of the picture' and that 'a composition is of value in proportion to the number of orderly connections which it displays'.[19]

The sort of thing I have in mind then, in looking at this kind of pleasurable response, which is typical for great painting,[20] is such matters as the relationships of balance and symmetry in an image, and the way in which a unified response may be secured by the organization of disparate objects within the frame (and any tensions with that in an implied breaking-out of it). As Diderot remarks when confronted by Chardin's *The Smoker's Case* (c.1737): 'How can one fail to be moved by the perfect diagonal of the pipe stem, the long shadows falling on the stone, or the subtle arrangements of horizontals and verticals?'[21]

Fig. 6 Chardin, *The Smoker's Case* or *Pipes and Drinking Vessel* (c. 1737). The art of making an entrancing geometry by the arrangement of real-life objects. And then painting them.

The same kind of tension and balance can be seen, as we noted, in the Picasso *Three Dancers,* where the formal configuration expresses the tension between the calm balance of the dancer and the agonized restraint of the crucified sufferer, and in Cubism there is a far more complex exploitation of interlocking, ambiguous geometrical or perspectival relationships as in Juan Gris's *Still Life before an Open Window, Place Ravignan* (1915).

It is finding unity which seems to count as a great pleasure for understanding here.[22] As Braque put it,

So when you ask me whether a particular form in one of my paintings depicts a woman's head, a fish, a vase, a bird, or all four at once, I can't give you a categorical answer, for this 'metamorphic' confusion is fundamental to what I am out to express. It's all the same to me whether a form represents a different thing to different people or many things at the same time. And then I occasionally introduce forms which have no literal meaning whatsoever. Sometimes these are accidents which happen to suit my purpose, sometimes 'rhymes' which echo other forms, and sometimes rhythmical motifs which help to integrate a composition and give it movement.[23]

Mary Acton asserts that 'Composition is about making relationships between objects in order to make a satisfying whole.' Like Fry, she thinks that different kinds of satisfying formal orders can have different types of emotional tone and effect.[24] And so she says that Piero's *Baptism,* thanks to its composition, 'radiates a feeling of stability and peace combined with spiritual tension and mystery' which is achieved in large part by the way in which the composition emphasizes vertical and horizontal lines. (She also sees a golden section here, and believes that the rigidity and monotony of the mathematical quality of the image is offset by its curves, which 'create movement and variety for the eye'.[25] (See Fig. 8.)

All sorts of images can be analysed in this way, at different levels of sophistication, and often to extraordinarily revealing effect. As David Sylvester argues,

Fig. 7 Juan Gris, *Still Life Before an Open Window, Place Ravignan* (1915). Cubist paintings generate many ambiguous diagonals. How can they be brought into a unity?

The basic assumption of modern art [he is thinking of Matisse, Bonnard, Braque, Picasso, Soutine, Klee, and Mondrian] is that the first concern of art is to present a configuration of shapes and colours and marks which in and of itself stimulates and satisfies, and that only after this condition has been fulfilled can the subtlety of observation, the depth of human feeling and insight, the moral grandeur, expressed in the work, have validity: before the work conveys reality it must achieve its own reality, before it can be a symbol it must rejoice in being a fact, and the more it affirms its autonomous reality the more will it contain the possibility of returning us to the reality of life.[26]

From the point of view of our pleasure, it is the emotional effects of such formal arrangements (beyond the pleasures we get from notic-ing them and attending to their ingenuity) which count. That is why a relatively 'stable' geometry as in Piero will indeed seem more 'calm and balanced' (partly because that is the way our metaphors in language interlink) than an unstable, mannerist one, as in the Picasso *Dancers* or the curvaceous but expressively agitated surface of a Jackson Pollock. But this kind of analysis can only point to highly gen-eralized effects—it doesn't discriminate between emotions at all well. This is not to say that the different types of harmonic relationship in Piero and in Vermeer are not in themselves just as variously and exquisitely enjoyable as are different kinds of chord sequence in music. But as for chords, it is difficult or eccentric to ascribe particular different emotions to them. And again like chords, pictures can go to work on us in this way without our needing to be able to analyse their underlying mathematics or grammar.

In any case, pictures are often enough not open to any very specific formal analysis, even in the most obviously geometrical cases. When C. H. Waddington tried to analyse the secret of the relationship between the mere 'Static Balance' and the 'dynamic movement in equilibrium' which Mondrian looked for in his beautifully balanced but far from boringly symmetrical geometrical abstractions, he found that no mathematical formula would do. Although there is a systematic relationship of similarity between a number of Mondrian's solutions of a formal problem, of including, say, five

Fig. 8 Piero della Francesca, *The Baptism of Christ*
(*c.*1440–50). A geometrical stability which is
reassuringly peaceful for the spectator.

rectangles in a broadly square canvas; there seems to be no easily derivable mathematical convention here.[27] A 'genuine' Mondrian is arrived at, and enjoyed, by a kind of 'subjective' intuition; it has a dynamic balance which comes about by satisfying the demands of the eye rather than from any mathematical formula. Waddington concludes that the kind of 'balance' which we recognize here is 'more akin to the type of relationship which the biologist encounters in the overall body-form of a healthy animal than to anything expressible in mathematical terms as simple as the geometry seems to imply'.[28]

Our pleasure at the ways in which art puts things in order (from *To the Lighthouse* as a whole, to an image of a cup or a table, to the final cadence of a piece of music) has a double aspect: it gives us through mimesis a pleasure at the superior ordering of our experience, compared to our ordinary dealings with the world, and at the same time it prepares us for more art, as we become aware of the various ways in which art can do this, and so also makes us aware of the *relativity* of our modes of perception and ordering. This can give us a double pleasure—one to be derived from the material made intelligible to us within the work, and the other from an awareness of the use of the medium, which sets up comparisons and collations between ways of seeing. This is made very obvious if we look at different treatments of a subject, even one as basic as a jug on a table, as represented by Chardin, or Cézanne, or Braque or Gris or Morandi.[29]

In paying this kind of attention we are reacting to aspects of images that are not usually thought of as representational. But they often are, if ambiguously so, because they *are* e.g. an arm, which is also *balanced against* the orientation of the rest of the body in a certain way. The default position in our looking at form is always also looking at representational content, from an arm more or less suitable for Zeus, to a red square that represents nothing much but itself. As Sylvester pointed out in our quotation from him earlier, an attention to form allows for a particular psychological refocusing of attention, which on the evidence of many responses, gives us pleasure, most particularly when it interacts or oscillates in an interesting way with an emotionally significant subject matter.[30] This attention has the typical feel of calm contemplation rather than of dramatic involvement or problem-solving. Fry thus speaks of 'the pure contemplation of the spatial relations of plastic volumes' which gives what is 'the purely formal meaning' to him.[31]

The distinction I have tried to make so far, between what one might call pleasure in design and the pleasure or pain caused by the emotional import of a subject matter, is not an easy one to make; and it can lead to its own painful contradictions. It seems that the formal pleasures I have discussed above depend on a mental set, which may be very different from, and even opposed to, the mental set likely to be brought about by the content of the image; in the Piero *Flagellation*, there is a hidden incongruity between the pain of the subject matter—flagellation—and the formal balance and the apparent calm of Christ, and so the 'form' here has to be interpreted as emphasizing the theologically redemptive rather than the humanly suffering aspect of his nature. Particularly where strong emotional responses to sex and pain are concerned, there can be a real tension between (calm) formal demands and (arousing) representational ones.

This tension is particularly apparent when we consider the relationship between design and the erotic subject, for example in Edward Weston, who made photographs of nudes with modernist formal attributes. There can be little question about mimetic commitments here. The erotic effect is strong enough, particularly given the (generic) signs for it; that is, their intertextual relationships to other, more 'popular', types of photography of the nude. There is an enjoyable tension between an erotic sense of the body and its formal arrangement, between its plasticity (the spectator's imaginative apprehension of the body as an object to be touched)[32] and its static, less 'amenable' sculptural form, particularly when the design of such photographs can make the naked female body come to resemble the biomorphically rounded natural objects of some of the modernist sculpture of its time.[33] And in Weston's *Nude on*

Fig. 9 Edward Weston, *Nude on Sand* (1936).
The photographer creates a graceful line to
rival those of the Modernist painter.

Sand (1936), for example, the shadowing on the edges of the body mimics the delicacy of outline in painting, and also aims at abstraction:

These simplified forms I search for in the nude body are not easy to find, nor to record when I do find them. There is that element of chance in the body assuming an important movement; then there is the difficulty in focussing close up with a 16″ lens; and finally the possibility of movement in an exposure of from 20 seconds to 2 minutes—even the breathing will spoil a line.[34]

Weston sent this, one of his favourite images from the *Nude on Sand* sequence, to the painter Charles Sheeler. His response: 'I am greatly enjoying the print you generously sent me. If there is a more beautiful photograph of the naked figure anywhere I haven't seen it. One associates it with a quality of drawing such as Ingres set forth in the Odalisque.'[35]

All this may give the spectator pleasure, as he or she sees how the photograph helps to define contours and rhythms which are essentially to be thought of as contemplatively 'seen' rather than sexually 'touched' in the imagination.[36] As this formal interrogation gives pleasure to the spectator it is in a balance or tension between the imagined appropriations of the 'erotic' and an acculturation into the conventions of the 'formal', which is supposed to inspire a more detached contemplation of the body, which is presumably the achievement of the artist as well.[37] Bodily subject and significant form here can have distinctively different (aspectual) emotional effects, or enter into balance.[38]

Heterosexual and homosexual spectators can enjoy both of these aspects, and it seems that conflicts between the formal and the erotic tend to arise in disputes which turn on questions of morality rather than of pleasure.[39] From the point of view of pleasure-taking I am only concerned to point to the interacting aspects of this sort of imagery—an imagined erotic appropriation and a formal enjoyment. Although this distinction has come under political attack, there is little evidence that as a pleasurable response it is simply historically superseded, for men or for women, and the moral rights and wrongs of this appropriation lie elsewhere.[40]

Awareness of Technique

I have been arguing that there is a complex cognitive mediation here, between the mimetic effects of sensory input and our more or less discriminating formal enjoyment of the work of art. But there is a problem here. How far do we need an explicit awareness of such formal considerations to facilitate our pleasurable response? I have suggested that the formal aspects of a painting may have a subliminal calming effect, as for example in Piero's *Baptism*. And for music I have suggested that we can rely upon the procedures of much tonal Western music as a kind of system for erotic tension and release. But what kinds of interpretation are involved in noting such things?

There seems to be in the literature on this subject a basic dispute about how 'immediate' an enjoying response can be or should be, and this is particularly acute for analysis of the form of artworks. Hanslick for example (with Wagner in mind) decried as 'pathological' any experience of music in which the listener did not understand the music as an imaginative object to be held at an aesthetic distance, and so allowed himself to simply react to the sound in a directly physiological or psychological sense. But what kinds of analytic representation should we be *able* to formulate to ourselves as we look or listen (or at least be able to do so consciously)? I have argued above that the most basic of these conditions for enjoyment, such as the harmonic tension and release model, can be picked up rather like a natural language, rather as we learn the possibilities of the system of perspective in drawing and painting,[41] and need not demand any conscious attention to those syntactic or formal procedures of which the creator may be aware.

But there can be a demand for a more technical approach to our experience, as in the responses which Kivy reports to a performance of Josquin's *Ave Maria*.[42] He resists any associative thoughts, narrative- or character-oriented, in favour of an awareness of the 'perfection of the part writing' here, which fits into a harmonious whole in 'consummate polyphony' with its 'wonderful voice-leading', its 'masterful preparation of cadences', and its 'building up of musical climaxes'. This is what he says he is 'emotionally excited about', and he is even more so when he realizes the 'difficulty' of the canonic procedure Josquin has chosen. This is, so to speak, the Meyer model, without the use of any emotional associationism, to which is added an apppreciation, in what Kivy calls 'music-theoretic' terms, of the formal syntactic aspect of the music. It is facilitated by a certain amount of technical knowledge.[43]

This seems the more plausible when music lies outside the mainstream of the eighteenth–twentieth-century classical harmony which seems 'natural' to us. For example, we can come to know about serialist methods, and indeed get some pleasure from analysing serialist music, given that we can understand its conventions of production. But there is a real doubt as to whether we can thereby come to enjoy the actual process of listening to serial (or atonal) music, in anything like the way that we can enjoy Beethoven or Wagner. If Scruton is right, our ingrained modes of perception would inevitably involve a frustrating attempt to impose our pleasurable, tonal, habits of listening upon such music.[44] I sympathize with his view, and accept that atonal music cannot easily give Meyerian pleasures, because it so often seems to be approaching and then receding from them in a frustrating kind of way. But it is all the same possible to create a different conceptual framework, in which the many excitingly sensational and emotional features of atonal music can be appreciated. It has timbre, tone, local effects, and emotional impact (if sometimes of an 'abstract' non-sequential kind) that can be enjoyed. Although the 'syntax' of atonal music may be largely conflicting for us (very much like the language of *Finnegans Wake*), it can offer many other, perhaps more local pleasures.

The general point then is that an awareness of the *'rules' of construction* of a work of art (which so to speak define the parameters of the form) may simply not correspond to the perceptual mechanisms by which we enjoy works of art of that type. For Josquin, there seems to be some kind of continuity between technique and perceptual mechanism—and for Stockhausen's *Carré*, a far more disruptive relationship. What we then risk enjoying is not the dynamic process of the work's performance, but our ability to impose some kind of conceptual analysis upon it. My aim here is not to evaluate different musical procedures, but to suggest their different relationships to our pleasure. It is consistent with this to say that once Berg's Violin Concerto is entirely familiar to perception, it can seem entirely inevitable, logical, and wholly pleasurable, beyond any explanation of tone-rows.[45]

We need to know in each case whether musical analysis, like the formal analysis of an image, can bring us closer to the pleasurable experience (like our paying attention to aspects of the taste of the wine). 'Musicological appreciation' can obviously add 'an extra dimension to the experience' because it 'helps to open the music up to reflective thought', as Cook puts it.[46] But this might just help us to think about musical procedures without having the effect of enhancing our appreciation of any particular performance of it.

I am working towards a distinction which will be discussed later: that between appreciation and interpretation, which is the practice and value (and the pleasures) of sharing in verbal discourse the meanings (plausible or otherwise) which are suggested to us by works of art. I am strictly concerned in this chapter with the immediate pleasurable response of the individual to the work, rather than the way in which an interpretative community may enjoy arguing about its larger significance, or its relationship to things outside it.

There is a difference then between our following a piece in 'technical terms' and listening to it 'in the ordinary way' for pleasure. For example, we can be technically trained to follow sonata form (first subject, modulation to the dominant, second subject, etc.) but if people who have been trained to make the analysis don't actually use it when listening, what are we to infer about the ways in which they are actually enjoying the music?[47] A Meyerian analysis is different from this, because it functions as a way of explaining how these background conditions may operate for us to be given that pleasing sense of continuity, order, and unity, which I suggested made for pleasure. We do not have to be consciously aware of such conditions, any more than we need to be aware of the 'laws' of 'good gestalt' in the visual case.[48]

Similarly, we need to command the grammar of a natural language to enjoy its poetry, but we need not be explicitly aware of the rules of that grammar to read the poem. (Even so, some explicit awareness of such rules, for example of the way in which syntactic and other ambiguities can be exploited in language, may be helpful, even necessary for reflexive works of art, for example in reading *Finnegans Wake*.) However, this seems to be different from the musical case because all competent listeners to language can also speak (are competent) and the exercise of this competence can make them more or less explicitly aware of their syntactical choices. But most listeners to music have nothing like this ability—they do not compose. They do not seem to need that productive competence for which they would also need some awareness of underlying structures. Of course you can't all the same learn to play even a simple piano piece, without some analytical awareness, because you would need to work out the hierarchy of its organization in various ways. And so an enjoyment of performance may well partly stem from an appreciation of the formal choices open to the performer. This suggests that some kinds of analytical approach may function like a variant performance, making us aware of the possibilities of the works's rhetoric, and so helping to 'refresh' our responses to a piece. It may have become for us (in Hanslick's terms) merely sensational, and that sensational response be fatigued—so that an awareness for example of Tchaikovsky's formal virtuosity in the first movement of the *Pathétique* may revive our attention to the detail of his music. And teaching someone to appreciate a generic musical procedure, like sonata form, may give the listener a mediating representation or formula that allows them to feel that they are more confidently mastering the experience ('here comes the second subject—it's in the dominant—five steps up etc'). But this rather self-congratulatory (if common) experience, although it is a successful act of labelling, isn't always well directed to an appreciation of the provocative rhetoric of this particular work as it presents itself to a listener.

Order

Our responses to the 'formal' properties discussed above ultimately depend upon a property which literature, painting, and music all tend to share to an 'unusual degree'—that of order, as opposed to disorder, unintelligibility, or irrational feeling (though all these are very significant *contrastive* properties in many works of art, particularly in Dada and Surrealist poetry, painting, and music, and in many post-modernist works).

A classic statement of this aim at ordering comes from Henry James, and it is underwritten by his own practice:

Really, universally, relations stop nowhere, and the exquisite problem of the artist is eternally but to draw, by a geometry of his own, the circle within which they shall happily *appear* to do so.[49]

This artistic ordering can lead to

A feeling we have all had: that the study of mediocre works of art remains a random and peripheral form of critical experience, whereas the profound masterpiece draws us to a point at which we seem to see an enormous number of converging patterns of significance.[50]

As we have seen throughout, the coherence of a work of art counts greatly for our pleasure: 'One thing leads to another; continuity of development, without gaps or dead spaces, a sense of overall providential pattern or guidance, an orderly accumulation of energy toward a climax, are present to an unusual degree'. And there can be a sense of completeness when 'The impulses and expectations aroused by elements within the experience are felt to be counterbalanced or resolved by other elements within the experience, so that some degree of equilibrium or finality is achieved and enjoyed. The experience detaches itself from the intrusion of alien elements.'[51]

Our being struck by the order within works of art is part of their rhetorical mode of being. Furthermore, the order of the work can give us an idea of the order of the world. Or of the world beyond this one, if the Last Judgement in the Sistine Chapel is to be taken seriously. You see *King Lear*, and you think, 'so that is the way the world might go' when evil comes to power. Or you read *To the Lighthouse* and you think, 'so that is the process by which someone could deal with grief. How they might get it into order.' This narrative order is as valid for us as the causal orders revealed by history and social science, and the physical sciences, for even these latter are ultimately to be understood as parts of a historical narrative of the doings of human doings.

And so, says Woolf, 'there is a pattern' out there in reality to be discovered. This is the faith of the scientist as of the artist. But the model that Woolf urges is not the scientific one. She asserts that 'the whole world is a work of art'.[52] Well, if works of art really do offer us some of our best models for ordering and understanding experience, this belief could indeed sometimes be useful. But Woolf is not considering the value of competing epistemological models here, rather the way in which, for example, the psychological experience of epiphany can be made 'real by putting it into words'. This articulation of experience into words is what we can most rely on literature to do for us. It 'makes it whole'—it satisfies a demand for the pleasure and satisfaction and relief of coherence in order. And pictures can do the same for us and the musical structures of operas as well. This is not just the search for a hedonistic reassurance; it is also quite reasonable and informative, because we could never effectively opt for the opposite—that is, for a sustained preference for different types of disorder.

This applies to all the rhetorical sequencing that I have so much emphasized in all the arts, and it is often most obvious in the fantasizing within mass art, which so often engineers the illusion of a connection between physical and artistic order. For example, when Gene Kelly is 'Singin' in the Rain'. Peter Wollen gives an excellent formal analysis of the sequence of ten shots used here, from the wonderfully regressive and childish splashing in the puddles, through to the typically fantasized reordering coincidences provided for Gene Kelly's pirouetting umbrella, which always seems to come to rest under a waterspout, and the use of some very well–placed puddles for him to splash in, and produce sound effects which fit in with the musical accompaniment, and so on. The structure here is one of 'escalation in the dynamics of movement, as it progresses from the initial still movement on the porch through the saunter and the ramp, to the song itself, inaugurated first by an acrobatic leap, then falling back to stroll, and eventually building again into the dance'.[53] Indeed the song and dance, and its peculiar appropriacy to its cinematic landscape, are an obvious superimposition of order, even upon the prose progress of the dialogue narrative of the film, as they escape from the (apparent) contingencies of the main plot to an exceptionally ordered exposition of Kelly's happy mood.

We enjoy these basic effects of order in art. The bitty, inconclusive, messy, and contradictory in work, say, like Burrough's *Naked Lunch,* are always to some degree frustrating of our pleasure. Of course the bits of order that our intellectual activities produce for us are always limited—to learn to boil an egg isn't to make a soufflé, yet, and even being able to make a soufflé doesn't make you a good all-round cook. And the orders we preserve and enjoy in the arts are often in conflict with others, for ideological and other reasons—an immersion in Wagner's emotionally satisfying religious order in *Parsifal* might well trouble the intellectual economy of a Catholic, and an atheist might admire but not accept the cosmic order of *Paradise Lost*, and so on. The soldier's narrative life-order is different from and in conflict with that of the rabbi or monk or of the left-wing intellectual. But the desire for *an* order, often of a satisfyingly indirect, difficult, intriguing kind (from the detective story to *Finnegans Wake*, Bach to

Stockhausen, Piero to Pollock), is a constant. Hence our pleasure, so often short-term, or even illusory, in the thought that what we think of as real-life experience has been satisfactorily (even if temporarily and sometimes, quite obviously illusorily) ordered for us in art.

If we need these kinds of formal order to be satisfied by our experience, then great works of art are our supreme examples of the ordering and making intelligible of miscellaneous materials. The finding of a hidden order (through an appreciation of the point of the apparently disordered techniques of the artist) is one of the greatest pleasures of a kind of puzzle-solving interpretation. It is this underlying (and largely narrative) order that we thus discover, for instance, in *Prufrock*, through Eliot's apparent gaps, lack of constancy in the speaker, juxtapositions, and allusions. What we want is a narrative, thematic, or metaphorical cohesion for the poem.

Of course there are deliberately disordered works, and the disorder and irrelevancies of the slapdash, or indeed the short-term order of merely conceptual art, can only give trivial pleasures. And there are works for which we cannot, at the beginning, grasp the order—the piece doesn't seem to hold together. The history of the avant-garde is also one of the frustrating of understanding followed by comprehension, if the work is to be successful and to last. The *Rite of Spring* baffled most of its first hearers, but it now sounds quite logical, its rise to climaxes inevitable, its melodic content obvious, and its rhythms complex, and violent, but clearly ordered. It gives pleasure by this. All artistic disorders, real or apparent, are in tension with our desire for conceptual order. (And so from the point of view of pleasure, we often look to the work of art and to its analysis and interpretation to help us to resolve or to overcome an apparent disorder; this will be discussed in Chapter 6.) You have to attain a very sophisticated level of Zen indifference to be able to accept, let alone enjoy, the contingencies which are let into some of the works of John Cage. Such disordering, questioning works of art can be immensely valuable for all sorts of (usually philosophical, moral, political) purposes. Many works of art indeed aim at disturbing us, at 'problematizing' issues, or asking questions. They have an immensely *useful* function (central even to tragedy) but they can't lead to a completely satisfying experience for us. Disorder and provocations alone cannot give us pleasure, whatever else they may have to contribute. But this book is not concerned with displeasing works of art.

Of course there are consequentialist justifications for the enjoyment of order (of the kinds, sensational, abstract, and formal), which we have looked at here and in Chapters 3–4, and they depend on a psychological theory or theories about the (instrumental) value of certain types of cognitive exercise and emotions—for example the state of mind advocated in some Aristotelian accounts of tragic catharsis. But, as we have seen, the notion that such states of mind are valuable because they are *enjoyable* need not depend at all on such consequentialist considerations.

Beyond this, some works on the right scale, and with the right degree of complexity,[54] further please our understanding by reason of their profundity. Of course I can be most pleased by learning those particular things that satisfy my expectations and desires, or which for one reason or another I want to know about, as well of course as those things which I find surprisingly useful to me. But I have already argued that the very process of the satisfaction of curiosity and the process of learning are pleasurable for us. And these satisfactions will of course vary according to their content—in particular their depth and explorability.

I have been looking here and in Chapters 3–4 at some technical and formal properties which are at least typical of and prominent in works of art and which are not (like the process of understanding or emotional response discussed earlier) so *obviously* to be found in everyday experience. The aspects of art discussed above, such as the pleasurable focusing of taste and colour and sound sensations, the technique of oscillation between surface and depth in painting, the music of poetry, the harmony of colours, the tensions and releases offered by musical forms, the balance and symbolism of formal ordering in the visual arts, are all encountered in experience as highly specific to particular works of art, though they can be found in usually less elaborated forms elsewhere. It is this idea, that the pleasures of works of art are somehow intrinsic to them, whereas their interpretative implications tend to float free of them into the world, that I wish to pursue in the following chapter.

Note

It will have occurred to some readers to ask if I haven't forgotten a peculiar pleasure to be derived from works of art—and that is the contemplation of the beautiful, or the 'aesthetic', in them. But we do not need 'the beautiful' in talking about the values for us of the arts. All we need, I think, are the true, the (ethically) good, and the pleasurable; and 'beauty' does no more in my view than point to our pleasure in the work of art, as typically provided by artistic conventions (and very often to our pleasure in a formal aspect of it, such as 'significant form'). It indeed suggests there is something intrinsically valuable about works of art. But it seems that the pleasures they bring about in us are the most plausible candidates for this attribute, and that the concept of pleasure can do all of beauty's useful work, without leaving an important aspect of art unanalysed.[55]

Notes

1. Peter Kivy, *Music Alone* (Ithaca, NY: Cornell UP, 1990), 100.
2. Of which Alan Rusbridger gives a hilarious account: *A Concise History of the Sex Manual* (London: Faber and Faber, 1986).
3. A kiss is usually both anticipated and then enjoyed. But when it is not anticipatorily wanted in the right way, it can seem to be no more than an (unpleasant) physical sensation. (The child who is not acculturated to these pleasures, or mature enough for sexual arousal, may say 'your kisses are all wet and your beard is too prickly. Ugh . . .'.)
4. Arthur Wheelock (ed.), *Johannes Vermeer*, exh. cat. (New Haven and London: Yale UP, 1995), 111.
5. Is this like seeing the duck/rabbit? Not really, because I don't think you can sustain contradictory mimetic illusions as you can this kind of medium/object

relationship. It is not a disconcerting choice that is involved here. Though something like it can be found in the work of Magritte and of course in Escher.

6. In all this one cannot but be impressed by the painting's use of scale, and its positioning of the viewer. The effects of light here are immensely augmented by the removal of varnish in 1994, and the handling of the relationship between shadow and sunlight can easily bring to mind Proust's marvellous thoughts through his character Bergotte, about this picture. (Updike thinks that Bergotte's 'petit pan de mur si bien peint en jaune' is 'most likely the bright roof just to the left of the Rotterdam Gate on the right'. John Updike, *Just Looking* (Harmondsworth: Penguin Books, 1990), 26.)

7. This is a kind of virtuosity which was traditionally appreciated, e.g. in the detail of Hans Holbein's *The Merchant John Gisze* (1532). It is now not valued since it led to a meretricious photographic realism, where I would say the texture of the painted medium too often lacks interest.

8. Elizabeth Prettejohn, *Interpreting Sargent* (London: Tate Gallery, 1998), 44.

9. Ibid. 52.

10. John Elderfield, in Sarah Whitfield and John Elderfield, *Bonnard* (London: Tate Gallery, 1998), 35 (citing Michael Baxendall, *Patterns of Intention: On the Historical Explanation of Pictures* (New Haven and London: Yale UP, 1985), 93). Compare the oddly disconcerting effect of the very sharp overall focus in the photorealist work of Estes and others.

11. Ibid. 36.

12. Ibid. 41. He also gives as an example what he calls 'a dramatisation of the attentional narrative' for Bonnard's *Young Women in the Garden* (1923; 1945–6), ibid. 42–3.

13. Ibid. 45.

14. Grodal, *Moving Pictures*, 53–4.

15. Elderfield, in Whitfield and Elderfield, *Bonnard*, 101.

16. I rely here on Richard Shiff's account of Fry in his *Cézanne and the End of Impressionism* (Chicago: Chicago UP, 1984).

17. Roger Fry, 'The Post-Impressionists II', *Nation* (3 Dec. 1910), in J. B. Bullen (ed.), *Postimpressionism in England* (London: Routledge, 1988), 130.

18. Roger Fry, 'Post-Impressionism', *Fortnightly Review* (May 1911), ibid. 178–9.

19. Roger Fry, 'An Essay in Aesthetics', in J. B. Bullen (ed.), *Vision and Design* (Oxford: OUP, 1990), 22.

20. Cf. the amazing structure of Bruegel's *Hunters in the Snow* as analysed by Walter S. Gibson, *Bruegel* (London: Thames and Hudson, 1977), 148 ff.

21. Pierre Rosenberg et al., *Chardin* (London: Royal Academy, 2000), 220.

22. This type of analysis is typical of books on art appreciation, like Clark's *Looking at Pictures* or Mary Acton's *Learning to Look at Paintings* (London: Routledge, 1997), where one of the things we are encouraged to look for in a picture is the

way in which composition, space, form, tone, and colour, 'echo' or 'rhyme' with one another (as in the Bonnard analysed above) and so go together to make a unity. We can sometimes follow this process through the artist's approach to a final version: cf. Clark's account of the formal organization of three different versions of Constable's *Leaping Horse* in *Looking at Pictures*, 118 ff.

23. Georges Braque, in Martin Gayford and Karen Wright (eds.), *The Penguin Book of Art Writing* (London: Viking, 1998), 313.

24. Acton, *Learning to Look*, 10. She does not rely, and nor would I, on the rarified and implausible mental state of '*aesthetic* emotion' as desiderated by Fry and others.

25. Ibid. 2. On this painting cf. Baxandall, *Patterns of Intention*, 105–13.

26. David Sylvester, *About Modern Art: Critical Essays 1948–97* (London: Pimlico, 1997), 150.

27. C. H. Waddington, *Behind the Appearances* (Edinburgh: Edinburgh UP, 1969), 39–44, compares four real Mondrians of this kind and a 'pseudo-Mondrian' made up by himself. The difference between the two, he says, is that the real ones are somehow more enjoyable for their mysterious unity.

28. Ibid. 42.

29. Cf. the examples of this kind of subject matter in Margit Rowell, *Objects of Desire: The Modern Still Life* (New York: Museum of Modern Art, 1997).

30. Cf. e.g. Armstrong's analysis of Bellotto's *Ponte delle Navi in Verona*, in *Philosophy of Art*, 50.

31. Roger Fry, *Vision and Design*, ed. Bullen, 197. Indeed Fry wants to distinguish between form and 'associated ideas'. My account of form in relation to emotion or mood (which may be more or less appropriate) does not fit with Fry's ideal of disinterested contemplation, which seems to be part of the legacy of Kant's implausible and idealizing account of 'aesthetic' judgement and pleasure as somehow detached from ordinary human interests. Zuckerman, *Wagner's Tristan*, 100, refers to this 'devastatingly harmful idea of will-less contemplation'.

32. 'When I've painted a woman's bottom so that I want to touch it, then the painting is finished' (Renoir to his son Jean cited in Martin Gayford and Karen Wright (eds.), *The Penguin Book of Art Writing* (London: Viking, 1998), 338.

33. Charis Wilson (ed.), *Edward Weston Nudes* (New York: Aperture Books, 1977), figs. 34 (1926) and 44 (1925).

34. Edward Weston, cited ibid. 49.

35. Cited in Theodore S. Stebbins (ed.), *Weston's Westons: Portraits and Nudes* (Boston: Little, Brown, 1989), 30: letter of 11 May 1937, in the collection of the Centre for Creative Photography in Tucson, Arizona.

36. Or whatever better distinction the spectator needs here. A conventional one is that proposed by Kenneth Clark, between the 'naked' (unclothed, defenceless) and the 'nude' (protected by artistic formal devices). But everyone seems to want

to make this distinction in slightly different ways, particularly in feminist art criticism. Cf. e.g. Lynda Nead, *The Female Nude: Art, Obscenity and Sexuality* (London: Routledge, 1992), 14–16, who sees Clark's distinction as a crude, philosophically suspect binarism.

37. This seems to be part of the intention behind Jaques Rivette's film *La Belle Noiseuse* (1991).

38. This is also the achievement of much of the ballet—in the modern context, those of Balanchine, e.g. Cf. Judith Mackrell, *Reading Dance* (London: Michael Joseph, 1997), 194 ff.

39. Indeed the evidence of the trial of Mapplethorpe's 'X Portfolio' photographs tends to suggest that the distinction is still very much alive and kicking. Hence the conflict which Robert Hughes saw in the testimony given in this case. He points to two theoretical defences, one 'aesthetic' and the other concerned with the transgression of (consensual) conceptual boundaries. The first is exemplified for Hughes by Janet Kardon, who was 'reflecting on one photo of a mans's fist up his partner's rectum, and another of a finger jammed into a penis, and fluting on about "the centrality of the forearm" and how it anchors the composition, and how "the scenes appear to be distilled from real life", and how their formal arrangement "purifies, even cancels, the prurient elements". This, I would say, is the kind of exhausted and literally demoralised aestheticism that would find no basic difference between a Nuremberg rally and Busby Berkeley spectacular, since, both, after all, are examples of Art-Deco choreography'. But for Hughes this formalist approach is 'no worse than the diametrically opposite view', that such images are 'in some sense didactic': they teach us moral lessons, by 'stripping away the veils of prudery and ignorance and thus promoting gay rights by confronting us with the outer limits of human sexual behaviour, beyond which only death is possible. "This", wrote Kay Larson, "is the last frontier of self-liberation and freedom".' Robert Hughes, *The Culture of Complaint* (New York: OUP, 1993), 183. Kardon also seemed to think that formal considerations could obliterate the distinction between bodies and flowers: 'The forearm of one individual is in the very center of the picture, just as many of his flowers occupy the center' (cited in Wendy Steiner, *The Scandal of Pleasure* (Chicago and London: Chicago UP, 1995), 9). Consistently enough, when asked by prosecutor Prouty 'would you call these sexual acts', Kardon replied 'I would call them figure studies' (Steiner, *Scandal*, 33). Of what?

40. Does the formal 'justify' or merely 'sublimate' the erotic desire by giving it a 'higher' (cultural) motive (e.g. ballet)? Both. Does it neutralize our awareness of the autonomy of the man or woman (becoming a 'sexual object' in Berger's terms) by subjecting them to the inanimating demands of the conceptual object or still life? Or is this whole line of argument fundamentally misconceived?

41. These systems of perspective are more various than we might think, and not restricted to a one-point perspective. Cf. Alastair Fowler's *Renaissance Realism: Narrative Images in Literature and Art* (Oxford: OUP, 2003).

42. Peter Kivy, *Music Alone*, 159–60.

43. Cf. Nicholas Cook in *Music, Imagination, and Culture* (Oxford: OUP, 1990) on 'Appreciation and Criticism', 160 ff., pointing out a bit of canon in Schumann's 'Vogel als Prophet'. It is embedded and hardly noticeable, so what is the point of pointing it out? Is it important from the point of view of compositional technique, rather than of listening as Cook suggests, ibid. 164–5?

44. Cf. Scruton, *Aesthetics*, 281–5, 294–307. He points out that 'compositional grammar' and 'listening grammar' can be at odds (ibid. 294).

45. Cf. Anthony Pople, *Alban Berg: Violin Concerto* (Cambridge: CUP, 1991), 91–102 on the reception of the concerto.

46. Nicholas Cook, *Music*, 166.

47. Ibid. 3. Cook indeed cites evidence, ibid. 46–7, to show that even musically trained subjects do not keep formal track of the music they are listening to. He is not alone in arguing that what even musically well-trained listeners actually notice, as in Chopin's Prelude, Op. 28 No. 2 (cf. ibid. 26 ff.), is very different from the features that many analysts point to. Cf. Joseph Kerman's very similar thoughts about a Schumann song, 'Aus meiner Thränen fliessen', the second of the *Dichterliebe* songs, in Kingsley Price (ed.), *On Criticising Music* (Baltimore: Johns Hopkins, 1981), 38 ff. and esp. 47 ff.

48. For Schenkerians the various surface patterns represented by the traditional forms can only be understood when interpreted in terms of the basic linear-harmonic structures that they elaborate. Form only really exists when everything in the composition can be related to this underlying (syntactic) structure. But this might be just be a way of analysing things, and not a mode of hearing at all. Such deep structures may indeed be there, and even 'psychologically real' in the sense accepted by linguists for syntactic structures, but the empirical evidence cited by Cook nevertheless tends to show that we do 'not perceive musical structure as being fully coordinated' (*Music*, 72) in anything like the Schenkerian sense. The Schenkerian higher nodes are in many cases critical selections from the perceptual experience and there is no more reason to say that the selection represents the underlying sentence in such a way as to correspond to our 'pleasurable' experience of the music, than there is to believe that a single sentence or gerundive conveying the essential plot of *Hamlet* ('to kill the king') correlates to the readers' or spectators' actual responses to the play in the theatre or study.

49. Henry James, Preface to *Roderick Hudson* (1907), repr. in *The Art of the Novel: Critical Prefaces by Henry James* (New York: Charles Scribner's Sons, 1962), 5.

50. Northrop Frye, *Anatomy of Criticism* (Princeton: Princeton UP, 1957), 17.

51. Monroe C. Beardsley, *Aesthetics* (New York: Harcourt and Brace, 1958), 528.

52. 'From this I reach what I might call a philosophy; at any rate it is a constant idea of mine; that behind the cotton wool is hidden a pattern; that we—I mean all human beings—are connected with this; that the whole world is a work of art; that we are parts of the work of art. *Hamlet* or a Beethoven quartet is the truth about this vast mass that we call the world. But there is no Shakespeare, there is no Beethoven; certainly and emphatically there is no God; we are the words, we are the music; we are the thing itself. This intuition of mine—it is so instinctive that it seems given to me, not made by me—has certainly given its scale to my life ever since I saw the flower in the bed by the front door at St Ives.' Virginia Woolf, *Moments of Being*, ed. Jeanne Schulkind (London: Grafton, 1989), 81.
53. Peter Wollen, *Singin' in the Rain* (London: BFI, 1992), 16 ff., 27.
54. A characteristic demanded by Beardsley for works of art is complexity, which relates to the idea of magnitude. 'The range or diversity of distinct elements that . . . [the experience] . . . brings together into its unity, and under its dominant quality' counts for complexity' (*Aesthetics*, 529). Although Beardsley thinks of these features as giving rise to a number of instrumentally defined values for works of art, that is as having morally and otherwise desirable psychological consequences, I cite them here as characterizations of the kind of experience which is typically to be derived from works of art (i.e. with respect to their formal organization), which we tend to find valuable, because they are, for my view here, criterial for our taking pleasure in an experience of the artistic work which is ordered. When taken together, Beardsley believes that his three criteria (of intensity, coherence, and complexity) allow us to assess the 'magnitude' of what he calls the aesthetic experience.
55. But see further the Appendix on Beauty, below, on this subject.

6 | *Specificity, Fantasy, and Critique*

The architect Le Corbusier said that God lies in the details, and the same is true of the meaning in life to us, here, now. The smile of her child means the earth to her mother, the touch means bliss for the lover, the turn of the phrase means happiness for the writer. Meaning comes with absorption and enjoyment, the flow of details that matter to us. The problem with life then is that is has too much meaning.[1]

Consider the following not very detailed or comprehensive analogy between our learning to enjoy a work of art and learning to play a game, like tennis, where at least one of our aims is generally agreed to be that of enjoyment, rather than that of just 'getting fit', which would be like the pedagogic exercise involved in the challenge to understanding posed by works of art in the classroom.

1. When we are learning how to do something, like hit a tennis ball, we are learning how to do it best to satisfy our interests and for our purposes (e.g. to 'hit it out in front' and win the game). Now what counts as success in learning to play tennis and then enjoying playing tennis, is that there can come a point when you play it and you don't have to admonish yourself to 'hit it out in front'. You just *do* hit it out in front, and you get your satisfaction from hitting it the right way. The learning is reinforced, not by a silent obedience to the diagnostic command 'hit it out in front' but by the fact that we enjoy and are positively reinforced by the satisfaction of having hit it out in front. We begin to enjoy playing tennis in that way. And we hit the ball without any such accompanying verbal thoughts.[2]

2. This account contrasts with what I'd call a more 'Freudian' story. When you are hitting the ball out in front, are you 'really', secretly and maybe fearfully, obeying the (interpretative?) voice of

the father/coach, telling you to do something? So that the satisfactions of playing tennis may 'really' be described as the satisfaction of obedience to rules, obedience to the Law of the Father, and so on. We are on this view 'really' involved all along in all those kinds of interpretative orders and prohibitions which produce the cultural context for tennis and indeed help to create and sustain the desires for which that satisfying learning is devised.

Now these seem to be rival views: but they might both be partly true of the same activity.

3. So there is a problem about the 'autonomy' and specificity of such pleasurable experiences and the ways in which we can explain them. For it follows on from the thoughts above to ask—can our pleasure in tennis (and works of art) tend to show that we can learn to enjoy something 'for its own sake'? That's just how pleasure works for us—I am not *prescriptively* defining pleasure as 'that which one enjoys for its own sake'. I am aiming at an empirical generalization, worth paying attention to, that in learning to have pleasure in something, one is in fact very often learning to take pleasure in something, as we say, 'for its own sake'. But the sakes of works of art are going to vary, once we consider their mimetic commitments.

One might wish to explain the backhand in this light, even though, of course, these good backhands are also going to serve the further ends of obeying the coach's voice and, if he is right, of our winning the game. (And again you can cease to enjoy the actual playing of tennis, if this latter imperative comes to dominate your mind. You then can only enjoy competing and 'having won a game of tennis'.) We get pleasure from learning how to hit a backhand, and then from the use of the 'autonomous module' that our learning has created in us. And of course there are many different strokes to learn.

This story about backhands may help to explain the way in which we can emancipate the learning/obeying and coming-to-appreciate processes, from an end result, of being able to do/enjoy/understand/appreciate something, including works of art. Our growing understanding (see Chapter 1) has emancipated us into an emotive pleasure (see Chapter 2), derived from works of art, which include sensations, abstractions, and formal characteristics (see Chapters 3–5) which are specific to the individual work of art to which we pay attention.

This view of pleasure allows for a causal, even Freudian interpretation, notably in those cases where we have *failed* to make a pleasurable activity (which could of course be sexual activity) sufficiently autonomous, and perhaps have failed to make ourselves sufficiently autonomous, in pursuing the pleasure. We may have failed to free ourselves to enjoy doing whatever it is—making love, pursuing our profession, listening to Bach—'for its own sake' without its inhibiting interpretative shadow. That is, without the memory, repressed or not, of the learning experience, or of external imperatives. An obvious though revealing example is when we need to read a poem to pass an exam, or to make an interpretation of it, and this interferes with our enjoyment in just reading it.

This is all parable. It introduces some of the main themes of this chapter.

Pleasure and Specificity: 'Only this one will do'

Consider the physical presence of Vermeer's *The Kitchen Maid*. It has solidity, the basics of milk and bread, and stoutness. Is all this intended to signify 'virtue' for a seventeenth-century audience? But the enduring virtues of this painting *as a painting* aren't just in the way Vermeer expresses or brings to mind the pleasing or intimidating moral character of the woman, but also in his attention to her dress, to the tilt of her shoulders, the gathering of the apron, the graininess of the bread, and so much else.[3] All this gives some interpreters a paradoxical sense of the 'timeless'. How is it achieved? Is it a sense of stillness, arrested movement, meditation, basic recurrence? But it projects a contingent, historical, human situation—its 'timelessness' is not the timelessness of an abstraction (something that becomes 'timeless' by evading narrative associations). It is probably the time-

Fig. 10 Vermeer, *The Kitchen Maid* (c.1658–60).
How are the particularizing virtues of painting
different from the conventional moral virtues
attributed to servants?

lessness of paying attention to an unchanging particular. Is it not also something to do with endurance? Is it to do with classical purification and idealization? Not just that either; because here as I shall argue it is the particularity that counts. Quite apart from any devotional atmosphere, this is at the most manifest level the depiction of a woman in a corner of a room, with light coming down on her diagonally from the left, performing a simple task, with a barrier between her and the viewer, which reinforces the three-dimensionality of the whole. The orthogonals of the window converge on her right elbow, and yet this formal organization never degenerates into a geometric formula, because it helps to focus our attention to detail, which particularizes and differentiates.

In literature, music, and painting, I have argued that our enjoyments, and in particular the pleasures of understanding, have a great deal to do with the closeness and depth of our acquaintance with the work, and so with our submitting ourselves to just such perceptual processes as I have sketched above—and to the linear processes (and seemingly complete ones—as the pleasures of order and unity declare themselves) of hearing or watching a performance or reading a book, and looking at a picture, where we make our own performance, like the one I sketched above. We hear this joke, sit down to pay attention to *this* performance of a play, or to the reading of a novel or poem that we are making for ourselves now, just as we look in a certain way and appreciate the formal characteristics of this picture, hear this performance of a piece of music.[4] Those philosophers were not wrong who thought of pleasure as peculiarly specific to its object; and it can be the greater (and the better articulated) the more we appreciate the individuality of that object. In the end, 'only this one will do'.[5] It is as if we are in love with the work of art. There is no substitute for this Vermeer or that one, or for Keats's odes or Beethoven's last quartets, or indeed for Proust, George Eliot, Renoir, Picasso, Mozart, and Stravinsky, taken as a whole. Our pleasurable relationships to works of art tend to be incorrigibly promiscuous, despite frequent attempts by puritans to interfere.

The pay-off for learning to appreciate, of being well informed enough to notice what is there, can then be (from the sensation-emotion-cognition point of view advocated above) that we can listen to the music or see the picture or read the poem so that (paradoxically) it more fully (if temporarily) masters us, in all its detail. But we know where we are with it. This particularity of the work in relationship to pleasure is also emphasized by Roland Barthes:

I cannot apportion, imagine that the text is perfectible, ready to enter into a play of normative predicates: it is too much *this*, not enough *that*; the text (the same is true of the singing voice) can wring from me only this judgement, in no way adjectival: *that's it!* And further still: *that's it for me!*[6]

We are at the centre of our pleasures: it doesn't make them merely subjective, but it makes them literally egocentric. This is not to say that the 'intrinsic' value of a work of art wholly depends upon our paying attention to it 'as a work of art', concentrating only on its 'internal properties'.[7] What the work of art does for me as it gives me pleasure can at the same time carry with it valuable external, instrumentalist consequences, as we learn to problem-solve, discriminate our sense-impressions, and so on. The attending to a work of art, once we have learnt some of the things that help us to appreciate it, indeed provides an experience 'worth undergoing for its own sake'— rather like a game—because the 'own sake' really refers to our experience of its uniquely configured but relatively complete and satisfying formal and temporal order, as in a Keats ode or a Beckett play. But this doesn't amount to having anything like a unique 'aesthetic emotion', it depends as we have seen on variants of all the common-or-garden emotions we have in the real world. The process of our enjoyment is always going to be specific to its object, because it varies with it—and this applies to fish and chips and committee meetings as well as to works of art. So I can also enjoy my purely instrumental- or consequence-based moral and political responses to these—to the sheer reassuring worthiness of Vermeer's maid, and similarly to Crucifixion scenes, *The Triumph of the Will*, *Antony and Cleopatra*, and

Die Meistersinger just as much as my more intimately sense-oriented responses discussed earlier.

Nothing then, except perhaps God in some theologies, is really valuable in itself, and all the values we have arise in varying cultural circumstances for varying ends. The pleasures satirized in Huxley's *Brave New World* are very different indeed from those advocated in this book, but they are prophetic, and far from unintelligible. But within all that culture, pleasure can also open up a valuable private space—which I am going to characterize rather roughly, as 'intimate'. The work of art can create for me, and no one else, what I find I need at the moment.[8]

The consequences of this are not generally understood. An appreciative enjoyment typically arises from the cognitive and emotional processing that we go through as we experience art. But it is far from clear that all strategies to increase our understanding of works of art also increase our *appreciation* of them—that is, yield an enhanced pleasure—by cooperating with those sensational, emotional, and formal elements which we have discussed in Chapters 2–5.

This is because our cognitive processing of art (like our falling in love) may be *more or less object-specific*. In some cases this is obvious. The pride and pleasure I have in thinking 'That Picasso cost me six million', because I'm enjoying the thought of being rich enough to possess it, is different from my enjoying the painting because it has a certain style and content. The first of these undoubtedly pleasurable, and broadly object-related, thoughts is not directed to any appreciation of the specifics of the picture.

To get to the pleasures of particularity in art then, we have to learn to pay attention in a certain way. There may be much to be taken here from religious thought, in terms of the practices of prayer and meditation, which allow for a close attention, and even a mental attitude of subordination to another, in the interests of a 'higher' mental state, though mere pleasure is admittedly not usually the aim in such cases, as the tradition of misapplying such exaltedly religious thoughts to some abstract painting tends to show (for example, the Blavatskyan cosmology 'behind' Kandinsky and Mondrian). A significant number of musical works also ask for this quasi-religious contemplative response—notably those of Messiaen (Catholic thoughts) Steve Reich (biblical cantillation), and Glass (Buddhism).[9] Michael Tippett's *The Rose Lake* (1995), which has interesting parallels to Debussy's *La Mer*, since it is intended to evoke the colour changes in the lake from dawn to dusk, has the advantage for me of being less theology-specific. It offers the pleasure of a meditation on space as a musical illusion, the beauty and symbolic evocativeness of its drum-inspired orchestral sound, and the suspensions of its harmony, which seem to arrest progress in time, and so to create a sense of calm that releases us from the tensed pursuit of complicated meanings. Tippet takes up an appropriately 'Eastern' contemplative attitude to the object which inspires his work.

Some of the most striking examples in painting of this focused attention to the particular come from still life and its cognates and derivatives. It is the realm of the unique object (or landscape) presented by the painter as implicitly and silently worthy of his transformation by observation into the unique object of his image (and sometimes by a recourse to one of the Platonic myths of creation—that of the artist-god's ordering of reality by geometric arrangement). It is this balance between the object in itself and the ordering of the visual space of the image that is realized in so much great painting, and most obviously for contemplation in the greatest still life—in Chardin's and Morandi's domestic objects, in the still life as landscape of Cézanne, in the Cubist analysis of objects and persons in Gris and elsewhere.

I have already noticed the reactions of Diderot to Chardin's paintings as being (to him) exceptionally truthful. But there need be no moralizing or allegorizing of objects here. For Pierre Rosenberg, his still lifes have a 'contemplative quality' and a 'peaceful harmony' within 'an ordered constrained world'. Within their empty space there is ' a certain gentleness'. In the *White Teapot* of 1759, 'the teapot, bottle and grapes stand in mysterious half-light, which invites contemplation and gives a sense of calm'.[10] In Norman Bryson's terms, they are 'figural' rather than 'discursive'—they don't let in too much verbal response and so tend towards abstraction.[11] Indeed he sees in these images 'surfaces', which are those of objects 'sanctified by contact with the human body'. They are polished, swept, solid, most obviously touched. 'From this', he says, 'stems a prime aesthetic value, of intimacy; body and material world exactly adapted to each other'[12] (see Pl. 11). If Baxandall is right, Chardin was also exceptionally attentive to the recording of visual sensation according to the theories of his time. He is particularly interested in our perception of surfaces and the sensation of 'momentariness'.[13]

Bryson argues that in images like *The Smoker's Case* (see p. 140),

Objects are arranged informally: they can be crammed together or moved about as required. Chardin allows a certain casualness of inattention to loosen his paintings and give them air. Tasks are not rushed: they succeed one another in a gentle rhythm of co-operation between hand and eye, in a low-plane reality of quiet duties and small satisfactions. And interpenetrating the tactile space inside the painting is the tactility of the painting itself. In his lifetime Chardin shrouded his technical procedures in secrecy—there is no record of anyone having seen him at work, and it was rumoured that he applied the pigment with his fingers. Which may well be true: paint in Chardin is trowelled and stroked, it mimics the texture of terra-cotta or of glaze, it dribbles; its texture is buttery, or like cream cheese, it is an almost comestible substance which everywhere announces that it has been *worked*.[14]

It is not just the safely inanimate object which can command this kind of attention and sense of intimacy. As Julian Barnes says of Courbet's *Origin of the World*:

No, it's not like that, it's like this, the painting seems to declare. And the fact that it continues to make this declaration when surrounded by twentieth century erotica, that it is capable of rebuking the future as well as its own past and present, is a sign of how alive Courbet's work remains.[15]

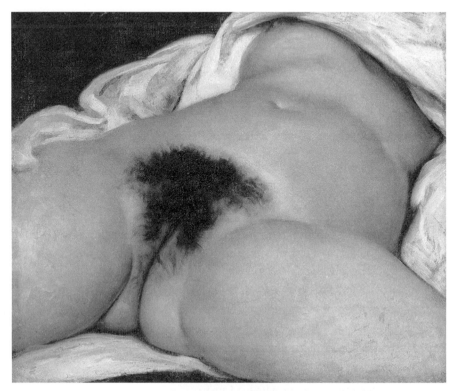

Fig. 11 Courbet, *The Origin of the World* (1866).
Forget the title. Are the pleasures of realism
ultimately what we want?

The title of the picture is probably not Courbet's own. But it has nevertheless prompted much quasi-psychoanalytical speculation concerning the 'real' focus of the painting, which was once owned by Jaques Lacan.

Intimacy and Company

Our attention to the specifics of the work of art considered in this way as expressive has a further consequence for an intimate relationship of the reader, hearer, or spectator to the particularity of the work. Our relationship to art can satisfy some of those interests and needs which give us pleasure in our relationships to persons.[16] People, like works of art, may inspire our gratitude by solving our problems for us, but they are also loved and desired for themselves. These are very different attitudes, as I shall try to show. As John Berger put it in his novel, *G*:

In an indeterminate world in flux sexual desire is reinforced by a longing for precision and certainty: beside her my life is arranged.

In a static hierarchic world sexual desire is reinforced by a longing for an alternative certainty: with her I am free.

All generalisations are opposed to sexuality.

Every feature that makes her desirable asserts its contingency—here, here, here, here, here, here.

That is the only poem to be written about sex—here, here, here, here—now.[17]

Although G stands for (Don) Giovanni here, I offer Berger's observations as not explicitly male or heterosexual in their implications. Much of what we are asked to appreciate here is that uniqueness which makes for difference: not a comforting resemblance to ourselves. Or as Jeanette Winterson puts it in *Written on the Body* (the gender of the speaker is indeterminate):

Why didn't I dump Inge and head for a singles bar? The answer is her breasts.

They were not marvellously upright, the kind women wear as epaulettes, as a mark of rank. Neither were they pubescent playboy fantasies. They had done their share of time and begun to submit to gravity's insistence. The flesh was brown, the aureoles browner still, nipples bead black. My gypsy sisters I called them, though not to her. I had idolised them simply and unequivocally, not as a mother substitute or a womb trauma, but for themselves. Freud didn't always get it right. Sometimes a breast is a breast is a breast.[18]

We also tend to be satisfied by our construction of a relationship to a single artist; this reaction is brilliantly and experimentally tested by Walter Abish in his 'What Else', where he asks 'who is the writer?'[19] The text is an arrangement of fifty unascribed segments from the diaries, letters, essays, and journals of writers ('all in my library'). It attempts 'to create from the disparate works of fifty authors an archetypal self-portrait of one', according to Abish's 'Introductory Note'. We know that one passage may qualify another across a gap, but we are not given any authoritative commentary to guide us. The text thus seems to get into contradiction by embracing opposed positions on either side of these gaps, and its 'Archetypal' writer to have no consistent psychology, as he is 'played through' by Abish's game with his library: 'My great strength, even in the past, was being very little concerned with opinion and not trying to construct myself consistently: writing as simply as possible and not trying to prove anything' (*99: New Meaning*, 21). This dialectic between inconsistency and coherence (so typical of the postmodernist text) is made acute by the conflict of voices here. Fifty writers are bound to contradict one another. . . . particularly if they are interested in projecting a unique vision. 'What Else' can therefore be read as a parody and *reductio ad absurdum* of the Barthes/Foucault notion of the author as the mere conjunction of socially available codes, or languages, or other texts (or, at least, of fifty of those available).

How do we take such an archetypal portrait? The tension between the eccentric and the typical, which haunts all artists in relation to tradition, is handed over to the reader to resolve here. We surely know what a text about writing should be like. But the author we *want* (as Barthes himself suggests)[20] is the individual writer, hidden behind his construction. The author-person we imagine 'Abish' to be lurks behind the idiosyncrasy of the texts he has chosen to possess, as 'the silliest images come down from the attic of recollections, while momentous ones remain there' (*99: New Meaning*, 13). We are challenged to imagine a hidden origin, so long as we can think of 'Abish' as responsible for using these passages to make a text. For this mythical portrait of Mr W.A. takes seriously the Barthesian attack on the unified authorial consciousness—and then demonstrates the aporias of that view by assenting to it. The arranger who copies and does not even write (except to record the word count of each passage) is indeed purely intertextual, but we are nevertheless driven to try to (re)construct him. (The 'Arranger' of Joyce's *Ulysses* is perhaps the most conspicuous of these sought-for figures, always hidden, but always implied.)

However much the social shaping of thought and perception may be necessary for our awareness of the implications between the passages, we can see that for all artists of any consequence such socially shaped perceptions are given a unique conformation within the individual.[21] To put it crudely, there are two distinct kinds of understanding for works of art here: a 'framework' understanding of the (logical, social, cultural) implications of what this person is saying, and what I will call a 'characterological' understanding, of the way in which what this person is saying fits into our uptake on the relationships between character, situation, and individuality.[22] The work of art is an individual then, in an extended sense—and only most obviously so—as the product of the expressive skill of highly original artists.[23]

When we are in contact with a work of art, we are usually in an implicit relationship with another person, most particularly through

Fig. 12 Titian, *The Entombment* (?1523–5).
This painting commands a universal emotional
response which has no need of religious belief.

the (inferred) intentions of the artist, who has used aesthetic and other conventions, and may have invented new ones, which are organized for us within that provocative rhetoric which we enjoy.[24]

This rhetoric is often going to be felt as expressive of states of mind—from God as the hidden cause of the natural sublime, to the ordinary pathetic fallacies of nature, and the domestic order of Morandi's jugs.

Our relationship to works of art is therefore, mediately, one to persons, and this is an important factor in our pleasure, as my arguments about sympathy and situation will have suggested. In enjoying them we are indeed choosing 'the company we keep' so that pleasurable feelings of intimacy, sympathy, and liking are (as we have seen) all involved.[25] It is these basic interactive human values (which also include a mediated solidarity with groups) which often underpin our enjoyment of all kinds of art. Hence, for example, Clark's remarks on Titian's *Entombment* (see p. 177): 'It is one of those obvious, eloquent appeals to our emotions, of which the great Italians, from Giotto to Verdi, have been the masters; and woe to him who cannot respond. He is cut off from one of the few artistic experiences which can be shared with the majority of our fellow-men.'[26]

Obvious examples of this appeal are the monologue and the portrait, written, painted, or musical (Fra Lippo Lippi, Titian, Marcel, Don Juan, Falstaff, the hero of *Heldenleben*). When we see a portrait we can have an emotional reaction to the character of the person as depicted. This will always be guided by all sorts of artistic conventions and the beliefs that underlie them, as 'framework' and 'character' interact in artist and sitter. The question then is the ways in which the mode or style of depiction can affect our sense of pleasure in relationship to another person. In Brilliant's analysis of the daguerreotype by Southworth and Hawes of *Daniel Webster*, for example,

The image corresponds to his reputation, and being a photograph, we imagine it to be true. Here is a character likeness; the stocky torso of a

Fig. 13 Southworth and Hawes, *Daniel Webster, 22 April 1851*. An American 'great man' idealized as Roman Senator.

middle aged man, forthright, erect, dressed in contemporary, formal costume, and nobly bald. But here is also an elaborate portrait iconography: the large cranium, indicative of the great mind within; the powerful and proper stance of a mid-nineteenth century gentleman; the grim, serious expression reminiscent of Roman Republican portraits, reflecting the patriotic dedication of this distinguished citizen of the American Republic; the column with its reference to the neoclassical architecture of Washington, where Webster served in the Senate, and its invocation of the noble portrait conventions developed in European art of the seventeenth century; the light from on high as a sign of divine revelation; and so forth.[27]

Brilliant is basically looking here at the (framework) conventions developed by artists in order to get the provocative rhetoric of the work (politically) 'right' for their audiences. Our pleasure in this representation is clearly supposed to come from putting us in touch with all the 'right' values, and an admiringly patriotic satisfaction that they are (even if rather subliminally) combined in this heroic figure.

This rather obvious example of idealization would contrast with the far more intriguing and perplexing sequence of Rembrandt self-portraits. The sequence is prized for its revelation of character and the supposedly introspective feelings of that character about himself,[28] and its emotional effects are situational; they depend on our compassion, our understanding of Rembrandt's facing up to the ageing process, and so on. And technically, on our appreciation of the unselfsparing detail with which he depicts his own changing face. Here too, variations in technique have a relationship to emotional effect. And so White and Buvelot say of the *Self-Portrait* of 1659, in Edinburgh (Pl. 12), 'There is no other self portrait of Rembrandt that gives the viewer such a sense of confrontation with the viewer', and they speculate that this may be due to the near photographic clarity of the rendering. 'In this picture Rembrandt adopted a . . . careful approach; fuzzy spots of paint, thin lines and transparent layers are juxtaposed or overlap, but nowhere is the paint applied thickly. The forms are modelled softly in a wide variety of hues, and the different parts of the face are forged into a whole without any abruptness of line'.[29]

The pleasures of art can then be, given our construction of a situation, the pleasures of admiration for someone else's feelings. This can be particularly close through the expressive performance of music, but it will often be mediated in a quite complex manner. I'm listening for example to Keith Jarrett playing the standard, 'Don't ever leave me' as a piano solo. His simple inflection of the melody brings the narrative associated with the words to mind—I identify with the feeling and message of the song—and I can associate that with my feelings for other people, because all standard songs adapt clichés in that way (for me)—indeed the whole disc from which this comes is an anthology of love songs. But what moves me and gives me pleasure is the extraordinary tenderness and delicacy of the playing of an improvisatory inflection of a tune which Jarrett and I love. Furthermore, by narrative association, prompted by the sleeve note, I can think of this playing as part of a tribute of affection (to Jarrett's wife, in this case). And I'm pleased by the thought that an exceptionally talented pianist can express that emotion in his playing. And the whole—for me—is a rather sad pleasure, like the distilling of love through experience in a poem like Williams' 'Asphodel, that greeny flower'. Although I've written this in the first person, I'd expect something very like the response I've described to be had by many of the people who hear the piece.[30]

My sympathetic identification here may be an idiosyncratic one, and have personal roots which go beyond that demand for reasonable assent on which I have so far based my argument. It is psychoanalytic theory which has most to say about the role of pleasurable or anxiety-inducing identification, and so I now wish to ask if it can give us insights into our emotional responses to the arts, which go beyond those offered so far. Maybe, too far beyond.

Fantasy, Freud, and Reductivism

My argument has been within a broadly philosophical tradition, which asks how reasonable or justifiable our responses to art may be.

For example, I have explained our emotional responses as tied to beliefs and attitudes, in such a way as to make it more or less reasonable, or more or less in accordance with realism of various kinds, to have a certain kind of emotion (and sentimentality seems for many to step over some of these boundaries). But what might lie beyond them? It has been the role of many who have looked at the fantasies and emotions which lie behind or within art (such as those we alluded to in discussing Cummings's poem, Larson's dog, Octavian's sexuality in *Der Rosenkavalier*, *La Bohème*, Millais's *Blind Girl*, and 'Singin' in the Rain') to say that it is possible to have a general theory of the ways in which they are irrational or subconsciously motivated. Preeminent among such theories are those influenced by various forms of psychoanalysis. I am concerned here, not with clinical practice, but with interpretations of art which might indicate the 'real' or hidden nature of our pleasure in it.

Such theories look for the underlying dynamics of our interest in persons in works of art. They also suggest that the work, like other cultural artefacts, works to disguise from ourselves the real nature of our emotional involvement, and hence our pleasure.[31] This kind of claim was very early articulated by Freud in his 'The Creative Artist and Daydreaming'. His idea is that the formal elements in a work of art constitute a 'bribe':

[an] incentive bonus, or a fore-pleasure . . . which is offered to us so as to make possible the realms of still greater pleasure arising from deeper psychical sources . . . In my opinion, all the aesthetic pleasure which a creative writer affords us has the character of a fore-pleasure of this kind, and our actual enjoyment of an imaginative work proceeds from a liberation of tensions in our minds. It may even be that not a little of this effect is due to the writers' enabling us thenceforward to enjoy our own daydreams without self-reproach or shame.[32]

You can see what he means: the joke as we saw can quite transparently 'mask' sexual agression, and so on. And if we like pornography or the erotic in the cinema, we may feel that a hard-core film like

Debbie Does Dallas[33] is too embarrasingly direct, and reveals our excessively prurient interest, but that if we watch a classically complicated
art-house movie like Nagisa Oshima's masterpiece, *In the Realm of the
Senses*, in which the sex is just as graphically depicted, we can indeed
feel better about ourselves. We can trade off our sexual voyeurism
against our serious consideration of the nature of sadomasochism.
But I am not sure that it any longer takes Freud for us to be made well
aware of the ambivalent nature of this contest between literary value
and obscenity or prurience, which has dogged legislators for some
time. And indeed one of the objections to the Freudian view is that it
is far too simply reductive: in its concentration on the sexual common
denominator, it prevents us from considering this kind of difference
properly.

I am not of course the first to point out that such theories can
sometimes be misleadingly reductive, and in the most obvious way
(to cite an objection going back to Jung's correspondence with
Freud),[34] because it sexualizes responses that may have other, better,
or at least simultaneous explanations.

For example, suppose we return to *To the Lighthouse*, which I
interpreted in Chapter 1 as a movingly elegiac celebration of Mrs
Ramsay's life as a loving mother, and a coming-to-terms (consciously
for Lily Briscoe, implicitly for Mr Ramsay) with her loss, ending in a
general mood of reconciliation and triumph for Lily Briscoe and the
reader at having arrived at a moment of vision. But for Daniel Ferrer
the hidden motivations and attitude to her parents beneath the story
(which are seen as Virginia Woolf's own) are very different. Woolf
said that 'writing The Lighthouse laid them [her parents] in my
mind'[35] and Ferrer interprets the book as an attack on her father
which masks a more insidious, less obvious one on her mother, which
is only accessible to the psychoanalytic approach. What seemed to
me to be praise, in Mrs Ramsay's triumphant realization of her
husband's love at the end of Part I, her satisfaction in the *bœuf en daube*
scene, and so on, really expresses what Ferrer calls Woolf's use of 'art'
as a 'discharge of aggressivity' against a woman who 'on a symbolic

level . . . embodies the mythical universal mother' (hence 'her caricatural obsession with the delivery of milk').[36] Lily's painting of Mrs
Ramsay really reflects, through the artistic medium of painting,
Woolf's act of aggression through Lily—she paints the picture to get
Mrs Ramsay out of the way, 'rolled up and flung under a sofa'.[37] That
is to say, Lily is not really expressing her likely failure as a woman
painter in this phrase, producing something that nobody wants; what
she (really) wants is a symbolic disposal of Mrs Ramsay as a piece of
rubbish. The act of painting itself is indeed fairly explicitly described
in sexual terms, and for Ferrer has an 'anal dimension', for as Lacan,
cited by Ferrer, notes, it is 'a succession of small dirty deposits juxtaposed', and manifests a 'sadistic aggressivity'.[38] Where Woolf claims
to have laid her parents to rest in her mind, Ferrer claims to have
shown that this can (really) 'be taken as murder'.[39]

Now it is clear, given the relevant psychoanalytic beliefs and the
psychologist's emphasis on patterns of behaviour which are set up by
the dynamics of early childhood, that this is the kind of interpretation that can emerge, just as it could for a Christian, a Marxist, or any
other theoretically elaborated point of view, given a Freudian view of
human nature and of the emotionally ambivalent role of the parent
in an upper middle-class family at the turn of the century. I mention
Ferrer's interpretation, not to dispute its background assumptions,
and certainly not to deny that we can have unconscious or repressed
aggressive motivations, but to point out that from the point of view
of our pleasure in *reading* (rather than interpreting) *To the Lighthouse*,
an interpretation like this would imply that the emotions we are
asked to discern here are very different from those which seem to
appear at the culturally endorsed—elegaic, Victorian, dignified, and
often comic—surface, and which seem to appeal to most readers and
critics. If the 'vision' here is 'really' one of vindictive dismissal, resent-
ment, and revenge, it is not easy to know how we would come to *feel*
this in response to the book, as opposed to merely comprehending
Ferrer's highly selective interpretation of it as there under the surface.
The motivating emotions here are literally not what we usually think

(or would easily admit) them to be, either for ourselves or even for Virginia Woolf.[40]

Susan McClary provides us with a more obviously challenging example, in her feminist account of sonata form: can we really always hear 'the thrusting masculine principle and the passive feminine principle' in many of its instances? She argues that in a symphony the masculine (first) theme will 'quash' the feminine (second) theme in a moment of triumphant 'climax'. According to her, the underlying fantasy here is 'the celebration of [male] sexual desire, which culminates in a violent ejaculation', and she believes that this is 'virtually a convention of nineteenth-century symphonic music'. The tonal system within sonata form does not just create all sorts of expectations and tensions and releases in varied ways internal to the music (as when we are listening in a 'music theoretic' manner); it is always the analogue representation of sexual desire. This is because 'the principal innovation of tonality is its ability to instil in the listener an intense desire for a given event: the final tonic cadence. It organised time by creating an artificial need (in the real world, there is no reason why one should crave, for instance, the pitch E; yet by making it the withheld object of musical desire, a good piece of tonal music can within ten seconds dictate even one's breathing).' Furthermore, 'Tonal procedures strive to postpone gratification of that need until finally delivering the payoff—its violent release of pent up tensions—in what is technically called the "climax" which is quite clearly to be experienced as metaphorical ejaculation.'[41] It is the last part of this which is most troubling, quite apart from the relationship between the 'clear' and the 'metaphorical': Why just 'ejaculation'? What is the force of 'metaphorical'? How do women respond to this kind of music? Do men like to be 'overcome' too?

This analysis claims to reveal a *causal* account of our pleasure, by seeking to show that a single, dominant, and largely hidden narrative association, or unconscious fantasy, of which we are not necessarily aware, and which many of us are inclined to suppress or deny, more or less secretly conditions our response. Many of these fantasizing emotional responses are part of our pleasure in works of art by now, and they hardly need much repression, for men or for women. The sexual parallels are fairly obvious, though I'm still inclined to differentiate my responses to Bruckner from those of sexual climax, while realizing that they may well have a good deal of neurophysiological excitation in common. And in any case *Tristan* and many other works seem to offer a better model for sexual excitation. But how Freudian, or idiosyncratic, can these more hidden ranges of our pleasure in emotional engagement be conceived to be? For example, when Stuart Feder sees Mahler's 'Abschied' as a 'reunion fantasy' of return to the maternal security of the womb?[42] Even if getting to the top of a mountain, or the end of the Bruckner, or the final release of the heroine from the clutches of a villain (or her return to them), or Lily Briscoe's act of painting, may suggest an ejaculation to some, they are very much more like themselves, just indeed as masturbation or lovemaking is like itself.

Psychoanalytic criticism, various though it is in its forms, has been most influential in trying to show how works of art depend upon our (often indirect) emotional commitment to fantasies, and subconscious motivations, which the critic attempts to specify.[43] This is because literature can indeed 'transform our primitive wishes and fears into significance and coherence, and this transformation gives us pleasure'. And further, 'The fantasy psychoanalysis discovers at the core of a literary work has a special status in our mental life that moral, medieval or Marxist ideas do not. These are conscious and adult and intellectual. Fantasies are unconscious, infantile, and fraught with emotion.'[44] I have no doubt that this process indeed occurs in many cases; I am less sure that psychoanalysis has the best account of it. Why do so many of us read lurid novels about serial killers—by such as Thomas Harris, Kathy Reich and Patricia Cornwell—which at least must arouse a kind of (pleasurable?) anxiety about violence to women. It is very difficult to know how far the psychoanalytic gets us in understanding the varying phenomenology of the pleasures brought about by works of art. (Though of course some such explanation of the dynamics of fantasy as it affects a particular *individual* may be necessary, to explain why he or she only, or predominantly, reads books about serial killers. Or writes them.)

Noel Carroll makes this point about differentiation very persuasively in relation to horror movies (which would seem to be excellent candidates for psychoanalytic interpretation, and of which he offers a very interesting general account, which I follow).[45] Such movies arouse a pleasurable response to things that ought to be unpleasurable, as we have seen. It is an ambivalent attraction–repulsion type of response. At one point Carroll refers us to the psychoanalyst Ernest Jones's explanation of vampires, which sees them as 'standing for the relatives' longing for the loved one to return from the dead'. But this longing is combated by terror at the bloodsucking, which Jones says, is nevertheless associated with seduction, so that the relationship to the vampire disguises an incestuous relationship. 'In short, the desire for an incestuous encounter with the dead relative is transformed, through a form of denial, into an assault'. The loving portray themselves as the innocent victims of this aggression, thus permitting themselves incestuous pleasure without blame. Jones also connects this bloodsucking 'with a regressive mixture of sucking and biting characteristic of the oral stage of psychosexual development'. So that our secret and anxiety-provoking incestuous desires underlay our involvement with vampire fictions.[46] Horror fictions in general could be seen in this way, even in the more sophisticated interpretations of a later psychoanalysis than Jones's,[47] if our 'ambivalence towards the objects of horror derives from a deeper ambivalence about our most enduring psychosexual desires'. This search for ambivalence is, as we have partly seen, typical of the psychoanalytical view. The repulsive features of such fictions just 'satisfy the censor' and are a means to a (secret) pleasure ('given the structure of repression'); that is, we are having a pleasure without being consciously aware of its true nature.

The 'liability' of any such theory, Carroll argues, is that it requires an 'animating wish' which has to be understood as sexual—and it is 'at least not easy to discern a latent *sexual* wish behind each and every one of the monsters in the gallery of horror fiction'. Vampires may be plausible candidates because they 'seduce'; but how can one see the fantasy 'of being trampled by big gorillas or possessed by vegetables', as gratifying a sexual wish? The chain of association in the explanation gets too stretched, Carroll suspects, just to make the data fit the sexual wish-fulfilment theory.[48]

It is true that the cephalopods come from the deep, but it is hard to gloss this as repression of psychic material, since one cannot specify the content of whatever repressed material they might be supposed to represent. One might say that since the cephalopods devour people, they represent repressed, infantile anxieties about being devoured. But, on the other hand, since some deep-sea creatures do devour humans, and since being literally devoured is a legitimate adult fear, and since there is nothing in this story [H. G. Wells's 'The Sea Raiders'] to suggest a connexion with the child's putative fear of being eaten by a parent or parental surrogate, there is no real force to claiming that the cephalopods are some sort of parent figure and that the story manifests a deep-seated, infantile fear of being gobbled up by Mom and Dad.[49]

But suppose one says that such figures 'manifest repressed anxieties' which are less obviously to be connected to the (highly disputable) psychoanalytic model of our early development? (For example, the fear of destructive aggression, of castration, of abandonment, of loss of identity, etc.) But all sorts of such anxieties may be repressed, rather than sexual wishes. Carroll thus suggests that 'telekinetic nastiness' (as in *The Exorcist*, *Carrie*, and so on) 'might be explained as gratifying the infantile conviction in the unlimited power of repressed rage' (it is a fantasy about 'the omnipotence of thought') which conveys it in the disguise of horror. For Carrie, looks really can kill. She is a monster who allows a guilty fantasy to surface.[50] And we both fear her and identify to some degree with the motives for her revenge.

All this counts, not against an explanation of our responses which refers to repressed sexual wishes (if you are convinced, you can have it, as I show below) but against an unduly reductive explanation of the (rather obvious) but various fantasy pleasures to be derived from works of art, including horror movies.

For even if *all* pleasures are 'really' sexual ones at base, there would still be point, if we are to learn to appreciate works of art in the ways described in earlier chapters, in differentiating them in many ways other than those favoured by even the later developments of psycho-analysis. It seems not very informative to think, for example, about our fantasy involvement in heroic and immensely powerful and indestructible figures, from Don Giovanni to Superman or Arnold Schwarzenegger as 'just' or 'basically' displaced sexual fantasies, even if at some fantasy level or another, muscle power and penis power are indeed (for men and women) more or less disguised equivalents for one another, and both bring with them fantasies of easy domination. It is differences, even in sexual activity, which seem to count for our everyday pleasure when we are reading books, given that heroic figures are so various—Don Giovanni, Julien Sorel, Walter's *My Secret Life*, and Proust's Marcel.[51] So far as our pleasures are concerned, the test of psychodynamic thinking should be the way in which it can dis-criminate on the 'surface' level, by pointing out all sorts of things within the flow of narratives whose emotional and erotic implica-tions we might not otherwise notice or appreciate. And this includes our introspection into the hidden basis of our enjoyment (though this may prove inhibiting, if it conflicts with our moral intuitions). But then we already know that fantasy (and indeed much art) is often designed to give us pleasure by bypassing our moral codes.

I have built a large part of my explanation of pleasure on the idea that works of art satisfy our curiosity and give us understanding in various ways, and this process of understanding can also be given a broadly psychoanalytic interpretation, as for example when Peter Brooks asserts that *all* quests for knowledge are disguisedly erotic.[52] The 'desire to know' for him is constructed from sexual desire and curiosity.[53] He applies this model to literature and painting by paral-lelling knowledge in general with knowledge of the body. (Indeed, 'In modern narrative literature, a protagonist often desires a body' as an 'ultimate good', so that in Don Juan there is 'a wish for mastery which is in essence a desire to know'.[54]) So all the narrative understandings analysed in Chapter 1 are in some way 'really' driven by sexual desire.

A quest of this kind certainly seems to underlie much of the work of David Lynch. 'Every film is like a waking dream', he says,[55] and his *Blue Velvet* is a good example of cultural Freudianism. It is deliberately dreamlike, and it provokes plenty of anxiety through all sorts of Surrealist incongruities, for example the severed ear, the beetles, and the mechanical robin at the beginning—which are, as Atkinson points out, 'all images that tug between pure dream and an undecipherable narrative logic, half Freudian and half bughouse qualm' (*BV*, 10). As Michael Atkinson, who is an exception amongst critics in being acutely aware of pleasurable response, comments, Lynch can 'squeeze astonished humour out of the routine moments. Everything is a little bit off, off from reality *and* off from the rhythms movies usually engender to enfold us in their reality. As a result we have a special relationship with *Blue Velvet*, half in and half out, half agog and giddy at its off-kilter universe and half creeped out by its alienness, half slave to the narrative's potent liquor and half dazzled spectator' (*BV* 26).

The basic narrative here is interpreted by Atkinson as an 'Oedipal schema' which dramatizes 'the shock of a child trying to come to grips with the adult cosmos' (*BV* 21), and I don't think that one has to buy the whole Oedipal myth to see the point of this child–adult dynamic. This shock for Jeffrey when he comes to witness a 'primal' scene from the sex life of the heroine while hidden in a cupboard, also involves, in Freudian terms, a castration anxiety, which, Atkinson supposes, is passed on to the equally voyeuristic (male) film viewer (though this presupposes that a fear of being found out is really a threat to our sexuality). The question that analysis then poses is this: how far is our pleasure at this point really coloured by the negative emotions claimed for our subconscious *identification* with such Freudian *loci classici* as the primal scene or castration anxiety, or can we explain our emotional involvement with this scene, not so much through an *identification* with Jeffrey as a child, as by the already frightening enough *logic of the situation* he confronts, as outlined in previous chapters?

For when we follow Jeffrey to the Deep River Apartments we see Dorothy 'lounging around her ill-decorated apartment in a flimsy scarlet lounge dress and a sluttish wig'. She is 'another archetype, or rather, several twisted into one unhappy knot' of 'an aging harlot and classic Jocasta figure' (*BV*, 3). Indeed for Atkinson, 'Dorothy represents the sexual force of the mother because she is forbidden and because she becomes the object of the unhealthy, infantile impulses at work in Jeffrey's subconscious' (*BV*, 38). How does he know? This is a test assertion for Freudian interpretation. Is she 'really' a mother to Jeffrey and to us, or is she an attractive woman, played by Isabella Rosselini, who is being blackmailed by a pathological gangster, of whom Jeffrey has every reason to be afraid, and who frightens us too? When Jeffrey is discovered in Dorothy's closet she goes down on him, and when the psychopathic gangster Frank enters, Jeffery indeed finds himself observing Frank acting the 'baby' to Dorothy's 'mother' (*BV*, 46). As he whiffs on nitrous oxide he whines, 'Mommy Mommy baby wants to fuck' and 'Baby wants blue velvet' (*BV*, 48). Dorothy obligingly tucks a bit of it into his mouth.[56] How can we know that we share Jeffrey's unhealthy infantile impulses in this 'primal scene', except by detaching ourselves from the progress of the narrative, and accepting for ourselves a Freudian interpretation of our behaviour?[57] Even those of us who are older and more experienced than Jeffrey would be making a return to our earlier, infantile, more 'Oedipal' selves. It is this fantasy regress to an infantile state that psychoanalytic critics are inclined to insist on. But from the point of view of our pleasure, what emotional responses to the film would they be inclined to predict? Presumably a 'practical' anxiety (what will the gangster do to me?) which is really deep down a sexual anxiety. It certainly seems to depend to some degree on a rivalry for Dorothy's attention, but I think that I would be more concerned about my general physical safety.

This is at the very least a classic instance of cultural Freudianism.[58] There is no more difficulty in 'acting Freud' than there is in acting Dostoevsky or Kafka or *Ubu Roi*. Acting up as a baby to a prostitute mother can easily be Frank's thing, as this kind of role playing is not unheard of in the life of prostitutes. Its Oedipal source may be far from certain; but the fantasy here is quite convincing enough on the surface: the threatening man wants to pretend to be a powerless baby—he is funny and menacing and pathetic all the way through—as Denis Hopper magnificently acts it. But I doubt whether a knowledge of the supposed aetiology of such behaviour as promoted by psychoanalysis will really reveal much more about the pleasures (if you share the fantasy, like to see Dorothy threatened, and so on) or the disgust, and fear of Frank, involved in our emotional responses to the scene. All this is part of a larger satisfying narrative structure of suspense and resolution. The plot of the film finally turns on the attempt by the child-detective (though the extent to which Jeffery is a child at all is debatable) and his girlfriend accomplice to rescue Dorothy, which climaxes when Jeffery shoots Frank, liberates Dorothy, and finds his way back to his girlfriend Sandy in a return to order, in a 'recovered suburban paradise' with the two Moms, a mechanical bird (eating a beetle!), and Dorothy playing with her son on the grass. This seems to be the kind of case where the phenomenology can carry on quite well without any help from an interpretation which involves our identification with the subconscious motivation behind this scene (that is, as derived from such putative early childhood events as the 'primal scene') which stirs the emotions associated with it. Some of us may indeed identify with Frank, and some of us be disgusted by him. And that is just a sketch of a male response—would women, thinking about Frank, feel the same, or have quite different emotional responses?

Are we really to see all this as part of an Oedipal family romance, and what is more, do we inevitably (according to psychoanalysis) experience it through our own represssed Oedipal feelings? And how would this count for our pleasure? Will a more 'Oedipal' viewer feel more conflicted and get less pleasure than a less 'Oedipal' one? One problem is that all this is an explanation of our varying unconscious responses which lie below the surface phenomenology. So how are they manifested? It would require a specifically Freudian self-recognition (or a self-recognition within some other neo-Freudian system) to sustain them. But we all introspect differently, according to our beliefs and the emotional predispositions they confer on us—and these indeed may include those of psychoanalytic therapy, with its distinctive approach to the unconscious motivation of pleasurable and unpleasurable emotions.

At this point, psychoanalysis becomes an ideological framework for interpretation like any other—Marxist or Christian or otherwise. For a Jungian, there would be a Jungian film, and so on for Kleinians, Winnicottians, Lacanians, and many others. A proper investigation of the phenomenology of our responses might help us to decide between such theories, were it not for the fact they all rely on the presupposition of occult, indeed unconscious or repressed, causes based in childhood.[59]

The key issue here lies in the phenomenology of those empathic or sympathetic responses which we first discussed in Chapter 2. For Freudians and their successors, we indeed identify, and thus let loose a contradictory series of inner subconscious emotions and conflicts.[60] From the point of view developed in this book, we are far more likely to be concerned with the protagonist's choices within the logic of the situation, and any much closer identification will indeed be highly personal or even pathological—and none the worse perhaps for that, from the point of view of pleasure. But the difference between the two analyses raises serious empirical questions.[61]

Some psychoanalytically inclined critics make the claim that our pleasures in art are always going to be in some specified way disappointing, or anxiety-provoking, because the representative system of a work of art can never (quite) give us what we want. As Roland Barthes puts it,

So-called erotic books . . . *represent* not so much the erotic scene as the expectation of it, the preparation for it, its ascent; that is what makes them 'exciting'; and when the scene actually occurs, naturally there is disappointment, deflation. In other words, these are books of Desire, not of Pleasure. Or more mischievously, they represent Pleasure *as seen by psychoanalysis.* A like meaning says, in both instances, that *the whole thing is very disappointing.*[62]

Of course any work of art will defer and defuse our desires, in so far as our desire is typically directed to real *objects in the world*, like real lovers, good food, and enjoyable possessions. But no work of art can provide that kind of object. It is indeed disappointing to many that a sex magazine is not an actual naked body, and of course such a conclusion is reinforced by the thought that in the case of sex, which for many is relatively hard to come by, we often stimulate ourselves with or even settle for substitutes and imaginary satisfactions anyway. On the other hand, we can't desire such 'real life' objects without antecedently knowing something about them—the sexual experience of many adolescents has had to be largely literature or film-derived in the earlier stages. In essence the Freudian (and latterly the Lacanian) claim about disappointment is a revived form of Platonism, combined with the story of the Fall—away from the mother's breast—the fruit in the still life isn't the fruit that you can eat, and it isn't Ideal Fruit either. We have to live with such claims just as well as with the Platonic one, given the obvious limitations on the fantasized, the imagined, and the merely represented—you can't travel in the picture of a bus. Societies develop systematically misleading representations in this respect (advertising the most obvious) and works of art can be a good deal more reliable than that. In any case, such limitations do not cancel out the pleasures described in previous chapters, and we can still *differentiate* between the pleasures we so receive—even if we do want to see them in relation to their more or less frustrating nearness or distance from the (largely) non-imagined reality in which we find ourselves. (A man or woman might like to sleep with someone *like* Weston's model, or to walk over a beautiful landscape as depicted by Cezanne.) We can still distinguish, between more or less successful and unsuccessful erotic quests if we compare Julien Sorel, Madame Bovary, the main characters in D. H. Lawrence's *Women in Love*, and those in John Updike's *Couples*; between more or less scary monsters; and more or less satisfying wine. Château Latour is one of the best wines in the world, better than plonk, and drinking it is a remarkably satisfying experience, and one has to go on a very long and perhaps unnecessary detour to relate my desire for such a wine to the ways in which I was or was not breast-fed as an infant.[63]

Can such psychoanalytic arguments always really be bypassed in this way? Not if they have something substantive to say about the phenomenological feel of our pleasure in the arts, with which I have claimed to be concerned. The Freudians tend to say 'But at a deeper level. . . . This is going on.' And I can say, ' if you believe that, and you can get in touch with the appropriate feeling, do so and see if you enjoy it. (You may not.)' As in my tennis example, where you may indeed be 'obeying the voice of the Father', or not, and this realiza-tion may be more or less satisfying to you. And since this 'deeper level' psychological process is *ex hypothesi* better 'known' to the informed analyst than it is to the uninformed experiencer, we can say that the really convinced Freudian analyst or critic or patient will indeed tend to get different kinds of emotional pleasure from works of art, in the light of their different beliefs and their sense of them-selves. But in this they are no different from the convinced Christian, feminist, or Marxist.

I am not sceptical then of the attempt to find particular underlying or unconscious fantasies as a source or cause of our pleasure in the arts. As I have suggested, these can be very important. I have assumed throughout that many cultural materials, like jokes and popular movies, depend upon unconscious, unadmitted, and undeclared emotional motivations of a fantasized kind, and that the primary model for these will often be sexual. One of Freud's central insights was that culture asks for repression in order to make us conform to social demands, but that repression will often fight back through fantasy. Hence the political joke.[64]

Such wish-fulfilling fantasies (or frustrations), if we differentiate them in relation to the particularity of the individual work, can be seen to have an illuminating relationship to the historical and cultural situations of the producer and consumer. Frith thus reports Levine on popular songs of the 1950s:

In a period when divorce rates were rising, family stability declining, pastoral life styles disappearing, bureaucratic impersonality and organisation increasing, popular music constructed a universe in which adolescent innocence and naivete became a permanent states. Men and women (often referred to as boys and girls) dreamed pure dreams, hopefully waited for an ideal love to appear (the gift of some beneficent power that remained undefined and unnamed) and built not castles but bungalows in the air complete with birds, brooks, blossoms, and babies.[65]

Fantasy movies, like the *Wizard of Oz* or *Les Enfants du paradis* or *Citizen Kane* or *Blue Velvet*, arise and are enjoyed under particular social conditions (including those of a general cultural belief in broadly 'Freudian' accounts of human nature) and the pleasures they give may indeed be best understood in relation to them.

Pleasure versus Critique

I have been mostly concerned above with (the phenomenology of) the 'primary' or basic processes of our interaction with individual works. I have not been concerned with the pleasures to be derived from the *proof* of our understanding them—by, for example, our making interpretations. These typically *restate* the terms of the work of art, or supplement them, or rewrite them, or defend them or attack them, in relation to the interests of a particular community surrounding the work. Of course even our primary understanding of anything always involves (bottom-up) interpretative mental events, in resolving ambiguity, or the relationship between surface and depth, for example.[66] But these are interpretative decisions which are internal to the process of appreciating the work.

All the same, there come points when we think we understand matters well enough for our own purposes—we can at least or at last listen to Stravinsky or Stockhausen or Wagner without being unpleasantly baffled. It is obvious that our current understandings can give us enjoyment, even though we know that our appreciation (or our understanding of the way to make a soufflé, or make love) can always be improved. In such moments further concerns about matters of general interpretation would interfere with our enjoyment of the work of art—as opposed for example to an immediate apprehension of performance variation, or awareness of technique, or of ambiguity and provocative rhetoric, as discussed above.

I think then of much interpretation as coming after, as a declaration of some more general significance for the meaning we grasp. Even though the processes of interpretation and understanding are mutually reinforcing (and at the most basic level of perception), it is worth making a functional distinction between these two types of activity.[67] And so I wish to distinguish between understanding as 'primary interpretation' (which I define as being involved in the psychological processes of appreciation and enjoyment) and 'secondary interpretation' (which I define as a subsequent reflective declaration of some general significance for the work, which may or may not have become apparent in the primary process).

This contrast can be clarified by an extended example, Manet's *Bar at the Folies Bergère* (Pl. 13).[68] Our primary understanding of this image surely involves our grasp of what Kivy calls its 'manifest representational content'. Anyone who could not see—in Manet's *Bar at the Folies Bergère*—a woman behind a bar with bottles on it, with her back and a man reflected in a mirror, would be illiterate with regard to visual representation. (Though Kivy wisely says that it is not really easy to 'explicate with logical rigour, the boundary between manifest and hermeneutical content in the visual arts of representation or in literature'.)[69]

Nor is the extent of our knowledge of the *historical context* as relevant for the production of pleasure easy to specify. We can for
example fill in a 'background' of historical-cultural narrative to
explain to ourselves the presence in the image of much of what we
manifestly see. For example, why is there a pair of legs hanging down
on the left? Because this is the Folies Bergère in Paris. What period
does the woman's clothing belong to? (The late nineteenth century.)
And so on. So far, this background story can fit very well with a
primary understanding of the nature of the place represented. We go
a bit beyond what is manifest when House tells us that the *promenoir*
part of the Folies Bergère which we see here was the 'unequivocal
province of the flaneur and the prostitute', whereas ordinary bourgeois families who wanted to see the show sat in the stalls, just visible
down below.[70] Stop's caricature of Manet's painting alludes to this
arrangement when it labels the barmaid a 'merchant of consolation'.
But, says House, the 'barmaids were able to chose their sexual partners', unlike the prostitutes of the *promenoir*. None of this is to be *seen*
here and so it is far from clear that we need to infer it from the painting alone.

Many interpreters nevertheless use this kind of contextual knowledge to offer an even broader interpretation of the 'cultural construction of Parisian class identity' as they say it occured within the
Parisian café concert. And so they tell us that the Folies Bergère was a
'social and cultural institution that operated across class divisions,
tested ideological limits, and threatened to destabilise any normative
representation of class relations'.[71] But the most I would expect from
the picture alone is that the woman and the man in front of her
would come from different social classes. The picture may be a
symptom or exemplification of the sort of thing that gave rise to the
social stresses of modernity, but it is hard to see how it expresses that
stress. And yet we are led to believe by such interpreters that 'just
looking' at it would be a far less sophisticated activity than interpreting it in this way. It is somehow 'wrong' (that is, politically or morally
insensitive) to refuse to 'read' the image for the political implications

that it has beyond itself. 'Read' gives the game away. It is the interpreter with a history book who provides the 'reading', and is far from
'just looking' to use Updike's phrase.[72]

This tension shows up when critic interpreters turn to what we
would have thought to be pretty well manifest; that is, the expression
on the barmaid's face. This would be part of a 'primary' understanding, and pleasurable or not because of the considerations above
concerning intimacy. But the interpreters' understanding of *her socio-
historical–sexual situation* seems to condition what they claim to see,
or project on to the painting; for they can't all be right.

James D. Herbert cites Paul Alexis in 1882, previewing the canvas
for *Le Reveil*, who takes a fairly simple view; for him she is a 'beautiful
girl, truly alive, truly modern, truly "Folies Bergère" '.[73] 'Modern' and
'truly Folies Bergère' are judgements that no one could endorse with
confidence a hundred years after, but 'beautiful' and 'alive' seem
candidates for the primary understanding of the image; but then
Louis de Forcaud saw her in 1882 as pouting and disgusted;[74] and
in recent accounts, such as Hanson's history of art, she is seen as
'detached and touched with melancholy'[75] as she is for Werner
Hofmann, who sees her eyes as having an emptiness that goes with
melancholy; and Levine finds three or four other critics who see indifference and boredom. (And Schneider in 1932 kindly thinks that this
barely hides her exhaustion.) Robert Rosenblum sees 'loneliness or
apathy' here, Linda Nochlin an image of alienation in an 'empty
stare', Honour and Fleming see 'that sense of isolation and alienation
so typical of the modern sensibility'. But Robert Herbert sees her as
dignified and self-contained, with a matter-of-fact, cool glance.[76] As
I do.

All of these interpretations, except for those which diagnose 'alienation', seem to me to depend, more or less plausibly, on the manifest
content of the image, and to leave us in a direct relationship to the
woman in which our sympathetic and stimulating responses to these
varying possibilities will condition our emotional response (and
hence our pleasure). But other interpretations attempt to get even

further behind her expression to a reconstruction of the mental states which they take to motivate it.

Albert Boime thus thinks she is detached, and 'meditates the transaction that positions her as one more item on the counter for sale'. 'It is possible', he fantasizes, that she 'dreams of owning her own establishment'.[77] And Bradford R. Collins sees a good deal further along this line (for him, the background explains the face): 'If Manet's barmaid is a clandestine prostitute, her uncongenial response to us, while still surprising, might, at least, have an explanation. Rather than unwilling to smile, she might simply be unable. If we see her as a victim of a complex patriarchal system of economic and sexual exploitation, as Clayson does, it also becomes easier to read her mood as tired, dispirited, glum.'[78]

The use of 'read' here and above indicates an interpretation of the image which is hardly a response to the manifest content. For many interpreters, then, she appears not so much as a person with an emotional expression, but as an object for sale.[79] She 'appears before us more as a commodity similar in shape and objective appearance to the bottles on the counter than as a consumer'. She, 'like the painting of which she is a part, is presented as an object of public consumption'.[80] This 'seeing' of the barmaid as part of an economic system in which women are commodified *à la* Marx, and are sold along with drink, is disapproving and guilt-inducing without being terribly informative: it is like interpreting a Crucifixion scene as symptomatic of a society in which torture is common. It posits a quite reasonable historical narrative, some way behind the picture. This narrative has its own interest and value, but it is not at all closely related to an enjoyment of the picture itself. It may be true as a generalization but miss the point of the picture.

Nor am I sure about the commodification metaphor. There are plenty of pictures in which people are offering their services for sale, and plenty of sexually provocative pictures, and the Marxist notion of commodification is a very general one; behind it lies the notion of a 'person as an object', and so the real underlying consideration

involves our sense of the autonomy (or the apparent moral autonomy) of the person depicted.

If we sexualize the barmaid in this way we may have trouble with
even more subtly resistant objects within the picture space. Freudian
allegories of unpleasurable frustration here proliferate, so that 'Our
masculine gaze, which at first seems to penetrate the depths of the
establishment's interior space (the sexual connotation is real, I think)
is actually rebuffed by the mirror and thrown back on itself.'[81] And furthermore, if we look at the opening at the bottom of the 'velvet redingote' we find that 'the provocative cut of the bottom of the barmaid's
velvet redingote opens not to something resembling the soft, aro-
matic flowers suggestively placed against it but to a shield-like area of
paint whose color and striations echo the cold, hard counter top that
separates us from her. The peculiar drama of invitation and denial
played out here seems a microcosm of the painting as a whole'.[82]

There seem then to be two ways of responding to the barmaid's
expression and clothing. One is as representing 'the ready satisfaction
of male desire'[83]—indeed for Griselda Pollock 'she is an embodiment
of bourgeois men's fantasies about female availability'.[84] The other
responds to her as more or less 'emotionally opaque' and resistant to
'the male gaze', so that 'the precise theme of Manet's work is an unex-
plained disappointment of carefully cultivated male expectations'.
Collins thinks that this interpretation has shown how 'Manet's Bar
throws new light on the question of erotic male fantasies'. And he
goes on to apply Lacan to this image, so that the barmaid is not (just)
an object of desire, she is the Lacanian Other, 'the mirror in whom we
males wish to see our "imaginary self"; whole, healed, complete,
perfect—in a word, desired'. But she fails to smile on us, and 'Her dis-
regard leaves us feeling alienated and insufficient'. The painting
'forces' us to feel our 'pathetic human deficiency, our essential "lack-
of-Being"'.[85] Not enjoyable at all; classically disappointing in the psychoanalytic sense.

I am not sure that *any* of these are any sort of direct response to the
person in the painting. Interpretations of these kinds bring into play

all sorts of political and ethical implications, which are not clearly manifest in the work of art, but which can emerge with more or less plausibility from a historical account of its institutional context, which constructs a kind of cognitive amplification. But in so doing they also try to use our knowledge of this context to *suggest a morally or politically correct cognitive-emotional response* for us. This attempts to deflect (male) pleasurable responses (in this little 'drama of invitation and denial') away from a certain intimacy and pleasure in the appreciation of a 'beautiful girl, truly alive, truly modern' towards a more anxious, guilty, alienated, politically correct doubt about any such appropriative erotic response. Pleasure is being repressed here, by the critics, rather than Manet. All this is in favour of a melancholy moral disapproval of typical male behaviour, so that 'we' can be got to feel what we ought to feel, not so much about her face, body, or even her person, as about what we imagine or believe to be her (historical) situation; perhaps, a generalized sympathy for a victim of prostitution. But she looks manifestly cool, dignified, and self-possessed. Many of the critics cited above obviously don't want us to respond to a fantasy of her desirability which would give a pleasure of which these interpretations would have us feel ashamed or guilty. Fantasies about her 'availability' presumably don't really apply, for historical reasons, anyway. But even if we try to put ourselves as viewers into the historical situation of her commercial availability, we would find that very difficult on the evidence of the picture alone (particularly, in my view, given the support of the unattractively mustachioed gentleman to the right, who is supposed to be the male's stand-in).

The differing implications for the male's pleasure here reverberate in the feminist discussion of the 'male gaze'. But the questions such interpretations raise are not directly the ones with which I am concerned, though they manifest a guilty awareness of them. I have used this example to show up the contrasts, and the hostility, between an actually occurring and pleasurable sexual response, directed to the appreciation of a work of art on its own terms—even if they are by now historically a bit disreputable—and a critique of it, for failing to live up to the moral standards and political perceptions which became the property of academics in the period after the work's creation.[86]

The naturally discursive and conceptually associative medium of language makes it almost impossible to distinguish between the primary understanding and the secondary interpretation of literature; but the distinctions I am trying to make are important here, too. George Eliot, for example, is generally agreed to have powerful arguments against egoism in *Middlemarch*, and indeed she does, often far better than those current in moral philosophy. She promotes the situational awareness of an 'equivalent sense of self' in others, and as we have already seen, fictions are peculiarly well suited to this task.

George Eliot herself is partly aware of this, despite her tendency to make not always successfully entertaining and ironic moral generalizations and reflections in her narrative, as we can see if we go a bit further into the passage quoted in Chapter 1:

The greatest benefit we owe to the artist, whether painter, poet or novelist, is the extension of our sympathies. Appeals founded on generalisations and statistics require a sympathy ready made, a moral sentiment already in activity; but a picture of human life such as a great artist can give, surprises even the trivial and the selfish into that attention to what is apart from ourselves, which may be called the raw material of moral sentiment.[87]

The surprise is the provocation; the moral sentiment the pleasure (or anguish); the raw material the specificity of the narrative. Reflection and generalization are different from this; we have plenty of it from outside art, and plenty of reminders of it within it. But the immediate engagement for George Eliot seems to be emotional, and so a matter of pleasure or pain. Indeed, for her, the sympathetic character as opposed to the detached and reflective one is precisely the kind of person who runs these emotional risks; which we are encouraged to run by art. Indeed she tells us that 'those who read [my writings] should be better able to *imagine* and to *feel* the pains and joys of those who differ from themselves in everything but the broad fact of being struggling erring human creatures'.[88] Her novels should never 'lapse from the picture to the diagram'.[89]

A further reflection concerning egoism is therefore not necessarily part of the original process of our enjoyment in reading the novel, of the kind that I tried to specify in Chapter 1: though it can indeed give us pleasure, if we are moralists of a certain kind, to be realizing that such authors are *developing* such good arguments, and ones that we ought to go on having the pleasure of mastering, and perhaps observing. The primary experience of reading *Middlemarch* will indeed help us to engage in a highly and perhaps uniquely detailed simulation of others' situations,[90] and to appreciate the place of altruism in human relations—as when Dorothea finally attempts to confront and 'save' Rosamund Vincy in chapter 81. In this way we are pleasurably moved by the ways in which human beings can come at moral understandings and resolutions of a certain kind (for example, when we understand George Eliot's metaphor about a candle before a scratched mirror in chapter 27, and grasp its implications for our own egoism). But as I have shown, the primary *pleasure* we get from the text derives not from those of a secondary philosophical reflection, but from the rhetorically provocative processes by which we come at and acquire those understandings. It's the process of mastering the metaphor, and of sharing a sympathetic emotion, of being held in suspense and then pleased or satisfied by outcomes (when she confronts Rosamond, Dorothea learns that Will loves her) that *inter alia* we enjoy or deplore. In the process we indeed think many things that might be useful to us, or morally good for us, in terms of our understanding of interpersonal relations as they might affect us outside the text. But that is only secondarily the pleasure *of* the text.

Immediate and Associative Responses

Unfortunately, the argument sketched above seems to be true by definition—the pleasure of the work is that of the work of art, and nothing else, in so far as we can give any sense to the 'nothing' that supposedly surrounds the work. And yet as we have seen in previous chapters, there do seem, quite apart from such matters of ethical and political reflection, to be two quite contrasted ways of listening to music, of looking at paintings, and of paying attention to literary narrative, and they have very different relationships to our pleasure.

One of these modes of getting pleasure I have called 'associative'. There is a cognitive process which usually adds some kind of narrative derived from a context external to the work, to the music or the painting, such as the (sexual) aggression of sonata form, or the story of the barmaid as victim of patriarchy. Indeed it is typical of many biblical, Christian, Freudian, Marxist, and other politically critical interpretations that they compare the work with another master-narrative which is not its own—they deliberately read 'against the grain'. This interpretative-associative mode naturally tries to dominate our responses to any mimetically commited or representational art, since its content can the more easily lead us from work to world, and so to a moral or political relationship between the two, which interpretation often tries to articulate, in favour of what the interpreter (rather than the work of art) sees as the truth. This sort of thing can be an extremely valuable exercise, and is what most interpretation involves, but it often has very little to do with our *enjoyment* of works of art.

In more abstract art forms and works of art indeed, it is the very non-referential character of their 'languages' that seems to tempt critics to try to assimilate them to this narrative-associative understanding. As we have seen, in looking at Monet and Rothko, and Beethoven and Shostakovich, the borderline between mimetic and abstract art can be very difficult to locate, and it is often the site of a battle for the redemption of art through interpretations which can associate it with the values of a linguistically expressible mimetic commitment. Kivy takes a very tough line with this sort of thing for music alone: 'if for any reason, I let myself be induced by the music to start thinking about the things and persons I am angry with, if it is angry music, or sad over, if it is sad music, I have lost concentration. If I am thinking about all the things that make me angry, I have stopped listening to and enjoying the *grosse Fugue*; or, if I can do both at once, the former is irrelevant.'[91]

For many people, nevertheless, the more or less abstract work is appreciated through the amplifying emotional dynamics of narrative association, which can provide, reinforce, or amplify the emotional effect of the work (as we saw in the case of painting, by suggesting that the abstract work is 'really' related to a particular type of emotionally laden mimetic landscape: hence Rosenblum's comparison of Rothko to Friedrich, and Polcari of Rothko to a classical tomb). And for many interpreters of Manet's Bar, just confronting or contemplating the appearance of the barmaid, which is the appearance of the picture, is not enough: some political narrative has to lead us into and away from the image.

Some of these associative interpretations are, as we have seen, designed to correct or guide our emotional responses. Should we shudder at the suppression of the female in Beethoven, disapprove of or pity the alienated barmaid as prostitute? In such cases painting and music are given a semantics which assimilates them to literature, and to the demands and pleasures of a historical or ideological understanding within which some other privileged narrative, such as that of the patriarchal suppression of women, is made paramount. There are many variations on this 'real narrative' approach to the work—in the case of opera production, for example, we often encounter contradictory but parallel historical narratives, which are supposed to enhance or emphasize or reinterpret aspects of the original narrative, but also often enough contradict them. Such paranarratives can be as distracting as any others from what we may understand as the 'originally intended' narrative of the opera—and they nearly always have a divergent moral or political directorial purpose, judged to be more relevant and so more pleasing or instructive to the interests of a contemporary audience. What we often enjoy or deplore here are two (metaphorically related) narratives running in parallel. (As when

Melisande sings of being lost in a forest, when she is clearly on the beach outside a Californian condominium.)

Or Hans-Jurgen Syberberg's film of *Parsifal* (1983), which begins with postcards of Germany in ruins after the war. The basic studio set is a huge rock and mountain-like death mask of Wagner, which is also Klingsor's Tower, and divides in two to reveal a flowery meadow. Parsifal is played by a boy and later after Kundry's kiss, by a girl, the ideal of the Grail turns out to be an androgyne 'paradisal man', and the final holy relic to be a model of Wagner's Festspielhaus. Mathilde Wesendonck and Judith Gautier are glimpsed among the flower maidens, and the approach to the Grail is along a flag-lined corridor which evokes the history of Germany. What we often enjoy or deplore here are two (metaphorically related) narratives running in parallel, which are often derived from contrasting or coinciding historical periods. (In the Covent Garden production directed by Bill Bryden and conducted by Bernard Haitink, the opera was presented as an end-of-term play put on in a 1930s public school with Gurnemanz as Headmaster.)

I'm not of course denying that one of the indirect or subsequent pleasures of art indeed arises from our ability to create interpretative communities of various kinds around it, which give us the pleasure of talking about or alluding to art with others who matter to us. A feeling of solidarity and community can arise from having a common interpretation and a common political or ethical commitment as well as from a common enjoyment. (But such solidarities all too often arise from a common disapproval.) But there is a big difference here, between the demand for the 'right kind of conceptual association' for a work, and the aim at giving us pleasure of a more 'internal' kind, for the obvious reason that moral or political discourses are all too rarely aimed at enhancing the pleasure of their audiences (except when parodic or humorous as in *Beyond the Fringe*, or when aiming at a relatively banal morale-raising uplift, as in *Land of Hope and Glory*).

A typical example of such a double framework is the oscillation we are so often asked to make between an abstract, often rather contentless and minimalist art object, and the 'conceptualist' *theory* which is supposed to accompany it—so that the work *exemplifies* the theory. This theoretical atmosphere may or may not compensate us for the lack of pleasurable (intrinsic) interest offered by the work, because its provocative rhetoric lies elsewhere, in the pleasure of domination by interpretation rather than by an understanding of the work. This sense of 'knowing how the art world goes' can supersede our direct relationship to the work. This is not to deny, as Danto says, that 'To see something as art at all demands nothing less than an atmosphere of artistic theory, a knowledge of the history of art.'[92] I agree that our perceptions of art can be theory-dependent. I have followed such a theory in the earlier parts of this book. So we need to distinguish between good and bad, inhibiting and fruitful theories, in relation not to the politics of art, but to our pleasurable responses to it. I think of much conceptual art and its accompanying theory as very bad objects to spend time with, if one is interested in the kinds of pleasure theorized in this book. The trouble here is that when the interest of the ideas surrounding such artworks diminishes, they can leave the work high and dry. Think of the utterly obvious things that we can say *about* Warhol's Brillo Boxes, about the 'questions they raise' about 'the nature of art' and of 'representation' and 'the banal nature of reality' and so on, and their amazing lack of visual interest, when (perhaps unfairly) compared to a sculpture by such as Anthony Caro; about whom there is in fact a good deal more to say concerning the nature of art and of representation.

There are then many cases in which we are encouraged to enjoy being able to give a very general 'theoretic' interpretation, rather than to enjoy (and talk about) the internal articulation and rhetoric of the art object. There is also an obvious alliance, and difference, between enjoying talking about wine and an appreciative drinking of it. It is all the same difficult for us to come to terms with the fact, significance seekers and communicators that we are, that the pay-off in many of our pleasurable experiences may be a non-interpretative, even a non-verbal one—kissing *without* telling.

Some listeners and lookers and readers seem to have a considerably lesser need for this kind of linguistic or conceptual accompaniment, which is so essential to the business and politics of academic exegesis. They can listen to 'music alone', contemplate an abstract painting without real-world associations, and have strong feelings about them, and read a poem simply as evoking a world, without any conscious awareness of any interpretative conceptual accompaniment, other than that which brings them closer to the object—noticing things, seeing aspects, knowing about the historical content of the work rather than interpreting it, and so on. They can get 'inside' the various versions of abstract painting by getting inside the geometry of the relationship between the shapes in it (relationships which might be very similarly based, to judge by the language used to describe it, to the grammar of harmony in music). They can also, if they wish, take a more technical approach, and try to see the work as a kind of game with rules—and so be made aware of the restrictions that Mondrian and other painters in De Stijl imposed on themselves—only right angles, only primary colours, and so on. Nevertheless, just as in the case of purely instrumental music, such abstract paintings are in the end just as they are, they go together more or less well (they harmonize more or less, in a very common judgement) and that is that, and we may then go on to see 'that' as an expression of a personality. Then the pleasure of a Mondrian or a Rothko or a Beethoven piano sonata just is the pleasure of Mondrian or Rothko or Beethoven, and 'the way their works go', from this point of view. And the music and articulation of the 'Ode to Autumn', or *Four Quartets*—or *Hamlet*, indeed—can hold together for us in just the same way. The work, at this pleasurable stage, does not need any associative cognitive differentiation—our relationship is to the understanding of complex individuals. We can trust the artist and our knowledge, rather than the critic, to give us what we want (including of course all the complex intricacies of thinking discursively about difficult matters, to be found in paintings, musical works, and literature).[93] We do not go back to Sophocles to correct or rewrite him but to think about the fate of Antigone (or Cleopatra, or Isolde, or Anna Karenina, Elizabeth Bennett, Dorothea Brooke, Isobel Archer, or Mrs Dalloway) in the exciting sequence and detail, and with the explanations, provided by their creators, who are uniquely authoritative in these areas, and whose thoughts on such matters have in general been thought worth preserving for longer than those of any of their interpreters.

There are, as we have seen, many interpretations (call them 'intimist' or 'primary') which can facilitate this pleasurable appreciation. They may help us to understand the historical connections and conventions within the work of art, and so bring us back to this particular work, with an increased understanding and appreciation of its complications. (For example, the analysis of the photograph of Daniel Webster cited above.)

The principal pleasure for this second (hedonist) group perhaps lies in cultivating a more direct cognitive-emotional response. What the work is saying, rather than the opinion of a critic, is good enough. Someone in this group might say that they like this particular poem of Mallarmé, this painting of Picasso, this piece by Stravinsky, and that the pleasure they get from such work consists in submitting themselves to it, and enjoying being in its company rather than in attempting to play beyond it, into the multiple possibilities or contradictions that it somehow fails to see. From this point of view, it is the way in which works of art are determined to particular repeatable enjoyable configurations that counts, and it is the (relative) constancy and reliability of the stimulus to thought of the work of art under these varying circumstances which constitutes a large part of its value as pleasurable. The canon is what we go back to: a newspaper may last a day, and academic criticism like this, if it is lucky, five years in a limited market.

On the other hand, so far as the value of deriving pleasure from art is concerned, I do not see any need to adjudicate between the two approaches I have outlined. I have written this book in the thought that specificity and intimacy can yield the most constant and sustained pleasure—from the first work or bar to the last—and in every smallest part of the intricately related picture plane or building or narrative. But the associative method clearly works, in giving pleasure, though obviously in a more selective, and perhaps satisfyingly controlling fashion. We can even oscillate between the two approaches in listening to or looking at or reading the same work. Some may need to associate stories with it—these can make the experience seem richer perhaps, facilitate an emotional response perhaps. But others don't want this, including Julian Bell, for example, who gives an account of painting which has been trying to 'steer a path through the maze of words, towards the complex, but largely wordless pleasures of looking—that is the broad intention of this text, because it comes from a painter, someone committed to producing objects specifically for viewing'. And so he thinks the associations suggested by the titles of Howard Hodgkin's paintings are 'preposterous'. How can a 'jungle of colours' communicate the private memory indicated by a title such as *Dinner in Palazzo Albrizzi* (Pl. 14)? He says, 'The only memory I can read into it is a cultured nostalgia for the glaring intensity of turn of the century modernist painting . . . the swipes and splodges of colour thrill, seeming to promise "meaning", though meaning no one thing.'[94]

My main aim has been to put into focus the enjoyment of art, partly because it is positively discouraged or obscured by our present obsession with interpretative criticism and with political and moral considerations, fascinating though they are. In this context, Susan Sontag's attack some while ago on interpretation still makes some sense: 'In a culture whose already classical dilemma is the hypertrophy of the intellect at the expense of energy and sensual capability, interpretation is the revenge of the intellect upon art'.[95] It is the enemy, not so much for its insistence on intellectual speculation about art, rather than on sensory experience and the understanding and enjoyment of it in all its detail (including its exciting and arousing, because emotional, conceptual implications), as for its joyless effects on the institutional context in which art is approached.[96] As

Sontag put it, 'Interpretation takes the sensory experience of the work of art for granted and proceeds from there. This cannot be taken for granted now. . . . What is important now is to recover our senses. We must learn to see more, to hear more, to feel more. . . . In place of a hermeneutics we need an erotics of art.'[97] That is what Bell is saying about Hodgkin's wonderfully enjoyable painting.

There are many people who would not approve of the subjectively orientated and often erotic view of pleasure advanced here. They would prefer that there should be more significant moral and political intervening variables in the process. For them, such hedonism is an evasion of moral responsibility.[98]

If we prefer values other than those of pleasure or enjoyment of course we can find various ways of promoting them and adjudicating between them. Of course such epistemological and moral concerns are of prime importance—shouldn't we be paying more attention to Soviet Realism than to Rothko? Why not?—and they often have consequences for the pleasures we (think we) can (allow ourselves to) have in practical contexts. University syllabuses are not usually constructed on hedonist criteria. But such moral issues seem to be as straightforward as moral issues ever are, as in the critique of the 'male gaze'. It is surely then a matter of moral judgement, how stern this prohibition of a pleasurable self-indulgence should be through *The Rokeby Venus* right on to Manet's barmaid, and all those outrageously violent and exploitative hard-core pornographic films.

We often do morally reprehensible things because we enjoy them so much, and so moral considerations will always more or less license or enhance or inhibit our pleasures ('I feel really guilty enjoying a bathe in Rothko rather than engaging with some more politically correct art'), or suggest that we ought to be doing something else entirely. But they are really not to the point in getting at the nature of our pleasures, and that has been my concern. There are plenty of moralizing defences of pleasure to be made, but that is not my theme in this book.

I have attempted to distinguish between those kinds of under-standings of works of art which seem to reinforce the pleasures analysed earlier; and to contrast to that the kind of interpretation that makes a critique of the work, and so may lie to one side of apprecia-tion, by pursuing further epistemological, moral, or political ends. The critique may terminally contaminate the pleasure, by making us feel guilty about it. My distinction between these approaches here has only been designed to clarify what might lie on the 'pleasure' side of this division of values, and not to do any justice to the range of ethical and political interpretation, or indeed to give an account of the many ways in which there is a tension between such concerns and those of pleasure. I have looked at the hedonist aspect of art, because it seemed to me to be an exceptionally interesting challenge to under-standing, and because it is neglected in current writing about the arts.

We can afford to be tolerant about any conflict between associative and non-associative responses to art, in so far as I have been con-cerned, not with a maximally accurate perception of the work of art, or with a 'morally correct' interpretation (desirable though these both are), but with understanding the ways in which we all can be quite variously intellectually and emotionally engaged by them. Were I to like Rothko partly because for some odd reason he evokes for me the pleasure of eating Mars bars, that would be OK for me, so far as my pleasure is concerned, even though I may not be being par-ticularly intelligible to other people, or even rational in this respect. That's the way I put it together, and my claim to enjoy what I enjoy in that way will probably stand up. Of course, I can still be introduced to 'better' ways of enjoying Rothko, of a more internal, discriminating kind (given in particular that Mars bars are pretty unvarying in their appeal if deeply satisfying at the top of a mountain; whereas Rothkos differ from one another).

I have been concerned above with the more likely, and indeed the more reasonable, of our pleasurable responses to art. These allow, as I have tried to show, for very different types of 'going concern' rela-tionships to the work, and so for many plural and conflicting values to be derived from them. So I have no final prescriptions about pleasure. Only a pluralist theory can do justice to the divergent phenomenology of our feelings about art. Like those of Margeurite:

'What is your favourite painting in all of Paris?' I ask Margeurite. . . .
'Let me think,' she says. She names Géricault, van Gogh, Picasso.
'All the Os,' I say.
'All the Os! Actually, at the d'Orsay, there's a pastel of Madame Monet, with the ribbons of her hat all untied. That's probably my favorite. She's sitting on a bright blue sofa—the most beautiful blues you've ever seen—and she is looking straight out of the drawing, as if to say, "I married a painter, and I still got this sofa." I like that one. Very French.'[99]

Great works of art are inexhaustible, in the sense that we will never fully absorb all the possibilities of their rhetoric and 'performance variation', including all the performances of our own looking and reading and hearing; they can all come off in so many different ways. We will never encounter the essence of a work direct (though we may have that wonderful illusion) but we can always find out or reaffirm something of its content. In the finale to *Le nozze di Figaro*, the Count and the Countess can be reconciled again and again, in subtly different ways, but always under the guidance of Mozart and Da Ponte's supreme invention. And how will Don Giovanni confront the Stone Guest this time? With what kind of defiance?

The pleasures given by works of art are specific and individual. We can love Mozart's *Don Giovanni* or Bronzino's *Allegory of Venus and Cupid* or Dickens's *Great Expectations* and, in *those* respects, for those features, nothing else will quite do. It's individualism that counts here, for our pleasure, just as it does for so much else. We may desire all women or all men and enjoy that, but, as I invited John Berger to remark above, you fall in love when you really get to know *this* one. And so far as our pleasure is concerned, this is all for us, whatever more we can make of it in interpretation, or shared conversation. Our relationship to artworks is very like our personal relationships: and so there is indeed a canon—of our relationships with a number of works of art and their implied creators, and they can be very varied and mixed, and go up and down in their intensity. As Wallace Stevens once put it,

> A little less returned for him each Spring
> Brahms, his dark familiar, often walked apart.[100]

But we can always rely upon or hope for some constancy from our own canon, along with lots of exciting and (usually early) flashes in the pan. (We can't blame Tchaikovsky and Puccini for once having seemed so very good to us.)

Antecedent knowledge obviously helps, since it's ultimately, I have argued, the pleasures of an emotional understanding that we aim for. But no particular amount of such information can be legislated for. This isn't an exam. And too much information, or the wrong kind (scholarly pernickety footnoting, nagging deconstruction, a deluge of related historical facts), can be deeply inhibiting of our pleasure, if not of our cultural standing.

It's the combination of realism and fantasy that so often gives us pleasure. But simple realism is all the same as good a place to start as Aristotle suggested it should be. If you've ever just looked at a river and trees and enjoyed that, you are on the way to enjoying much of Monet. The people who go to picture galleries and look for the flowers in their gardens or appealing houses are far from doing the wrong thing, certainly so far as their pleasure is concerned. Conversely a fantasy that lacks an interesting relationship to our world can be thin or pointless. That is why *Lord of the Rings* is for many a more reliable source of pleasure than *Terminator 1, 2,* or *3* or more.

On the other hand, pleasure doesn't have to be difficult. Getting at pleasure, as opposed to rocket science, involves our use of a very elementary and strongly motivated human kit which it is well worth developing. After all, sex and food work for us in very similar ways—but serious libertinage and gourmandise will take a bit of application, knowledge, and skill, and so does art. I have written above about the 'sophisticated' pleasures to be derived from canonical art, but my appetite for Monet or Chardin or Beethoven or Bruckner was all the same first fed by children's book illustration, Disney cartoons, Elvis Presley, and Johann Strauss, all of which I still enjoy.

All the way through, the arts can help us to cultivate our senses, and to find our place on the cline from oversensitive aesthete to brute. Tennis players and wine connoisseurs, and lovers of the arts, like other lovers, live a little better inside their own bodies.

And we all want to feel that we can understand our own experience and cope with it. Works of art can offer us a wonderful series of graded exercises of this capacity, as many members of reading groups will know, since it is also a communally negotiated interpretation that helps us to assimilate such experiences.[101]

Nevertheless we usually think about works of art in various forms of privacy, and it is more than ever important to cultivate this private space with its private tastes, in an invasive and politically conformist world. It is not at all surprising that oppressive regimes have so often censored the arts as a locus of private freedom. While we are outside such social concerns, we can find that artworks can tolerate our sometimes excessive, pornographic, vindictive, and other attitudes to them without answering back.

And unlike most things, except perhaps human individuals, works of art repay a constantly renewed and lifelong attention. They are the emotional and intellectual counterparts of love affairs, marriage, friendship, gardening, and good design. The house of fiction in all the arts, whether Funhouse, Valhalla, or Paradiso, can be an exceptionally well-proportioned one to live in. In exploring it we should not allow ourselves to be inhibited by external ethical or political demands. We probably have plenty of such beliefs already, anyway, and they may be vital for real life, but they are not always so good for the development of the imagination, as it expresses itself in art, particularly in that which invents liberating alternatives. In this area pleasure is as good a guide as anything.

Notes

1. Simon Blackburn, *Being Good* (Oxford: OUP, 2001), 80. Blackburn continues: 'In other moods, however, everything goes leaden. Like Hamlet, we are determined to skulk at the edge of the carnival, seeing nothing but the skull beneath the skin. It is sad when we become like that, and we need a tonic more than an argument. The only good argument is, in a famous phrase of David Hume's, that it is no way to make yourself useful or agreeable to yourself or others.'

2. All this discussion is relevant to the contention at the beginning of Ch. 3 that you can enjoyably play with bricks, make love, enjoy music and painting, without thinking in words (and even, perhaps enjoy a poem without thinking discursively away from the words—i.e. without thinking of any *words* other than those of the text, though there are huge problems in describing our comprehension of language without appealing to associated ideas which may be verbalized).

3. Or consider the little *Street Scene*—with its textures of red brick façades, the wood of window shutters, and the outlining of leaded glass windows. A house to which the figures are clearly subordinated but at home. They are separate, anonymous—it's difficult to see that they are supposed to exemplify virtues, such as 'diligence with house cleaning', the vines symbolizing love, virtue, and fidelity. 'Signatures of all I read', as Stephen Dedalus says on the beach. But we don't need to read such works in this moralizing way. The value for us may partly lie in our nostalgia for a 'simpler' way of life, but also in the virtues of mere solidity and presence. As when Vermeer is conveying the weathering of the building, and the worn surface of the object and the worked surface of the painting are in harmony, e.g. the painting of the whitewash on the walls, as repainted by Vermeer (Cf. Wheelock (ed.), *Vermeer*, 102–3.)

4. I am not asking for the peculiar kind of quasi-religious submission demanded at Bayreuth, as a kind of church and pilgrimage site. Cf. Joseph Kerman's article on this in the *New York Review*, 9 Aug. 2001, 37.

5. 'As John Stuart Mill insisted, the only evidence for whether an experience is worth having for its own sake is the verdict of those familiar with the experience.' Malcolm Budd, *Values of Art* (London: Allen Lane, 1995), 12.

6. Roland Barthes, *The Pleasure of the Text* (New York: Hill and Wang, 1975), 13.

7. As Malcolm Budd seems to argue, *Values of Art*, 5–6.

8. Though being with an audience can help to amplify our unmediated responses—notably in laughing at comedy, and for the actor, some audiences are too quick and some fatally slow for their timing.

9. Cf. K. Robert Schwarz, *Minimalists* (London: Phaidon, 1996), 84–5, 117–18.

10. Pierre Rosenberg et al., *Chardin*, 33, 35, 278.

11. Norman Bryson, *Word and Image* (Cambridge: Cambridge UP, 1981), 13.

12. Bryson, *Word and Image*, 117–18.
13. Cf. Rosenberg et al., 84–6, *Chardin*, and Michael Baxandall, *Patterns of Intention*, 102.
14. Norman Bryson, *Looking at the Overlooked* (London: Reaktion, 1990), 94.
15. Julian Barnes, *Something to Declare* (London: Picador 2002), 120.
16. There is a deconstructive paradox here which arises in any interpretative account of a work as individual. You can't specify its particulars except in a highly generalized language, but you can, as Bryson and Baxandall show, focus our attention on aspects of them by description. The same applies to our general descriptions of valued persons. Some suggest that there is an ontological relationship that can get through this distancing effect, i.e. that the valuing of the human individual comes from a unique need to be in relation to that person. There may be something in this. I shall argue that there is a great deal to be gained by thinking of our relationship to works of art as like one to persons, because in both cases we can focus on the values of individuality and autonomy.
17. John Berger, *G: A Novel* (London: Weidenfeld and Nicolson, 1972), 110–11. And compare ibid. 130 ff. where G makes love: 'You are being seen as you are'.
18. Jeanette Winterson, *Written on the Body* (London: Cape, 1992), 24. John Updike knows about this sort of particularity as well.
19. Printed in *99: The New Meaning* (Providence, RI: New Directions, 1990), 13–32. Further refs. will be given in the text.
20. Barthes, *Pleasure of the Text*, 27.
21. And artists who are not much good, who merely articulate, in a best-sellerish or modish or theoretical kind of way, the social commonplaces of their time, tend to fall into neglect. It may be a merely sociocultural fact that the Western cultural canon seems to value this kind of individuality, but it will be an important cultural fact for most readers of this book, and one which strongly conditions our pleasure.
22. This characterological method, in so far as it can be thought of as independent of the first, may also obey a moral principle: that of respect for the autonomy or integrity or individuality of the other. The framework method on the other hand can lead us to see how the individual is in fact articulating general (public) matters whose implications she or he may or may not wish to accept.
23. Of course there are collectively produced yet stylistically unified artworks which test this generalization—most obviously in architecture, or the *Yellow River* piano concerto, written by a committee, and which sounds like an imitation of bits of many of the popular piano concertos which preceded it; or indeed the Bible, where a single author has been hard to find and a God has had to be imagined who can make the text as consistent as possible; or the attempt to define a single 'Homer'; or in the study of the assisted studio works of great

artists, which are anxiously scrutinized for the stylistic diversity and inconsistency of the less good work that may rob them of the highest (individual) value.

24. I believe that our uptake on intention is always at issue in understanding human communication, following e.g. Dan Sperber and Deirdre Wilson, *Relevance: Communication and Cognition* (Oxford: Blackwell, 1986), 21–38, 54–64.

25. Cf. Wayne C. Booth, *The Company We Keep: An Ethics of Fiction* (Berkeley and Los Angeles: University of California Press, 1988), esp. 157–224.

26. Kenneth Clark, *Looking at Pictures*, 25. He also cites Handel, Beethoven, Rembrandt, and Bruegel as similarly universal.

27. Richard Brilliant, *Portraiture* (London: Reaktion, 1991), 56–7.

28. Cf. Christopher Wright, *Rembrandt Self Portraits* (London: Gordon Fraser, 1982), 21.

29. Christopher White and Quentin Buvelot (eds.), *Rembrandt by Himself* (London: National Gallery, 1999), 204.

30. It is commonplace in the analysis of popular song, that audience identification with the singer is a prime element in the enjoyment they give. This may be one of the biggest differences between the reaction of the fan and the more detached appreciation I have described so far in this book. Cf. Simon Frith, *Performing Rites* (Oxford: OUP, 1996), 67.

31. How anxious is the writer above when listening to Keith Jarrett's 'Don't ever leave me'? Why did he choose this tune? Does the choice and the reaction to Jarrett's playing of it reflect an identification with it and him, in nostalgia, or guilt? Or is the reader being invited to question his responses in this way by this example?

32. Sigmund Freud, 'Creative Writers and Daydreaming', *Standard Edition* (London: Hogarth Press and the Institute of Psychoanalysis, 1953–74), ix. 153.

33. Cf. Linda Williams, *Hard Core* (London: Pandora, 1990), 170 and *passim*.

34. Cf. *The Freud/Jung Letters*, ed. William Maguire (London: Picador, 1979), 14, 285 ff., 299, and *passim*.

35. *The Diary of Virginia Woolf*, ii. *1925–1930*, ed. Anne Olivier Bell (Harmondsworth: Penguin, 1982) 208.

36. Daniel Ferrer, 'To the Lighthouse', in Maud Ellmann (ed.), *Psychoanalytical Literary Criticism* (London: Longman, 1994), 146, 145, cf. 152 on milk.

37. Ibid. 155. Ferrer is very illuminating, ibid. 156, on the sexual passage concerning painting in *To the Lighthouse* (Oxford: OUP, 1992), 215.

38. Ferrer, 'To the Lighthouse', 152, 156. Again, this is presumably a generalizable claim. But clearly some painters are more 'anal' than others. I'd start with De Kooning. Cf. Wollheim's Freud-inspired response to him, cited in Ch. 2, above.

39. Ferrer, 'To the Lighthouse', 156.

40. The tendency of the psychoanalyst is sometimes to say that if we can't feel it, we too are therefore disguising or cut off from our true feelings by the process of repression, etc. But this is a notorious 'heads I win, tails you lose' argument, which is sometimes also deployed against rational objections to psychoanalysis. The more you resist, the more you are just resisting.

    Hermione Lee, in her *Virginia Woolf* (London: Chatto and Windus, 1996), 80–3 and 477–8, gives a far more measured account of Woolf's recollection of her mother, including Vanessa's judgement that 'You have made one feel the extraordinary beauty of her character'.

41. Susan McClary, 'Comment: Getting down off the Beanstalk', *Composer's Forum Newsletter*, cited in Frith, *Performing Rites* (Oxford: OUP, 1996), 103. He also directs us to her *Feminine Endings* (London: University of Minnesota Press 1991), 77–8 (on the homosexual interpretation of Tchaikovsky's Fourth Symphony).

42. Cited in Hefling, *Mahler*, 118.

43. Including 'the parricide and incest that we all supposedly commit in fantasy'. Maud Ellmann, in Ellman (ed.), *Psychoanalytical Literary Criticism*, 8.

44. Norman H. Holland, *The Dynamics of Literary Response* (New York: OUP, 1968), 27, 30.

45. Carroll, *Philosophy of Horror*, 168 ff.

46. Jones, reported ibid. 169.

47. For some interesting speculations on the psychological attraction of horror, see James B. Twitchell, *Dreadful Pleasures* (New York: OUP, 1985), 65–104.

48. Carroll, *Philosophy*, 170–1.

49. Ibid. 173.

50. Ibid. 171.

51. Or even hard-core pornography; cf. Williams, *Hard Core*.

52. 'Sexuality develops as a swerve from mere genital utility, driven by infantile phantasies of satisfaction and loss; it involves a dynamic of curiosity that is possibly the foundation of all intellectual activity, which I describe under the rubric of "epistemophilia".' Peter Brooks, *Body Work: Objects of Desire in Modern Narrative* (Cambridge, Mass.: Harvard UP, 1993), p. xiii.

53. Ibid. 5. This claim is developed with reference to Melanie Klein. The mother's body, especially the breast, is the original object of symbolization, and is the field of exploration for the child's developing 'epistemophilic impulse' so that 'Bodily parts, sensations, and perceptions (including the notorious recognition of the anatomical distinction between the sexes) are the first building blocks in the construction of a symbolic order, including speech, play, and the whole system of human language, within which the child finds a libidinally invested place' (ibid. 7). There is a breathtaking confidence in the causal claims implied by this narrative; and it is such claims about cause and effect which most often

fail when psychoanalysis is brought to the test of verification by scientific standards.

54. Ibid. 8, 11. Though for Brooks, Walter's epistemophiliac quest in *My Secret Life* is rather simpler: he is intent on looking at women's genitals and this is 'really', i.e. according to Freud, not directed to women at all. It is (*per consonantia oppositorum*) a 'search for the missing phallus, motivated both by anxiety at its absence and by a need for reassurance that its absence in the other assures its presence in himself' (ibid. 97–8).

55. Cited in Michael Atkinson, *Blue Velvet* (London: BFI, 1997), 9. Subsequent references are in the text and notes as *BV*.

56. This sequence as a primal scene parallel is elaborated by Atkinson in *BV*, 49. I am using 'primal scene' in its Freudian cultural, that is mythical, sense. There is considerable doubt that the 'primal scene' in anything like the way in which Freud conceived it actually occurs, and so on for many of the other events he and others have posited for early childhood. So all speculations about its consequences may founder, given that they depend upon an empirical causal claim for which there is no reliable evidence. Cf. the by-now-standard objections to the scientific claims of psychoanalysis, as registered in Adolf Grunbaum, *The Foundations of Psychoanalysis: A Philosophical Critique* (Berkeley, and Los Angeles: University of California Press, 1984); Frank Cioffi, *Freud and the Question of Pseudoscience* (Chicago and La Salle, Ill.: Open Court, 1998); and many others.

57. To put it another way, do we need to be converted?

   Jeffrey's nice middle-class girlfriend Sandy says to him: 'I don't know if you're a detective or a pervert' (*BV*, 40) and he replies 'That's for me to know and you to find out'.

58. Also to be found in Laura Mulvey's account of *Citizen Kane*—which largely turns on the pleasure for the audience of the 'enigma of the meaning of Kane's dying word—"Rosebud" '. This leads to a view of the film as about 'Oedipal conflict and sexual difficulty', stemming from Kane's separation from his parents. Laura Mulvey, *Citizen Kane* (London: BFI, 1992), 16, 49, 50 ff. She also thinks the film is about 'the political unconscious of the United States', ibid. 31.

59. Hence the recent controversies about Recovered Memory Therapy and the legal testimony arising from it in cases of child abuse. Cf. Frederick Crews's abrasive account of this in his *The Memory Wars: Freud's Legacy in Dispute* (London: Granta Books, 1995).

60. This process is made fairly clear by Terry Eagleton, when he offers his own answer to the paradox of our pleasure in tragedy: 'Tragedy of this kind is sublime in both humanist and psychoanalytical senses—pleasurable, majestic, awe-inspiring, suggestive of infinite capacity and immeasurable value, yet also punitive, intimidating, cutting us savagely down to size. We see men and

women chastened by the Law for their illicit desire, a censure which with admirable economy satisfies our sense of justice, our respect for authority and our impulse to sadism. But since we also identify with these malcontents, we feel the bitterness of their longing, a sympathy which morally speaking is pity, and psychoanalytically speaking is masochism. We share their seditious passion, while reaping pleasure from castigating ourselves for such delinquent delight. Pity brings us libidinally close to them, while fear pushes them away in the name of the Law. But we also fear our own pity, alarmed by our own dalliance with destruction. Not all tragedy pitches insurrection against authority; but when it does, it satisfies the sombre demands of the superego while letting the death drive ecstatically loose. And this does nothing to alter the fact that the issues at stake remain ethical and political ones, questions of justice, violence, self-fulfilment and the like. Few artistic forms display such impressive erotic economy, and perhaps none caters so cunningly to our sadism, masochism and moral conscience all at the same time.' Terry Eagleton, *Sweet Violence: The Idea of the Tragic* (Oxford: Blackwell, 2003), 176.

61. Do serial killers really identify with fictional characters or not? Despite the millions of dollars spent on the analysis of the effects on audiences of TV and film, there does not seem to be a convincing answer to this question.

62. Barthes, *Pleasure of the Text*, 58.

63. Cf. Blackburn, *Being Good*, 76: 'it sounds miserable if the satisfaction of desire is fleeting, and desire itself is changeable and apt to give rise only to further dissatisfactions. But is it really something to mope about? Thinking concretely, suppose we desire a good dinner, and enjoy it. Should it poison the enjoyment to reflect that it is fleeting (we won't enjoy this dinner forever), or that the desire for a good dinner is changeable (soon we won't feel hungry), or only temporarily satisfied (we will want dinner again tomorrow)? It is not as if things would be better if we always wanted a dinner, or if having wanted a dinner we never wanted one again, or if the one dinner went on for a whole lifetime. None of these things seem remotely desirable, so why make a fuss about it not being like that?'

64. Some Marxists particularly like this point of view, since it allows them to argue that 'fantastic literature points to or suggests the basis upon which the cultural order rests for it opens up, for a brief moment, on to disorder, on to illegality, on to that which lies outside the law, that which is outside dominant value systems. The fantastic traces the unsaid and the unseen of culture: that which has been silenced, made invisible, covered over and made "absent".' Rosemary Jackson, *Fantasy: The Literature of Subversion* (London: Methuen, 1984), 3–4.

65. Simon Frith, *Performing Rites*, 162, citing Lawrence W. Levine, *Black Culture and Black Consciousness* (New York: OUP, 1977), 273.

66. But as Richard Shusterman (*Pragmatist Aesthetics* (Oxford: Blackwell, 1992), 130) points out, understanding is not just a matter of interpretation: 'if we could never understand anything without interpreting it, how could we ever understand the interpretation itself?' We would be involved in a frustrating infinite regress. (Of the kind made popular by deconstructive criticism, I might add.)

67. 'Since any putative fact or true understanding can be revised or replaced by interpretation, it cannot enjoy an epistemological status higher than interpretation; and interpretation is paradigmatically corrigible and inexhaustive. This is sometimes what is meant by the claim that there are no facts or truths but only interpretations.' Ibid. 121.

68. In what follows I take advantage of the fascinatingly engaging and various interpretations, by many distinguished critics, of Manet's painting, brought together in Bradford R. Collins (ed.), *12 Views of Manet's Bar* (Princeton: Princeton University Press, 1996).

69. Kivy, *Philosophies of the Arts*, 181–2.

70. John House, *12 Views*, 237.

71. Richard Shiff, in *12 Views*, 3.

72. John Updike, *Just Looking* (Harmondsworth: Penguin Books, 1990)—one of the few books that is seriously discriminating of the pleasures to be had from paintings. e.g. concerning Cezanne: 'Blue, green, and ochre—these basic shades never bore him, and are observed and captured each time as if afresh. In the intensity of the attention they receive, the painter's subjects shed their materiality' (ibid. 11). And perhaps less seriously, 'the numerous paintings in Boston [in an overcrowded Renoir exhibition], dutifully consumed by the eyeball as one shuffles past in a slow pedestrian choo-choo, begin to deposit on the retina an accumulated taste of artificial sweetener' (ibid. 82).

73. James Herbert, in *12 Views*, 214.

74. As cited by John House, ibid. 240.

75. As Steven Z. Levine reports, ibid. 265.

76. Ibid. 266. Herbert's response comes from his *Impressionism: Art, Leisure and Parisian Society* (New Haven and London: Yale UP, 1988), 88.

77. Albert Boime, in *12 Views*, 57.

78. Bradford R. Collins, ibid. 123. (Phew! That's *much* easier.)

79. 'In pursuing the question of whether her body is for sale or not, we lose sight of the fact that she is a kind of prostitute; she is selling something of herself, if only her smile.' (Collins, ibid. 123). Her customer is involved in 'the overt buying of drinks, and yes, perhaps the covert buying of sex as well' (Carol Armstrong, ibid. 38).

80. Armstrong, ibid. 39, 42.

81. Collins, *12 views*, 120. And the mirror with its vaguer image is part of 'an identification with femininity represented as indeterminate, double and divided' (Armstrong, ibid. 35). This for Collins would be disappointing because a mirror in painting is usually supposed to help you see, as he coyly puts it, 'a more complete inventory of a female subject's charms' (ibid. 117).

82. Ibid. 120–1. Flam on the other hand is rather repelled by this detail: 'this triangular area very much resembles a pudendum—a reading that is reinforced by the insistent vertical of the seam. A kind of pudency almost blocks out this perception, but it is so obviously suggested, underlined as it were by a bold horizontal brushstroke, that it is difficult to ignore' (ibid. 167).

83. Richard Schiff, ibid. 11.

84. Griselda Pollock, ibid. 283. How does she *know* this?

85. Bradford R. Collins, ibid. 121, 124, 130 ff.

86. Although I would not be surprised to learn that Manet had a reasonably humane attitude to young women in the barmaid's position, I cannot imagine that he could think about his picture in the way that many of these critics do. He probably couldn't 'see' alienation as we can, any more than virtually any painter before 1700 should be thought to be imagining the enjoyment of his or her image from the atheist's point of view.

87. George Eliot, *Selected Critical Writings*, ed. (Oxford: Rosemary Ashton OUP, 1992), 263.

88. George Eliot, in *The George Eliot Letters*, ed. (London: Gordon S. Haight OUP, and New Haven: Yale UP, 1954–5), iii. 111.

89. Ibid. iv. 300–1. Kerry McSweeney, in citing this passage in his *Middlemarch* (Unwin Critical Library; London: George Allen and Unwin, 1984), 30, refers us to another crucial passage in the *Letters* (vii. 44): 'My function is that of the *aesthetic*, not the doctrinal teacher—the rousing of the nobler emotions, which make mankind desire the social right, not the prescribing of special measures, concering which the artistic mind, however strongly moved by social sympathy, is often not the best judge.'

90. It is relevant to this part of our discussion at least to to note Martha Nussbaum's insistence on the specificity to be found in literature, in her *Love's Knowledge* (Oxford: OUP, 1990) and the conclusions she draws from it. Literature is complex, allusive, and attentive to particulars (ibid. 3) and some truths can only be stated in this kind of language (ibid. 5). Since values arise out of the particular, we need to be able to follow particularized narratives, rather than to consult general principles, and so on. Nussbaum cites James as an example of what she finds in literature: his characters manage a 'richness of reflection' and an 'intuitive perception' and an 'improvisatory response' and have a willingness 'to alter his or her prima facie conception of the good in the light of the new experience'. This is 'likely to clash with certain classical aims and assertions of

moral philosophy' which claim to 'extricate' us from the very kind of 'bewilderment' which James goes to work on (ibid. 141). For James and for Nussbaum 'a responsible action . . . is a highly context-specific and nuanced and responsive thing, whose rightness could not be captured in a description that fell short of the artistic' (ibid. 154). In such circumstances 'Rules' alone would be 'obtuse' (cf. ibid. 156). Literature captures something that philosophy cannot. (It is also good at demonstrating to us how circumstances alter cases.)

91. Peter Kivy, *Music Alone*, 168.

92. Arthur Danto, *The Transformation of the Commonplace* (Cambridge, Mass.: Harvard UP, 1981), 135.

93. George Steiner's account, in his *Antigones: A Myth in Western Literature, Art and Thought* (Oxford: OUP, 1984), of the history and reception of the *Antigone* and its different versions, is immensely instructive in this regard.

94. Julian Bell, *What is Painting?* (London: Thames and Hudson, 1999), 172.

95. Susan Sontag, *A Susan Sontag Reader* (Harmondsworth: Penguin, 1983), 104, 198. The essay dates from 1971. She says also that we can't 'retrieve that innocence before theory' (ibid. 98).

96. Here the performance arts (of music, theatre, film) have an advantage, as the rhetoric of performance is designed to coerce our attention. But we do not always know how to perform a novel or a poem or a picture convincingly to ourselves, and so too often take refuge in thinking interpretatively about it, rather than thinking through it.

97. Susan Sontag, *Reader*, 104.

98. But cf. J. C. B. Gosling, *Pleasure and Desire* (Oxford: OUP, 1969), esp ch. 8, and L. W. Sumner, *Welfare Happiness and Ethics* (Oxford: OUP, 1996).

99. Lorrie Moore, *Who Will Run the Frog Hospital?* (London: Faber, 1994), 82.

100. Wallace Stevens, 'Anglais mort à Florence', in Stevens, *Collected Poetry and Prose* (New York: Library of America, 1900), 119.

101. Cf. Jenny Hartley, *Reading Groups* (Oxford: OUP, 2001).

Appendix on Beauty

The concept of the beautiful arises partly because it has seemed to many (and in particular to Kant) that we ought to be able to point to a property of (some) natural objects, and of all works of art, that could be made the basis of a universalizable 'aesthetic' judgement. I am not concerned with this problem, of how we can get other people to agree with us, or to allow for such a property in aesthetics, largely because I am willing to settle for developing a pluralist theory of responses, which are bound to conflict, and are inherently open to debate. But the relationship of the pleasurable to what many writers call 'the beautiful' is still of importance—for if works of art did possess this rather occult property, it would surely be one of the properties they have, which most obviously gives us pleasure. There are really two questions here. First, is 'beauty' really just a popular label for some generally recognized pleasure-giving *aspects* of art? (Such as a complex formal property, a holding together in some way, of the kind that I have been trying to analyse.) But then should we not look for descriptions by which the forms of art can be clearly analysed without appealing to this overall, occult emergent property? And secondly, are there really (some) artistic conventions which are so unique to works of art that they give rise to a kind of pleasure which is *only* to be derived from contemplating them, and which we might as well call 'beauty', or even 'aesthetic value' because they are supposed to arise from purely 'aesthetic' properties?

Clearly enough, to claim that a work of art is 'beautiful' is usually to claim that one is pleased by it in some way.[1] For to say that something is beautiful but not *ipso facto* pleasurable seems odd.[2] Now, even if it may be that the property beauty, in some sense as defined by its defenders (for example as 'the pleasurable contemplation of those formal properties which are unique to the arts'), may help us to (ostensively) define the nature of art, or even to defend some typical pleasure-giving properties of art, like 'significant form' in painting, saying that these very various conventions also give rise to the 'beautiful' in so far as they are pleasure-giving won't much advance our purposes. A far more analytical account of the ways in which we get pleasure from such formal aesthetic conventions (e.g. sonata form, or Mondrian's division of the picture space) can surely be given. All I am concerned with at this point is to ask whether there is a particular kind of pleasure (that of the contemplation of 'beauty') that I have failed to account for.

My feeling is that calling things 'beautiful' can only damage our notions of pleasure in the arts. We may know how to handle the 'agreeable' or notions of pleasurable horror, or enjoy our seeing a fit between picture and world, or feel the tension or release of a harmonic progression, or get the point of a joke or a poem, as I have tried to show. Why then introduce the occult predicate 'beautiful' to label both the object and the pleasure-giving effect of such an experience? Or worse, to say that we are 'really' experiencing 'beauty'? We have plenty of other non-occult predicates for the description of our responses to works of art, just as we do for our purposes in relation to blankets, motor cars, scientific experiments, etc. To say that one or other of these is also 'beautiful' may indeed be to suggest that things which are not works of art can have properties which are most usually to be found in works of art—like a certain sort of elegant coherence (in a scientific proof, say) or a strong emotional effect (that car looks elegantly powerful to me: but that is a result of its visual design). These may be relatively harmless uses of the word, but as my examples show, we still don't need to apply it to the analysis of works of art and their effects. Most importantly, it neither supplements nor usurps the sense of the pleasurable which I am trying to analyse. My feeling is not so much that we need to look at the beautiful as a formal property within, or as causing a valued mental state arising from, our contemplation of works of art, as to ask how that would square with their instrumental value, in being true or morally good or pleasurable for us, or most typically a combination of all three, and what is more in ways which are also familiar to us from our 'non-aesthetic' experience. As we have seen, pleasure may well promote the first two values. Having such kinds of pleasure may indeed be consequentially morally good or bad for us—and our delight in seeing how things fit together may also be a valuable cognitive exercise. The values involved here are the same as those which apply outside the realm of art in our reactions to other kinds of object. They are not peculiarly 'aesthetic'.

I may well, once I've analysed out the reasons for other people wanting to call a work of art 'beautiful', indeed arrive at values that I would think it rational or useful for others to share or agree with, and to get pleasure from contemplating in that sort of artwork (if that is the verb—the more active 'understanding' and 'feeling about' is what I have gone for above). But no more. I do not believe that another category of value, that of beauty, will emerge. Why should we want to complicate things further by asserting that some works of art are 'beautiful' or have an 'aesthetic value'? This is on the supposition that the latter means something more than 'have value by virtue of being works of art', i.e. by typically or generically exploiting a, b, c artistic conventions, and so possessing x, y, z valuable properties. (For example, the virtues of an organization that enable them to convey useful experiences to us more efficiently—such as the conventions of narrative of the horror film, which help it to deliver the pleasurable shock.) But even here I'm inclined to rely on the presence of conventions, for example of narrative, which are in fact never strictly confined to art, and so can't be purely 'aesthetic' because they are nearly always shared with things which aren't intended as works of art, like newspaper articles or political speeches. I do not expect to find any peculiarly 'aesthetic' narrative conventions.

Notes

1. Mary Mothersill, *Beauty Restored* (Oxford: OUP, 1984), 220, agrees that to judge something beautiful is to find it a cause of pleasure, but she also argues that not everything that is a cause of pleasure is thought to be beautiful. But to show the necessity of such a general concept, we have to do something more complicated—i.e. show that a haiku, a successful poem of Alcibiades, etc., all have an interesting common feature (cf. ibid. 249). Of course one can specify a (generically tied) value for anything—the 'dormitive' value of all sleeping pills e.g. is a bit like the 'aesthetic value' of all works of art. But this doesn't prove its usefulness. It's still circular.
2. Ibid. 85 and 107—'X is beautiful' implicates (tenselessly) 'It gives me pleasure'.

Picture Credits

Figures

1. Picasso, *The Goat*. © Succession Picasso / DACS 2004. Photo RMN / Béatrice Hatala.

2. Munch, *The Scream*. © Munch Museum / Munch-Ellingsen Group, BONO, Oslo, DACS, London 2004. Photo © Munch Museum (Anderson / de Jong).

3. Willem de Kooning, *Woman I*. © Willem de Kooning Revocable Trust / ARS / NY and DACS, London 2004. Photo © The Museum of Modern Art / Scala, Florence.

4. Millais, *The Blind Girl*. Birmingham Museum and Art Gallery / Bridgeman Art Library.

5. Mondrian, *Composition 10 in Black and White 1915*. Kröller-Müller Museum, Otterlo.

6. Chardin, *The Smoker's Case* or *Pipes and Drinking Vessel*. Photo RMN / Hervé Lewandowski.

7. Juan Gris, *Still Life Before an Open Window*. Philadelphia Museum of Art: The Louise and Walter Arensberg Collection.

8. Piero della Francesca, *The Baptism of Christ*. National Gallery, London / Bridgeman Art Library.

9. Edward Weston, *Nude on Sand*. Collection Centre for Creative Photography, The University of Arizona © 1981 Arizona Board of Regents.

10. Vermeer, *The Kitchen Maid*. Rijksmuseum, Amsterdam.

11. Courbet, *The Origin of the World*. Photo RMN / Hervé Lewandowski.

12. Titian, *The Entombment*. Photo RMN / R. G. Ojeda.

13. Southworth and Hawes, *Daniel Webster*. The Metropolitan Museum of Art, Gift of I. N. Phelps Stokes, Edward S. Hawes, Alice Mary Hawes and Marion Augusta Hawes, 1937 (37.14.2). All rights reserved, The Metropolitan Museum of Art.

Colour Plates

1. Vermeer, *The Love Letter*. Rijksmuseum, Amsterdam.

2. John Singer Sargent, *Mrs Hugh Hammersley*. The Metropolitan Museum of Art, Gift of Mr. and Mrs. Douglass Campbell, in memory of Mrs. Richard E. Danielson, 1998 (1998.365). Photograph © 1998 The Metropolitan Museum of Art.

Index